Penguin Education

Penguin Critical Anthologies

General Editor : Christopher Ricks

John Webster

Edited by G. K. and S. K. Hunter

D0907973

John Webster

A critical anthology

edited by G.K.and S.K.Hunter

Penguin Books   Baltimore · Maryland

Penguin Books Ltd, Harmondsworth,
Middlesex, England
Penguin Books Inc., 7110 Ambassador Road,
Baltimore, Md 21207, U.S.A.
Penguin Books Australia Ltd, Ringwood,
Victoria, Australia

First published 1969
This selection copyright © G. K. and S. K. Hunter, 1969
Introduction and notes copyright © G. K. and S. K. Hunter, 1969

Made and printed in Great Britain by
Hazell Watson & Viney
Set in Monotype Bembo

Contents

6   Contents

7 Contents

Preface

In the following anthology all quotations from and line-references to *The White Devil* and *The Duchess of Malfi* have been made to conform to J. R. Brown's 'Revels' editions – with one exception. Brown spells 'Bracciano' in the proper Italian way. We have restored the Elizabethan 'Brachiano' – where the 'ch' carries its usual English sound. All other Webster quotations have been referred to F. L. Lucas's edition of the *Complete Works*, but the spelling has been modernized. Footnotes in extracts dated before 1800 are the work of the present editors; later than this the footnotes are the work of the original authors, unless otherwise designated.

We wish to express our gratitude for permission to reprint. One exception is noted below (p. 101). We must also thank George Rylands and Henri Fluchère who generously searched their memories to answer questions, and various colleagues in Coventry and Berkeley who responded to queries in lifts and corridors with patience and accuracy. The General Editor and the editorial staff of Penguin Education have given consistently helpful advice and accurate information.

Table of Dates

1604   Webster writes an 'Induction' to Marston's *The
       Malcontent* and perhaps some small additions to make it
       suitable for adult actors: it had previously been played
       by the boys. The play was published in 1604 with an
       ambiguous title: *The Malcontent. Augmented by
       Marston. With the additions played by the King's
       Majesty's servants. Written by John Webster.*
       Webster and Dekker write verses for an engraved volume
       showing the allegorical arches which were invented
       by Stephen Harrison ('joiner and architect') to welcome
       the new king James I into the City of London.
       Westward Ho acted.

1605   [2 March] 'A comedy called Westward Ho, presented
       by the Children of Paul's' entered in the Stationers'
       Register 'provided that he [sc. the publisher] get further
       authority before it be printed'.
       Northward Ho acted.

1607   '*The famous history of Sir Thomas Wyatt. With the
       coronation of Queen Mary and the coming-in of King Philip.
       As it was played by the Queen's Majesty's servants.
       Written by Thomas Dekker and John Webster . . . 1607.*'
       [6 August] 'A book called Northward Ho' entered in
       the Stationers' Register.
       '*Westward Ho. As it hath been divers times acted by the
       Children of Paul's. Written by Thomas Dekker and
       John Webster . . . 1607.*'
       '*Northward Ho. Sundry times acted by the Children of
       Paul's. By Thomas Dekker and John Webster . . . 1607.*'

1612   Second edition of *Sir Thomas Wyatt.*
       The White Devil acted.
       '*The White Devil; or, The tragedy of Paulo Giordano
       Ursini, Duke of Brachiano. With the life and death of
       Vittoria Corombona, the famous Venetian courtesan.*
       Acted by the Queen's Majesty's servants. Written by
       John Webster . . . 1612.'
       [25 December] 'A Monumental Column' entered in the
       Stationers' Register.

1613   '*A monumental column erected to the living memory of the*

Part One Contemporaneous Criticism

Introduction

'Contemporary reaction' to the plays of an author as far back and as little identified as Webster is not a matter that can be discussed in general terms. Unlike the London of (say) Browning, the London of the Elizabethan dramatists attached little importance to literary gossip; and in any case plays were hardly thought of as literature. The few pieces of evidence that exist are printed here; but these exist as separate comments on separate occasions; they do not give us enough to make possible the creation of a landscape of opinion about the author. Indeed the whole idea of 'the author' is a dubious invention, made by drawing tendentious lines between widely scattered points and inferring significances without objective warrant.

As a member of a merchant-tailor family in London (the total we know about him) Webster seems to have entered playwriting as a trade by something akin to the regular process of apprenticeship. Obviously he had been to grammar-school; and one would expect him to have been to the famous Merchant Taylor's School – but there is no evidence of this. It seems probable that he did not go to University; but it is clear that he admired those who had. He is first visible in the cloud of Henslowe's hacks, earning something like thirty shillings for one act of a play, written quickly and to order. He emerges as the particular associate of Thomas Dekker, and he first reaches publication as collaborator in plays which reflect Dekker's temperamental choices – citizen life and English history – rather than those we may suppose *ex post facto* to have been Webster's. That Webster had other interests and other ambitions about this time (and was known to have them) may be reflected by the fact that the King's Men (Shakespeare's company) gave him the task of adapting Marston's *The Malcontent* for performance by adult rather than child actors. By undertaking this work (as in his collaboration with Dekker) Webster may be judged to have joined with the popular side in the 'war' between the aristocratic private theatre of the boys and the public theatre of the men. But it is not at all

clear where Webster stood in this 'war'; and it is probable that
modern scholars have drawn over-simple lines of demarcation. As
co-author (with Dekker) of *Westward Ho* Webster was the object
of learned and aristocratic correction supplied in *Eastward Ho*,
in which Jonson, Chapman, and Marston collaborated; and in
Northward Ho Dekker and he seem to have replied, defending their
own vein. But Webster's aspirations seem to have lain with the
Eastward Ho group rather than with Dekker. Marston was the man
whose plays helped him, more than the work of any other man,
to acquire his own voice – by which we mean the voice of
The White Devil and *The Duchess of Malfi*.

   The Preface to *The White Devil* – his first published independent
play (1612) – should be read, it seems, as the manifesto of this
hard-won independence from his past. For he not only defends his
play but places it in relation to the main playwriting tendencies of
his own day. The master playwrights are Jonson and Chapman
(Marston had fled from the stage about 1608) and the
aristocratic Beaumont and Fletcher. The 'good' popular
playwrights, Shakespeare, Dekker, and Heywood, are also praised,
but with less particularity and less warmth.

   Jonson's Preface to *Sejanus* (1605) is the obvious model in front of
Webster; and Webster (very typically) seals his admiration by
borrowing several lines. The resounding failure of Jonson's *Catiline*
(1611) may also have been in Webster's mind; under these auspices
popular failure becomes something like a guarantee of artistic
integrity. The antithesis between the learned and the popular
writers that the preface contains may also have a bearing on the
slowness with which the tragedy seems to have been composed.
The antithesis which the seventeenth century set up between Jonson
and Shakespeare emphasized the contrast between

The sweat of learned Jonson's brain
And gentle Shakespeare's easier strain

(as Suckling defines it), between the flow of Shakespeare's 'easy numbers' and 'slow-endeavouring art' (as Milton phrases it). In these terms there can be no doubt where Webster saw himself.

Webster's borrowings in his plays confirm this estimate of what was most important to him in the contemporary dramatic scene. Jonson and Chapman gave him more than any other practising dramatists. But an aristocratic closet dramatist – Sir William Alexander, the Earl of Stirling – gives even more. Webster's effort seems to have been to cling to the literary coat-tails of those he most looked up to, and with this aid to escape from the citizen world of popular playwriting. .

The failure of *The White Devil* when first performed may be attributed in part (as the Preface suggests) to the nature of the theatre where it was presented. The Red Bull in Clerkenwell was a rowdy house with little taste for subtle poetry. On the other hand, Webster offers what almost seems to be a retraction of the Preface, at the end of *The White Devil*. He says that the acting by the Queen's Men was very good 'for the true imitation of life', and he singles out 'my friend Master Perkins' (who seems to have played Flamineo) as notably worthy.

Webster's next play, *The Duchess of Malfi* (written 1613–14) was performed by the King's Men, who were favourites at Court and played to an aristocratic clientele at the Blackfriars' 'private' theatre as well as at the public 'Globe'. There is every sign that *The Duchess* was a theatrical success. The play was performed at both houses, the cast-lists imply revivals, and it remained unprinted till 1623 – when, presumably, its theatrical cash-value was beginning to wane.

In spite of all this Webster returned to the Queen's Men. They acquired a 'private' house – the Cockpit in Drury Lane – in 1617; it was there that *The White Devil* was performed later in the century; and it may have been for this theatre that *The Devil's Law-Case* was designed. But the theatrical history of these decades is stormy and complex. The Queen's Men returned to The Red Bull and it was there that *Keep the Widow Waking* (see below) was performed in 1624. In this as in other respects Webster's career describes a circle back to its origins.

The printing of *The Duchess of Malfi* in 1623 may give us a further indication of Webster's literary reputation at this point. Three prefatory poems are prefixed to the play; but they do not come from the pens he had praised. Middleton's involvement in citizen life, and the absence of oppressive learning in his plays make him unsatisfactory as a witness. Rowley is a bit of a hack. Ford, it is true, was a gentleman by birth and a member of the Middle Temple; but at this point he seems to have been in penury and (like Webster at an earlier point) surviving under Dekker's tutelage.

The evidence (such as it is) suggests that Webster's attempt to escape into the world of fashionable learning was only partly and briefly successful. That he was for some time a notable figure in the milieu of the Blackfriars' theatre is indicated by his inclusion in *Notes from Blackfriars* by Henry Fitzjeffrey (1617). Webster's desire for 'weight', his desire to load every rift with somebody else's ore, is well caught in the poem. If our interpretation of his career is correct, his laborious assertiveness would be hard for those living easily in higher social or literary levels to bear. His dedicatory epistles show the same prickly independence of those he is supposed to be praising. The lost play of *The Guise* belongs to this period, and presumably it is a major loss to English literature. But already by *The Devil's Law-Case* (probably to be dated 1617–19) there is a decline from the intransigently dense allusiveness of the tragedies, and an acceptance of the thinner texture and undemandingly episodic structure of Beaumont and Fletcher tragicomedy.

When we meet Webster again, in 1624, his return to his bourgeois origins seems complete. In this year he produced his longest

occasional work, a description of the Lord Mayor's show for Sir
John Gore, which Webster not only devised but also produced. The
expenses for the whole affair were paid for by the merchant-tailor's
company to which both Gore and Webster belonged. That by 1624
Webster was also returning to his theatrical origins is strongly
suggested by what we know about *A Late Murder of the Son upon
the Mother*. The Master of the Revels licensed this play in September
1624, attributing it to Ford and Webster. More recent research has
shown that the planning and writing of the play was the
responsibility primarily of Dekker and secondarily of Rowley. The
play, called in fact *The Late Murder in Whitechapel, or Keep the
Widow Waking*, cashed in on two recent and local scandals, a (tragic)
matricide and a (comic) forced marriage. It must have been
written in a great hurry to catch the public while the scandal was
still hot, and Dekker called in two of his assistants, Webster and
Ford, to write something like an act apiece. This was very much the
Henslowe mode; and the sordidness of the whole affair, performed
almost while the victims were bleeding, certainly while they were
smarting, is very remote from the dignified stoicism of Webster's
best verse.

Appius and Virginia is usually supposed to belong to the thirties
and to be Webster's last recorded work. If so, it reflects a final point
in that process of simplification (or 'thinning') which has been
noted above. The evidence cannot be leant on; but a believable
pattern is created by the idea that Webster returned to this quiet
unassertive competence at the end of a career in which individual
assertion and social expectation achieved tension but no resolution.

There is some evidence that Webster's tragedies were known, as
part of the general heritage of Jacobean drama, up to and into the
Civil War. James Shirley, that notable magpie of the Jacobean past,
obviously remembers Webster at a number of points. He seems to
have been especially impressed by the last scene of *The White Devil*,
which he glances at in *The Gentleman of Venice* (1639), *The Cardinal*

(1641), and *The Brothers* (?1641). Nathaniel Richards in his play
Messalina (1640) and his *The Celestial Publican* (1630) draws on the
same scene. Robert Baron, in the curious playlet *Gripus and Hegio* –
included in his Ἐροτοπαίγνιον (1647) – embodies a fair number of
quotations from *The Duchess of Malfi*. Commonplace books of the
period, both manuscript and printed, confirm this meagre but
undoubted survival of Webster's plays. Only one vocal admirer
stands out: Samuel Sheppard not only writes an epigram on
The White Devil, in 1651, but includes Webster in the hall of literary
fame in his manuscript epic *The Fairy King*. It is worth noticing
that he appears in the latter as an anti-Jonson figure.

If editions of plays are indicative of popularity, it is significant
that *The White Devil* and *The Duchess of Malfi* were the only plays
by Webster that had any reprints in the seventeenth century.
The White Devil was reprinted four times and each printing
indicates a separate place of acting. We infer from this that the play
had a fairly continuous stage-history. The theatrical records of the
post-Restoration period tell us that it was performed on 2 October
1661 and again two days later, on 11 December 1661, and in
August 1671.

It may also be worth notice that the title-pages of these editions
imply a gradual emergence of Victoria herself as the undisputed
central figure. The 1612 and 1631 editions call the play: *The White
Devil, or the tragedy of Paulo Giordano Ursini, Duke of Brachiano, with
the life and death of Vittoria Corombona, the famous Venetian
courtesan*. This seems designed to be a just expression of what a
tragedy formally requires. If a tragedy is the fall of a noble person
then the tragedy that the play shows is that of Brachiano. By 1665
however the title-page cares more for what it takes to be the chief
attraction of the play than for formal propriety. It sets forth *The
White Devil, or Vittoria Corombona, a lady of Venice. A Tragedy*.
The 1672 edition goes one stage further: *Vittoria Corombona or the
White Devil. A Tragedy*. This centering of attention on the *femme*

fatale from Venice is evidenced further by the Latin epigram by
J[ohn] W[ilson] (1617?–96) added to the 1665 and 1672 editions:

In Mentem Authoris
Scire velis quid sit mulier? quo percitet oestro?
En tibi, si sapias, cum sale, mille sales.
[The purport of the author: Do you want to know what a woman
is? with what power she stings you? Here it is for you, if you
wish to know, not only witty, but wittily put.]

1661 seems to have been a bumper year for Webster. We have
mentioned the performances of *The White Devil*. *The Duchess of
Malfi* was performed on 30 September with the best actors in
town (Betterton as Bosola and Mrs Betterton as the Duchess,
Harris as Ferdinand). John Downes, the historian of Drury Lane,
tells us: 'This play was so exceedingly excellently acted in all parts,
chiefly Duke Ferdinand and Bosola, it filled the house eight days
successively, it proving one of the best of stock tragedies.' In the
same year Francis Kirkman brought out *A Cure for a Cuckold* with
a preface we may be tempted to believe: 'As for this play, I need
not speak anything in its commendation, and the authors' names,
Webster and Rowley, are (to knowing men) sufficient to declare its
worth.' The attachment of the same repute to Rowley as to Webster
must make one doubt, however; so must the affixing of Webster's
name to *The Thracian Wonder*.

The peak of reputation in 1661 was followed by a slow decline.
The Duchess of Malfi was performed again on 25 November 1668,
31 January 1672, at court on 13 January 1686, and under the title,
The Unfortunate Duchess of Malfi, or the Unnatural Brothers in 1707.
Appius and Virginia had a revival in 1679, in a revision by Thomas
Betterton. Now called *The Roman Virgin or the Unjust Judge* it
had Betterton as Virginius, Mrs Betterton as Virginia and Harris
as Appius. Downes tells us: 'all the parts exactly performed, it
lasted successively eight days and very frequently acted afterwards'.

The unsold sheets of the first edition (1654) were given a new title-page in honour of Betterton's revival; but the interest aroused was not great enough either to cause Betterton's version to be printed or the original to be reprinted.

When next we hear of Webster, in 1707, we hear in spite of silence. In this year Nahum Tate, famous for his version of *King Lear* with a happy ending, published a play, *Injured Love: or the Cruel Husband*, making no mention of the fact that this was a rewriting of *The White Devil*. It seems likely that Tate kept quiet because he assumed that no one would know the original well enough to recognize the theft. It would only be poetic justice if Tate's larceny brought him no reward. The title-page describes the play as 'designed to be acted at the Theatre Royal', but there is no evidence of the design being fulfilled.

Tate's adaptation documents a view of the play that might well have been expected to make it tolerable to post-Restoration audiences. Vittoria becomes a high-spirited but not essentially wicked destroyer of the married state. Isabella (the 'wronged wife') assumes a much greater importance than in the original – an importance that is even accepted by Vittoria. She is given an extended praise of Isabella's virtues to replace the sinister 'yew' dream in Act 1. The changes in Vittoria, and in the whole play, interestingly parallel those that Dryden's *All for Love* imposes on Shakespeare's *Antony and Cleopatra*. The highly ambiguous female lead, powerfully destructive, dangerous, even murderous, yet with a blaze of splendour and magnificently seductive self-confidence, is toned down into something more acceptably feminine. No doubt the change is connected with the theatrical switch from boys to women as portrayers of female roles. But even more it is connected with the onset of sentimentalism.

Nahum Tate's appropriation of *The White Devil* is, if anything, less blatant than Lewis Theobald's theft of *The Duchess of Malfi*, which he published in 1735 under the title of *The Fatal Secret*.

Theobald seems to have been at work on the play in the summer of
1731. His letter of 18 December 1731 to Dr William Warburton
(printed below) not only tells us this, but indicates that he had no
fear that even Warburton (one of the prime scholars of his age)
would recognize the plot. The play was planned to appear in 1732,
but there were difficulties at the theatre. He writes in March 1733
that it 'is to make its appearance immediately after Easter holidays';
it was in fact acted twice, on 4 and 6 April 1733. It is pleasant to
record that at some point before the performance Theobald was
obliged to admit that the play was originally Webster's. He remarks
somewhat disingenuously, in his Preface:

Though I called it *The Fatal Secret*, I had no intention of disguising from the public that (as my friend has confessed for me
in the Prologue [see p. 42 below]) John Webster had preceded
me, above a hundred years ago, in the same story.

Theobald seeks to remove one glaring fault that always strikes
neo-classical critics of *The Duchess of Malfi* – the point that children
are conceived, born and grow up in the course of the action. In
Theobald no children are born; Ferdinand interrupts the marriage
before it is consummated. Tautness of plot-development is thus
secured; but only by sacrificing the various complexities of
Webster's scene. Theobald also reduces the spectacular horrors of
the play. When Ferdinand visits the Duchess in the dark, instead of
a dead man's hand he leaves her Antonio's ring. The Duchess is led
off-stage to die in her bed-chamber:

And expiate there your sin, where't was committed.

Theobald's most radical change, however, is in the ending. The
Cardinal and Ferdinand kill one another in a manner not too
remote from Webster. Bosola (more plainly virtuous) is captured
and charged with the death of the Duchess. But all is well. Bosola,
instead of killing the Duchess, had deceived Ferdinand with a

'beauteous waxen image so admired | Framed by Vincentio di Laureola' (which he happened to have by him). The Duchess, Cariola, etc., emerge from hiding and join Antonio, Delio, and the young Duke of Malfi.

Theobald's regularization of the plot involves the loss of many of the most splendid passages in the play (for example, the Duchess's wooing of Antonio). There is little evidence that he had much taste for the splendours that were left; instead of the famous

Cover her face: mine eyes dazzle: she died young,
(IV ii 264)

he writes

Cover her face; my eyes begin to dazzle.

However, where he can he compensates with lines taken from Shakespeare. Thus Ferdinand, hearing about the Duchess's marriage, is given Brabantio's lines about love philtres; and Bosola, taking up his role as spy in the Duchess's household, remarks:

I'm here in double trust . . .
                         The hot Duke
Bribes me with gold to be his spy o' the time.

John Webster

Preface to *The White Devil*   1612

To the Reader

In publishing this tragedy, I do but challenge to myself that liberty,
which other men have taken before me; not that I affect praise by it,
for, *nos haec novimus esse nihil*,[1] only since it was acted, in so dull a time
of winter, presented in so open and black a theatre, that it wanted
(that which is the only grace and setting-out of a tragedy) a full and
understanding auditory: and that since that time I have noted most
of the people that come to that playhouse resemble those ignorant
asses (who visiting stationers' shops, their use is not to inquire for good
books, but new books) I present it to the general view with this
confidence:

Nec rhoncos metues, maligniorum,
Nec scombris tunicas, dabis molestas.[2]

If it be objected this is no true dramatic poem, I shall easily confess it –
non potes in nugas dicere plura meas: ipse ego quam dixi[3] – willingly, and
not ignorantly, in this kind have I faulted: for should a man present to
such an auditory the most sententious tragedy that ever was written,
observing all the critical laws, as height of style, and gravity of person,
enrich it with the sententious *Chorus*, and as it were liven death in the
passionate and weighty *Nuntius*: yet after all this divine rapture, *O
dura messorum ilia*,[4] the breath that comes from the uncapable multitude is able to poison it, and ere it be acted, let the author resolve to fix
to every scene this of Horace,

. . . Haec hodie porcis comedenda relinques.[5]

To those who report I was a long time in finishing this tragedy, I

1 'We know these things are worth nothing' (Martial, XIII 2).
2 'You [the poet's book] will not fear the jeers of the malicious, nor supply
fiery jackets for mackerel' (Martial, IV 86).
3 'You cannot say more against my trifles than I have said myself' (Martial,
XIII 2).
4 'O strong stomachs of harvesters' (Horace, *Epodes*, III 4; alluding to their
love of garlic).
5 'What you leave will make today's pigfood' (Horace, *Epistles*, I vii 19).

confess I do not write with a goose-quill winged with two feathers, and if they will needs make it my fault, I must answer them with that of Euripides to Alcestides, a tragic writer: Alcestides objecting that Euripides had only in three days composed three verses, whereas himself had written three hundred: 'Thou tell'st truth,' (quoth he) 'but here's the difference: thine shall only be read for three days, whereas mine shall continue three ages.'

Detraction is the sworn friend to ignorance: for mine own part I have ever truly cherished my good opinion of other men's worthy labours, especially of that full and heightened style of Master Chapman, the laboured and understanding works of Master Jonson: the no less worthy composures of the both worthily excellent Master Beaumont, and Master Fletcher: and lastly (without wrong last to be named) the right happy and copious industry of Master Shakespeare, Master Dekker, and Master Heywood, wishing what I write may be read by their light; protesting, that, in the strength of mine own judgement, I know them so worthy that though I rest silent in my own work, yet to most of theirs I dare (without flattery) fix that of Martial:

... non norunt, haec monumenta mori.[1]

Henry Fitzjeffrey

[Crabbed Websterio] from *Notes from Blackfriars, Satyres and Satyricall Epigrams* 1617

But hist! with him,[2] crabbed Websterio,
The playwright-cartwright[3] (whether either!). Ho!
No further. Look as you'd be looked into;
Sit as ye would be read. Lord! who would know him?

1 'These [literary or funerary] monuments do not know how to die' (Martial, x ii 12).
2 I bring in Webster to accompany the previous character – a fantastic singing man.
3 One whose playwrighting was lumbering and slow-moving. One John Webster in London at this time had a brother who hired out carriages; and it is possible that the reference picks up this point.

Was ever man so mangled with a poem?
See how he draws his mouth awry of late,
How he scrubs,[1] wrings his wrists, scratches his pate.
A midwife, help! By his brain's coitus
Some centaur strange, some huge Bucephalus,[2]
Or Pallas, sure, engendered in his brain,
Strike Vulcan,[3] with thy hammer once again.
This is the critic that of all the rest
I'd not have view me, yet I fear him least.
Here's not a word cursively[4] I have writ
But he'll industriously examine it,
And in some twelve months hence, or thereabout,
Set in a shameful sheet[5] my errors out.
But what care I? It will be so obscure
That none shall understand him I am sure.

Orazio Busino[6]

from *Anglopotrida* 1618

The English scoff at our religion as disgusting and merely superstitious; they never put on any public show whatever, be it tragedy or
satire or comedy, into which they do not insert some Catholic
churchman's vices and wickednesses, making mock and scorn of him,
according to their taste, but to the dismay of good men. In fact, a
Franciscan friar was seen by some of our countrymen introduced into
a comedy as a wily character chock-full of different impieties, as given
over to avarice as to lust. And the whole thing turned out to be a
tragedy, for he had his head cut off on open stage. On another occa-

1 scratches himself
2 Alexander the Great's bull-headed horse – a hybrid like the centaur.
3 Pallas (or 'wit') was engendered in Jove's forehead; Vulcan had to split this
open before she could be born.
4 quickly, carelessly
5 The white garment worn by those undergoing formal penance; also the
sheet of paper in which Webster will expose Fitzjeffrey's errors.
6 Venetian envoy in England.

sion they showed a cardinal in all his grandeur, in the formal robes
appropriate to his station, splendid and rich, with his train in attend-
ance, having an altar erected on the stage, where he pretended to
make a prayer, organizing a procession; and then they produced him
in public with a harlot on his knee. They showed him giving poison
to one of his sisters, in a question of honour. Moreover he goes to war,
first laying down his cardinal's habit on the altar, with the help of his
chaplains, with great ceremoniousness; finally he has his sword bound
on and dons the soldier's sash with so much panache you could not
imagine it better done.[1] And all this was acted in condemnation of the
grandeur of the Church, which they despise and which in this kingdom
they hate to the death.

From London
7 February 1618

John Webster

Dedication of *The Duchess of Malfi* 1623

To the Right Honourable George Harding, Baron Berkeley,
of Berkeley Castle and Knight of the Order of the Bath to the
illustrious Prince Charles

My Noble Lord,
That I may present my excuse why, being a stranger to your Lordship, I offer this poem to your patronage, I plead this warrant: men,
who never saw the sea, yet desire to behold that regiment of waters,
choose some eminent river to guide them thither; and make that as it
were, their conduct,[2] or postilion. By the like ingenious means has
your fame arrived at my knowledge, receiving it from some of
worth, who both in contemplation, and practice, owe to your Honour their clearest[3] service. I do not altogether look up at your title,
the ancientest nobility, being but a relic of time past, and the truest
honour indeed being for a man to confer honour on himself, which

1 Act III scene iv of *The Duchess of Malfi* seems to be described here; and Act V
scene ii, if we may suppose that Busino confused Julia and the Duchess.
2 conductor
3 completely dedicated

your learning strives to propagate, and shall make you arrive at the dignity of a great example. I am confident this work is not unworthy your Honour's perusal for by such poems as this, poets have kissed the hands of great princes, and drawn their gentle eyes to look down upon their sheets of paper, when the poets themselves were bound up in their winding sheets. The like courtesy from your Lordship, shall make you live in your grave, and laurel spring out of it; when the ignorant scorners of the Muses (that like worms in libraries seem to live only to destroy learning) shall wither, neglected and forgotten. This work and myself I humbly present to your approved censure,[1] it being the utmost of my wishes, to have your honourable self my weighty and perspicuous comment: which grace so done me, shall ever be acknowledged

By your Lordship's in all duty and observance,

John Webster

Thomas Middleton, William Rowley and John Ford

Poems prefixed to *The Duchess of Malfi*   1623

In the just worth of that well deserver, Mr John Webster, and upon this masterpiece of tragedy

In this thou imitat'st one rich, and wise,
That sees his good deeds done before he dies;
As he by works, thou by this work of fame,
Hast well provided for thy living name;
To trust to others' honourings, is worth's crime –
Thy monument is rais'd in thy life-time;
And 'tis most just; for every worthy man
Is his own marble; and his merit can
Cut him to any figure, and express
More art, than Death's cathedral palaces,
Where royal ashes keep their court. Thy note
Be ever plainness, 'tis the richest coat:

1 tried judgement

Thy epitaph only the title be –
Write, *Duchess*, that will fetch a tear for thee,
For who e'er saw this *Duchess* live, and die,
That could get off under a bleeding eye?

In Tragaediam
Ut lux ex tenebris ictu percussa tonantis;
Illa, ruina malis, claris sit vita poetis.[1]

Thomas Middletonus
Poeta & Chron: Londinensis[2]

To his friend Mr John Webster upon his *Duchess of Malfi*

I never saw thy duchess till the day
That she was lively body'd in thy play;
Howe'er she answer'd her low-rated love,
Her brothers' anger did so fatal prove,
Yet my opinion is, she might speak more;
But never, in her life, so well before.

Wil. Rowley

To the reader of the author, and his *Duchess of Malfi*

Crown him a poet, whom nor Rome, nor Greece,
Transcend in all theirs, for a masterpiece:
In which, whiles words and matter change, and men
Act one another; he, from whose clear pen
They all took life, to memory hath lent
A lasting fame, to raise his monument.

John Ford

---

1 To Tragedy
As light is struck out of darkness at the blow of Jove, the thunderer,
So may it give life to famous poets and ruin their detractors.
2 *Chron: Londinensis* Chronologer of London (Middleton was appointed City Chronologer in 1620).

John Webster

Dedication of *The Devil's Law-Case*   1623

To the right worthy and all-accomplished gentleman, Sir Thomas Finch, Knight Baronet

Sir, let it not appear strange that I do aspire to your patronage. Things that taste of any goodness love to be sheltered near goodness. Nor do I flatter in this, which I hate; only touch at the original copy of your virtues. Some of my other works, as *The White Devil*, *The Duchess of Malfi*, *Guise* and others, you have formerly seen. I present this humbly to kiss your hands and to find your allowance. Nor do I much doubt it, knowing the greatest of the Caesars have cheerfully entertained less poems than this; And had I thought it unworthy I had not enquired after so worthy a patronage. Yourself I understand to be all courtesy. I doubt not therefore of your acceptance, but resolve that my election is happy. For which favour done me I shall ever rest

Your Worship's humbly devoted

John Webster

A[braham] W[right]

from a manuscript commonplace book   *c.* 1650

The Duchess of Malfi

A good play, especially for the plot at the latter end, otherwise plain. In his language he uses a little too much of scripture as in the first Act, speaking of a captain full of wounds, he says he [was] like the children of Ishmael [all in tents]. And which is against the laws of the scene, the business was two years a-doing, as may be perceived by the beginning of the third Act where Antonio has three children by the Duchess, when in the first Act he had but one [*sic*].

The White Devil

But an indifferent play to read, but for the presentments I believe good. The lines are too much rhyming.

The Devil's Law-Case

But an indifferent play. The plot is intricate enough, but if rightly
scanned will be found faulty by reason many passages do either not
hang together, or if they do it is so sillily that no man can perceive
them likely to be ever done.

Samuel Sheppard

On Mr Webster's Most Excellent Tragedy Called 'The White Devil',
from *Epigrams Theological, Philosophical and Romantic*   1651

We will no more admire Euripides,
Nor praise the tragic strains of Sophocles;
For why? Thou in this tragedy hast framed
All real worth that can in them be named.
How lively are thy persons fitted, and
How pretty are thy lines! Thy verses stand
Like unto precious jewels set in gold
And grace thy fluent prose. I once was told
By one well skilled in Arts he thought thy play
Was only worthy fame to bear away
From all before it. Brachiano's ill –
Murdering his Duchess hath by thy rare skill
Made him renowned, Flamineo such another –
The Devil's darling, murderer of his brother.
His part – most strange! – given him to act by thee
Doth gain him credit and not calumny.
Vittoria Corombona, that famed whore,
Desperate Lodovico weltering in his gore,
Subtle Francisco – all of them shall be
Gazed at as comets by posterity.
And thou meantime with never-withering bays
Shall crowned be by all that read thy lays.

Samuel Sheppard

from a manuscript poem, *The Fairy King*   1648–54

Webster the next, though not so much of note
Nor's name attended with such noise and crowd,
Yet by the Nine and by Apollo's vote,
Whose groves of bay are for his head allowed –
Most sacred spirit (some may say I dote),
Of thy three noble tragedies[1] be as proud
As great voluminous Jonson; thou shalt be
Read longer and with more applause than he.

(v vi 61 [fol. 66 v])

Samuel Pepys

from his diary   October 1661 to May 1669

2 October 1661: . . . we went to the Theatre, but coming late and sitting in an ill place I never had so little pleasure in a play in my life; yet it was the first time that ever I saw it – *Vittoria Corombona*. Methinks a very poor play.

4 October 1661: Then Captain Ferrers and I to the Theatre, and there came too late; so we stayed and saw a bit of *Vittoria* which pleased me worse than it did the other day. So we stayed not to see it out, and drank a bottle or two of China ale.

30 September 1662: . . . after dinner we took coach and to the Duke's playhouse, where we saw *The Duchess of Malfi* well performed, but Betterton and Ianthe[2] to perfection.

---

1 He may be thinking of *The White Devil*, *The Duchess of Malfi*, and the 'tragicomedy' *The Devil's Law-Case*; or he may be excluding the last, but adding the lost [tragedy] of *The Guise*.
2 Saunderson, subsequently Mrs Betterton.

2 November 1666: . . . and so home, I reading all the way to make end of the *Bondman* (which, the oftener I read, the more I like) and begun *The Duchess of Malfi* which seems a good play.

6 November 1666: . . . after dinner down alone by water to Deptford, reading *Duchess of Malfi* the play, which is pretty good.

25 November 1668: . . . my wife and I to the Duke of York's house to see *The Duchess of Malfi*, a sorry play; and sat with little pleasure for fear of my wife's seeing me look about.

12 May 1669: . . . my wife and I to the Duke of York's playhouse, and there, in the side balcony over against the music, did hear but not see, a new play, the first day acted, *The Roman Virgin* an old play and but ordinary I thought; but the trouble of my eyes with the light of the candles did almost kill me.

Lewis Theobald

from a letter to William Warburton   18 December 1731

I have applied my uneasy summer months upon the attempt of a tragedy. *Sit verbo venia!* I have a design upon the ladies' eyes as the passage to their pockets, if the town be not too depraved for any remains of sensation. And as I shall not in this enter upon any part of the preface I'll indulge myself in submitting a pair of soliloquies to you as a taste of my poor workmanship. I lay my scene in Italy. My heroine is a young widow duchess who has two haughty Spanish brothers that enjoin her not to marry again. She, however, clandestinely marries the Master of her Household on the morning I open my scene; and in the third Act I show her expecting her bridegroom's private approach to her. So much by way of argument.

Scene changes to the Duchess's bed-chamber. A bed seen and a table with papers. The Duchess is sitting undressed:

DUCHESS: How tedious is suspense that makes an hour
Move slow and heavy as a winter's night
When nights are longest! – I have strove, in vain,
By reading to beguile the lazy time;
But my unsteady eye and roving mind
Like two impatient restive travellers
Though bent the same way get the start by turns,
And will not keep each other company –
I know not what I read – What hideous noise?
It may be 'twas the melancholy bird
(The friend of silence and of solitude)
The owl, that screamed; or was it Fancy's coinage?
When once the soul's disturbed each little thing
Starts and alarms – the court's not yet at rest,
Or he would come – my breast is like a house
With many servants thronged, unruly all,
And all employed on tasks of differing natures;
Doubts, perturbations, thoughts of self-conviction,
Uncertain wishes and unquiet longings.
Debate the strife within – I've heard it said
Love mixed with fear is sweetest. I'm perhaps
Too much a coward, and that spoils my relish.

The next, dear Sir, is in the fourth Act. Her match is discovered;
her husband obliged to fly. One of her tyrannous brothers, a duke,
employs an agent to strangle her; and after the order given, I produce
him in the conflict betwixt Conscience and Remorse:

[*Enter Duke Ferdinand*]
FERDINAND: O sacred Innocence! that sweetly sleeps
On turtles' feathers whilst a guilty conscience
Makes all our slumbers worse than fev'rish dreams
When only monstrous forms disturb the brain.
'Tis a black register wherein is writ
All our good deeds and bad; a perspective
That shows us hell, more horrid than divines
Or poets know to paint it – Hark, what noise?
The screams of women ever and anon
Ring through my ears shrill as the Sabine cries

When Rome's bold sons rushed on their frighted virgins.
A thousand fancied horrors shake my soul
E'er since I dictated this deed of slaughter. –
There is no written evidence to proclaim
My order, and must coward apprehension
Give it a tongue? – The element of water
Drops from the clouds and sinks into the earth;
But blood flies upward and bedews the heavens. –
The wolf shall find her grave and scrape it up,
Not to devour the corse but to discover
The horrid murder. – Shall I let her live?
What says Revenge to that? – Or what says Nature?
Resentment preaches treason still to Virtue;
And to repent us of a blameful purpose
Is manly pious sorrow. – She shall live.

You see, my dear friend, I have feasted my own vanity at large: I wish
I may have consulted your entertainment in any proportion.

Lewis Theobald

from the Preface to *The Fatal Secret*   1735

The importunity of some friends whom I could no means disobey
has drawn from me the publication of this piece at a disadvantage . . .
Such was its fate . . . that, appearing at a season when the weather was
warm and the town in a political ferment, it was praised and forsaken;
and I had the choice comfort left me of hearing everybody wonder
that it was not supported . . . Though I called it *The Fatal Secret* I had
no intention of disguising from the public that (as my friend has confessed for me in the Prologue) John Webster had preceded me, above
a hundred years ago, in the same story. I have retained the names of
the characters in his *Duchess of Malfi*, adopted as much of his tale as I
conceived for my purpose, and as much of his writings as I could turn
to account without giving into too obsolete a diction. If I have borrowed Webster's matter freely I have taken it up on fair and open

credit, and hope I have repaid the principal with interest. I have no-where spared myself out of indolence; but have often engrafted his thoughts and language because I was conscious I could not so well supply them from my own fund. When I first read his scenes I found something singularly engaging in the passions, a mixture of the masculine and the tender which induced me to think of modernizing them. Another motive was that the distress of the tale was not fictitious but founded upon an authentic record. . . .

[Talks about Lope de Vega's *El Mayordomo de la Duquesa de Amalfi* (printed 1618) which he finds of little or no value.]

As to our countryman Webster, though I am to confess obligations to him I am not obliged to be blind to all his faults. He is not without his incidents of horror, almost as extravagant as those of the Spaniard. He had a strong and impetuous genius, but withal a most wild and undigested one; he sometimes conceived nobly but did not always express with clearness; and if he now and then soars handsomely he as often rises into regions of bombast; his conceptions were so eccentric that we are not to wonder why we cannot trace him. As for rules, he either knew them not or thought them too servile a restraint. Hence it is he skips over years and kingdoms with an equal liberty. It must be [admitted] the Unities were very sparingly observed at the time in which he wrote; however, when any poet travels too fast that the imagination of his spectators cannot keep pace with him, probability is put quite out of breath. Nor has he been less licentious in another respect: He makes mention of Galileo and Tasso, neither of whom were born till near half a century after the Duchess of Malfi was murdered.

Having been so free in characterizing the old bard, I may reasonably expect an inquisition into my own performance. But I am willing to be beforehand with censurers and allow all the faults they shall think fit to impute to it. What I have done is submitted to examination and I'll spare myself the odium of marking it out. If the piece has any praise it is, in my opinion, that it had power to draw tears from fair eyes. The poet who writes for the stage should principally aim at pleasing his female judges; for the best proof whether he can draw a distress is how far their nature and virtues are touched with his portrait.

Philip Frowde

from the Prologue to Lewis Theobald's *The Fatal Secret* 1735

An ancient bard a century ago
Chose out this tale of soft pathetic woe.
Then, as they say, beaux could attention keep,
And injured virtue force the Fair to weep.
He who could stir the passions knew no fears;
Sincere applause still crowned him with their tears.
Tonight's advent'rer the same powers would show
And tries his strength in Webster's nervous[1] bow.
Why should he then despair, since this his aim?
Nature should be in every age the same . . .
A waste uncultivated soil he found
O'er-run with weeds; yet in the fertile ground
Some flowers, almost impervious to the view
Fragrant and fair irregularly grew.
These was the modern's labour to display
In comely order, opened to the day;
With decent grace, arranged before your eyes,
He bids them in their genuine lustre rise.
The rude old bard, if critic laws he knew,
From a too warm imagination drew,
And scorning rule should his free soul confine
Nor Time nor Place observed in his design.
This wild luxuriance our chaste Muse restrains,
Binds him indeed, but 'tis with friendly chains . . .

If yet some taste for tragedy remains,
To you, ye fair, are meant the coming scenes.
Should your full eyes in soft compassion flow,
Your breasts with gen'rous indignation glow,
The fair example shall instruct the age
And banish farce and folly from the stage.

1 Strung with sinews.

Part Two The Developing Debate

Introduction

Neither Tate's nor Theobald's rewritings of Webster's tragedies succeeded in giving them new theatrical life; and the period which follows marks the lowest ebb of Webster's reputation. Though series like Dodsley's *Old Plays* (1744) were beginning the work of making the early drama available to the reader, only *The White Devil* was reprinted. On the other hand the second half of the eighteenth century was a notable period of antiquarian research into Shakespeare's contemporaries. Scholars like Malone, Steevens, and Capell were busy glossing, illustrating, and emending the text of Shakespeare, and were reading through whole libraries of Tudor and Stuart literature. So they knew the plays of Webster. But they were not interested in them for their own sake. Capell in his *The School of Shakespeare* (1783) – the third volume of his *Notes to Shakespeare* – prints the Preface to *The White Devil* and a number of short passages which contain words or meanings of a Shakespearian cast. Webster is present, but only as note-fodder. None the less it must be pointed out that the large collections of Elizabethan books that such men assembled formed the basis of the modern major libraries' holdings. Passing into the public libraries of London and Oxford and Cambridge, their texts provided the material on which much subsequent work depended. As Charles Lamb pointed out in the Preface to his *Specimens*:

More than a third part of the following specimens are from plays which are to be found only in the British Museum and in some scarce private libraries.

Praise for restoring Webster's plays to critical as against antiquarian appreciation lies, in fact, where it has always been supposed to lie – with Charles Lamb, in his *Specimens of the English Dramatic Poets* (1808). Lamb's book is, in some senses, an apologia for Romantic poetry. As he says in the Preface:

I have sought after ... scenes of passion, sometimes of the

deepest quality, interesting situations, serious descriptions, that
which is more nearly allied to poetry than to wit, and to tragic
rather than to comic poetry . . . My leading design has been to
illustrate what may be called the moral sense of our ancestors,
to show in what manner they felt when they placed themselves
by the power of imagination in trying situations, in the conflicts
of duty and passion.

The relationship of these aims to the view of poetry expressed by
Wordsworth in the Preface to *The Lyrical Ballads* should be noticed.
Lamb is anxious to restore to the reader of English poetry his lost
heritage of passionate and intensely individualized verse. He seeks
(like Hazlitt after him) to discriminate between the old dramatists
and modern theatrical experience, between wild and irregular but
'natural' genius and the artificial 'taste' or 'wit' introduced by
Dryden. It follows inevitably, though we do not think it was any
part of the original intention, that Webster and his contemporaries
come to be read as poets rather than playwrights. At the very
least their capacities are seen as criticisms of the contemporary
theatre; but it was probably more important that they should be
seen as symptoms of the Romantic vision.

It is worth noticing that the association of these dramatists with
the Romantic vision can operate outside England. Stendhal had in
his journalism indicated a general acquaintance with 'the old
English dramatists who were the predecessors and contemporaries
of the bard of Avon'; he made the general point that 'the English
know better than the French how to write tragedies which reveal
the depths of the human heart, which raise terror and excite all
the passions'. He displays his acquaintance with Webster (with
Lamb's Webster at the least) by using a passage from *The White
Devil* (Cornelia mourning for Marcello) as an epigraph to Chapter 31
   Armance (1827).
of Stendhal's *espagnolisme* is not unrelated to the anti-French slant

that an anonymous writer in the *European Magazine* for 1820 gives
to the revival of the old dramatists. The defence of the Elizabethans
is a defence against French taste (especially Voltaire's), a revival
of the genuine English genius. This article, like most in the period,
is largely taken up with extracts (all from *The White Devil* in this
case) linked by a brief commentary. The author admires especially –
and it is generally admired in the period – the interview between
Isabella and Brachiano (II i). The saintly virtues of a good wife
elicit powerful proto-Victorian approval. He does not quote the
Arraignment of Vittoria, because Lamb had already quoted it; but
clearly it is for him as for Lamb one of the great moments in the
play. Cornelia's dirge (v iv 95–111) appears here, however, as well
as in Lamb. Presumably it seemed too good to lose.

The author of the *European Magazine* article avoids questions of
structure on the whole, and the mode of the article allows this
very conveniently. 'The irregularity of the fable, the rapid change
of scene' etc. are mentioned, but not dwelt upon. This is true of
most periodical comments of the period. 'H.M.' (John Wilson)
writing a series of 'Analytical Essays on the Early English Dramatists'
devotes section v (published in *Blackwood's Magazine* in 1818) to
The White Devil (*the* Webster play at this time). He tells us that

This play is so disjointed in its action – the incidents are so capricious and so involved – and there is, throughout, such a
mixture of the horrible and the absurd – the comic and the
tragic – the pathetic and the ludicrous – that we find it impossible within our narrow limits to give anything like a complete
and consistent analysis of it.

But the rest of the essay ignores the valuations implied in this
paragraph. 'Few scenes in dramatic poetry surpass the following in
pathos' he says of Cornelia's mourning for the dead Marcello. The
pathos or the passion of short passages evidently creates a value
on its own account; and on this account Webster is valuable

enough to be worth reading. The anonymous author of 'Webster's Plays' in the *Retrospective Review* for 1823 seems able to dissolve even the 'structural faults' in his enthusiasm for individual scenes. 'Webster's plays', he tells us, 'are much better calculated for representation than most of our early dramas.' It would have been interesting to hear the proofs of this unusual statement; alas, none is offered.

The first flush of enthusiasm for the Elizabethans having faded, interest in Webster seems to languish. The plays had, however, been made more generally available. *The Ancient British Drama* reprinted *The Duchess of Malfi* in 1810; and in 1815 Dilke printed *Appius and Virginia* in his *Old English Plays*. Finally in 1830 came the Revd Alexander Dyce's *The Works of John Webster* – the standard text for the next hundred years. But the next phase of critical interest seems to arise from the theatre rather than the study. Samuel Phelps became licensee of the Sadler's Wells theatre in 1844, determined to 'offer an entertainment selected from the finest stock dramas in the world'. He staged many plays by the old dramatists, among them *The Duchess of Malfi* 'reconstructed for stage representation by Richard Hengist Horne' and performed on 20 November 1850. Horne's Preface and Prologue are full of interest and are printed below (pp. 58–60). His rewriting of the play, which is remarkably thorough, is worth sustained study. Above all he is concerned to tighten up connexions and motivations and to prune away the violent or 'offensive' particularity of the scattered passions and relationships with which the original play was crowded. Thus Julia (now Giuseppa) is bowdlerized into a minor instrument of the Cardinal's plot against the Duchess (now called Marina). Motives are supplied with startling explicitness:

BOSOLA: The provisorship o'th' horse. 'Tis a good place;
But evil in the earning. Why should this duke
Turn pale with passion at the very thought

Of's sister's second marriage? He is lord
Of Tarragona – hath a great estate
In Old Castile – a dukedom in Calabria –
And covets he succession of this duchy
Of Malfi? – [*pauses*] No; 'tis something in his blood
Of monstrous pride that would not have her wed
Save by his choosing. 'Tis not my affair.
So to my task.   [*Exit*]

The Cardinal is given a similar and parallel motivation in a speech
placed in the scene with Julia (II iv):

The great prince Malateste, who so lately
Hath made proposals to him: 'tis a choice
In all ways suited to me. Rich in lands –
Nobly descended – very old – 'tis certain
The prince's death will give large 'heritance
Which I may make my own, because the Duchess
Cares not for wealth . . .

Even the torments of Act IV (such as remain) are no longer
fantastic imaginings of Hell, but well-thought-out political courses.
The madmen are so placed that those who hear them will think that
the howling comes from the mad duchess, whose estate thus falls
into the administration of her brother. The labyrinth of plans and
accidents that fills Act V is sorted out into an easier progression;
and the memory of the dead duchess is dwelt upon to link this Act
to the preceding ones. The end may be quoted:

  [*The body of* ANTONIO *is carried in*]
FERDINAND [*bending forward*]: I must look closer at that
    sleeping man.   [*They assist him forward*]
His face is paler than the waxen mould
My sister once did stare at through her tears;

And I do seem to breed strange memories
Of passion and of sorrow in my brain,
Where thunder lately echoed.   [*He kneels beside the body*]
                    Shifting mists
Thicken between us. Poor Antonio –
A damp and heavy earth lies on our hearts –
The frost doth take our knees, so that I pray,

                                        [*Taking* ANTONIO'*s hand*]
But cannot rise – my thoughts lose government
And have no meaning – but stray all forlorn,
Seeking forgiveness – till some weeping ghost
Melt us into itself. Marina calls!   [*He dies*]

What we are left with is a tidy corpse of a play, disembowelled of all
the splendours and mysteries that give it vitality, written in a clear
but unresonant verse that some critics thought better than Webster's.
Indeed G. H. Lewes thought that Horne was wasting his time tinker-
ing with Webster; he should be using his genius to write his own
better plays.

   Horne's version made *The Duchess of Malfi* attractive to a
number of Victorian actresses; but it was superseded in 1860 or so
by another adaptation, which referred back to the 1850 production
but offered in fact quite a different text. This is printed in
Cumberland's Acting Plays as 'adapted from John Webster' and
'printed from the acting copy', and it is quite clear from the
Preface (p. 64) that D. – G. [George Daniel] who wrote the Preface
was also responsible for the adaptation. Daniel's version was
reprinted (without acknowledgement) in *Dick's British Drama*
(number 350, printed about 1883), which claims on the title-page
to be 'the original complete edition' and 'as revived at Sadler's
Wells theatre, 20 November 1850'. The truth lies somewhere
between these two falsehoods: Daniel's version is a cross between
Horne and the original, with a few novelties of its own. Thus where

Horne preserved Ferdinand's lycanthropy Daniel's version changes
this to 'hypocondriacism'; and where Webster's doctor says

> ... they imagine
> Themselves to be transformed into wolves
> (v ii 10–11)

Daniel's version has

> ... they imagine
> Themselves the sports of all sorts of maladies.

The dead man's hand, however – deleted by Horne – is returned to
the scene. In both versions the Duchess is strangled off-stage (as,
later, in Poel), but in both she *rushes suddenly out with the cord about
her neck and falls at* [BOSOLA'S] *feet in the agonies of death* (Daniel)
or *re-enters and falling in the centre of the stage utters the word 'Mercy'
and dies* (Horne).

The most damaging effect produced by these Victorian versions
is the loss of specific weight in the language. Few of the physical
details with which Webster's text is loaded survive the pruning
knife. Sometimes there is a moral objection to vivid physical fact
(like Bosola's account of the Duchess's pregnant 'longings');
sometimes there seems to be stylistic objection to what Dr Johnson
called 'low' terms. Thus where the original has 'Shall I die like a
leveret', Horne changes this to 'Shall I be slain like some dumb
animal'.

The reviews of Phelps's 1850 production, leaving on one side the
nature of the text involved, raise at once what was to remain one of
the two central issues in nineteenth-century criticism of Webster.
There is throughout the century (and into the next) a line of poets
and poetry-fanciers who see Webster as a great explorer of the
human soul and of the mystery of the world's iniquity –
Swinburne, Rupert Brooke, T. S. Eliot, Allen Tate all bear witness
to the pressure of Webster's poetic imagination. For Swinburne, as

for so many Victorian critics, an appreciation of Webster presents itself in the form of a comparison with Shakespeare; and Swinburne finds Webster closest of all to Shakespeare in his power of projecting personal attitudes like 'height of heroic scorn', 'dignity of quiet cynicism', 'deep sincerity of cynic meditation and self-contemptuous mournfulness'. This concern with the ethical attitudes of the author frees Swinburne from any need to talk about structure. He alleges that Webster's 'fame assuredly does not depend upon the merit of a casual passage here or there', but he does not try to prove this. After all his book is dedicated to the memory of Charles Lamb.

On the other side from the poets are the theatrical critics, who can only see ramshackle structure and improbable accidents. Every new production seemed to throw up new enemies for Webster; but the most implacable proved to be William Archer, the friend of Shaw, the translator of Ibsen and the editor of G. H. Lewes. Lewes had suggested that the resuscitation of the Elizabethan dramatists was an impediment in the way of theatrical advance. It is hard to know what he had in mind in 1850. Archer takes precisely the same line and it is easy to see what he means. The 'new drama' of Ibsen and Shaw can only win through to public acceptance if the public (and its literary mentors) are disabused of their unhealthy attachment to the 'old drama' in the mode of Shakespeare. 'Good plays' are for Archer of one kind only, obeying what he calls 'rational canons of dramatic construction'; they have to be well made, with believable characters acting in coherently motivated ways (which reflect the ways of real life), moving step by step towards rationally developed conclusions.

Poel's production of *The Duchess of Malfi* on 21 October 1892 was sponsored by the Independent Theatre Society, which was to promote many of the early London performances of Ibsen and Shaw. Archer was quick to point out the folly of this particular venture; and when the play was next performed – by the Phoenix

Society in November 1919 – his pen was already charged with vitriol:

The long-delayed reaction against the cult of the lesser Eliza-bethans ... is being powerfully promoted by the activities of the Phoenix Society ... The privilege of listening to its occa-sional beauties of diction was felt to be dearly bought at the price of enduring three hours of coarse and sanguinary melo-drama.

Finally he gathered together his views on 'the old drama and the new' and in the book of that title (1923) he had a final fling at the 'barbarous violence of effect' in Webster and his fellows and at the 'passage worship' of Lamb and Swinburne. He reprints with a few changes his 1920 essay on the Phoenix Society production. It is not clear why Shaw and Archer exempted Shakespeare himself from their strictures. Shaw says, 'Shakespear survives by what he has in common with Ibsen and not by what he has in common with Webster and the rest' (*The Quintessence of Ibsenism*, 1891). One feels that the 'Shakespear' who survived on these terms had lost more than his final 'e'. Certainly Shaw can find no words bad enough for his contemporaries, who are not to be saved by any diminution, however extraordinary:

What Shakespear got from his 'school' was the insane and hideous rhetoric which is all that he has in common with Jonson, Webster and the whole crew of insufferable bunglers and dullards whose work stands out as vile even at the begin-ning of the seventeenth century ... plays that have no ray of noble feeling, no touch of faith, beauty or even common kind-ness in them from beginning to end.
                    (*Our Theatres in the Nineties*, vol. II, 130–31)

Or again:

When one thinks of the donnish insolence and perpetual thick-skinned swagger of Chapman over his unique achievements in sublime balderdash, and the opacity that prevented Webster, the Tussaud laureate, from appreciating his own stupidity – when one thinks of the whole rabble of dehumanized specialists in elementary blank verse posing as the choice and master spirits . . . it is hard to keep ones critical blood cold enough to discriminate in favor of any Elizabethan whatever.

(vol. III, 317)

The other clearly marked dispute about Webster in the nineteenth century can be seen to be related to the one we have just looked at, but it centres on moral rather than theatrical categories (not that moral assumptions are far below the surface in Archer and Shaw). The first blow struck was struck powerfully by that muscular Christian, Canon Charles Kingsley. He published in the *North British Review* for 1856 an article called 'Plays and Puritans' which reviewed various modern attempts to revive the Elizabethan dramatists (including Dyce's *Webster*) (see below, p. 61). Kingsley revives against these the objections to 'licentious drama' made by Elizabethan puritans; he declares these to represent what was then and is still the only possible moral position. The plays as they are printed may be 'poetry' in the limited sense of containing anthology pieces, but in any larger consideration they are bound to reveal the barbarous origins and the undisciplined brutality of the audience to which they originally appealed. The claim that their exhibitions of vice may deter the would-be vicious is dismissed as cant:

As the staple interest of the comedies is dirt, so the staple interest of the tragedies is crime. Revenge, hatred, villany, incest and murder upon murder are their constant themes, and (with the exception of Shakespeare, Ben Jonson in his earlier plays and perhaps Massinger) they handle these horrors with little or no moral purpose, save that of exciting and amusing the audience

... We do not know of a complaint against the School of
Balzac and Dumas which will not equally apply to the average
tragedy of the whole period preceding the civil wars.

Kingsley's morality is related to Archer's Ibsenism (though in all
other respects the two men are poles apart) in the importance
both men attach to a literal idea of 'truth' in a play, in the distrust
of poetry they both display and in their desire to have 'real people'
on the stage. And if the defence of conventional morality goes
hand-in-hand on the one side with realistic stagecraft, on the other
side the praise of poetry is joined to a feeling for irrational and
bizarre forms of life as revelations of important truths. Webster's
concentration on what J. A. Symonds calls 'the essential qualities of
diseased and guilty human nature' seems to these men to be more
than mere morbidity or a flair for the commercial advantages of
Grand Guignol. The fascination that the Jacobeans exerted over a
Romantic poet like T. L. Beddoes is an early symptom of the
extent to which a taste for German Gothic fantasies and for the
Jacobean macabre could unite. The later admiration for the plays of
Webster, Tourneur, and Ford expressed by the theatrical theorist
Antonin Artaud (though outside the chronological limits of this
section), may be cited to indicate the nourishment for Romantic
agony that the Jacobeans continued to provide, well into the present
century. The revival of interest in the early dramatists noticeable in
the last quarter of the nineteenth century must be associated with
the anti-Victorian or decadent strain in the literary life of the time.
Swinburne, J. A. Symonds, Havelock Ellis, Vernon Lee (Violet
Paget) are critics for whom the exploration of past decadence is a
liberation from the present and a means of justifying their own
tastes. Renaissance Italy provided for scholars like Symonds or
Vernon Lee a mode of evoking and appreciating the world of
Webster's tragedies which avoided both technical and structural
questions about his stagecraft and mere passage worship. In these

terms one could say that Webster's vision was true not simply
because he had made it into poetry, but because (in the language
Lucas is still drawing on in 1927) it really happened; 'read the
history of the time'. This is the line that Poel takes, defending his
1892 production against the attacks of William Archer (see below,
p. 85). Vernon Lee denies (as does Symonds) that Renaissance Italy
was really like the Italy of Webster and Tourneur. None the less her
writings show that Renaissance Italy and Jacobean tragedies offered
the same escape from a modern Northern world of rigid morality,
cleanliness, and progress:

Old palaces, almost strongholds, and which are still inhabited
by those too poor to pull them down and build some plastered
bandbox instead; poems and prose tales written or told five
hundred years ago, edited and re-edited by printers to whom
there come no modern poems or prose tales worth editing instead; half-pagan, medieval priest lore, believed in by men and
women who have not been given anything to believe instead;
easy-going, all-permitting fifteenth-century scepticism not yet
replaced by the scientific and socialistic disbelief which is puri-
tanic and iconoclastic; sly and savage habits of vengeance still
doing service among the lower classes instead of the orderly
chicanery of modern justice.

But it is not simply a matter of judging that these things really
happened, or didn't. The Italy in the mind of Webster, or in the
mind of Vernon Lee, only has imaginative validity if it represents
a permanent (though perhaps hidden) condition of the mind.
Webster's fantastic world perhaps had to be called Italian in his own
day; and perhaps it was easiest for Victorians to think of its
un-Victorian qualities in Italian terms; but today the fantastic hardly
needs these geographical palliatives. It is perhaps no accident that
Havelock Ellis moved from Jacobean drama to psychopathology.
Certainly it should be noticed that the bestialities of war seem to

make Webster's worlds more generally credible. Part Three contains
Edmund Wilson's reaction to the production of *The Duchess of
Malfi* he met while touring the ruins of Europe (p. 150). F. L. Lucas's
introduction to his great edition is much concerned with the
relationship of Webster's theatrical horrors to the real horrors he
had lived through in the time of the Somme or Passchendaele. The
war-shadowed sensibility of T. S. Eliot's early poems reflects the
same combination of elements – the Jacobean poets, the final
collapse of the Victorian cultural and moral tradition in the Great
War, and the new Websterian landscapes of the inner life of man
and of society documented by Freud and Marx.

Charles Lamb

from a letter to William Hazlitt   November 1805

You send me a modern quotation poetical. How do you like this in an old play? Vittoria Corombona, a spunky Italian lady, a Leonardo one, nick-named the White Devil, being on her trial for murder etc. – and questioned about seducing a duke from his wife and the State, makes answer:

Condemn you me for that the duke did love me?
So may you blame some fair and crystal river
For that some melancholic distracted man
Hath drown'd himself in't.

(III ii 203–6)

Charles Lamb

'A Note on "The Arraignment of Vittoria" (*The White Devil*, III ii)', *Specimens of the English Dramatic Poets Who Lived about the Time of Shakespeare*   1808

This White Devil of Italy sets off a bad cause so speciously, and pleads with such an innocence-resembling boldness, that we seem to see that matchless beauty of her face which inspires such gay confidence into her; and are ready to expect, when she has done her pleadings, that her very judges, her accusers, the grave ambassadors who sit as spectators, and all the court, will rise and make proffer to defend her in spite of the utmost conviction of her guilt; as the shepherds in Don Quixote make proffer to follow the beautiful shepherdess Marcela 'without reaping any profit out of her manifest resolution made there in their hearing'.

So sweet and lovely does she make the shame,
Which, like a canker in the fragrant rose,
Does spot the beauty of her budding name!

Charles Lamb

'A Note on Cornelia's Dirge (*The White Devil*, v iv 95 ff)', *Specimens of the English Dramatic Poets Who Lived about the Time of Shakespeare* 1808

I never saw anything like this Dirge, except the Ditty which reminds Ferdinand of his drowned father in *The Tempest*. As that is of the water, watery; so this is of the earth, earthy. Both have that intenseness of feeling, which seems to resolve itself into the elements which it contemplates.

Charles Lamb

'A Note on *The Duchess of Malfi* (IV ii)', *Specimens of the English Dramatic Poets Who Lived about the Time of Shakespeare* 1808

All the several parts of the dreadful apparatus with which the Duchess's death is ushered in, are not more remote from the conceptions of ordinary vengeance, than the strange character of suffering which they seem to bring upon their victims is beyond the imagination of ordinary poets. As they are not like inflictions *of this life*, so her language seems *not of this world*. She has lived among horrors till she is become 'native and endowed unto that element'. She speaks the dialect of despair, her tongue has a snatch of Tartarus and the souls in bale. – What are 'Luke's iron crown', the brazen bull of Perillus, Procrustes' bed, to the waxen images which counterfeit death, to the wild masque of madmen, the tomb-maker, the bellman, the living person's dirge, the mortification by degrees! To move a horror skilfully, to touch a soul to the quick, to lay upon fear as much as it can bear, to wean and weary a life till it is ready to drop, and then step in with mortal instruments to take its last forfeit – this only a Webster can do. Writers of an inferior genius may 'upon horror's head horrors accumulate', but they cannot do this. They mistake quantity for quality, they 'terrify babes with painted devils', but they know not how a soul is capable of being moved; their terrors want dignity, their affrightments are without decorum.

George Darley

from a letter to Allan Cunningham   22 May 1831

Have you ever read Webster? Why, my good sir! there are passages in *Vittoria Corombona* almost worthy of the Angel Gabriel. Don't mind what Campbell says – his criticism upon this author is nearly as strong evidence against his own poetical genius as the *Pleasures of Hope* is in favour of it. There are passages in that play every whit as good as – No! deuce take it, that would be too bad! – but every bit as good as – damn it! that won't do either! – Well, Shakespeare and Milton excepted, there is poetry in Webster *superior* to that of any other English author. If you have not *The White Devil* by heart, get it.

R. H. Horne

Preface to his edition of *The Duchess of Malfi, Reconstructed for Stage Representation*   1850

When I first conceived the idea of bringing *The Duchess of Malfi* upon the modern stage, I thought that a considerable reduction of its length, by the erasure of a number of unnecessary scenes, and a little revision of certain objectionable passages, would be nearly sufficient. But, before I had got half through the first act, the futility of such a course became sufficiently apparent. Still I hope to accomplish the task, with due reverence to a work which I considered the most powerful of any tragedy not in Shakespeare, and equal in *that* quality even to him. For, if the two chief elements of tragic power be terror and pity, assuredly both of these are carried to the highest degree in *The Duchess of Malfi*.

The more, however, I examined the structure of the tragedy the more manifest did it become, that the only way to render it available to the stage must be that of re-constructing the whole, cutting away all that could not be used, and filling up the gaps and chasms.

Nor was this all that it required. The contradictions, incongruities, and oversights were of a kind that exceeded anything I had previously conjectured. In truth, until I came to scrutinize the scenes thus closely, I had overlooked these discrepancies as well as the author, and others have done. Let me give an instance. Antonio sends off his friend Delio, post-haste to Rome on a service of most vital importance; and the next time they meet on Delio's return, Antonio has forgotten all about it. Again: after the Duchess (in Act IV, Scene i, of the original) has seen, as she believes, her children lying dead in their shrouds – she, in the very next scene, has entirely forgotten this, and gives precise and affecting maternal directions concerning them both, as if they were alive. Several other extraordinary instances might be mentioned, but it would only confuse the mind between the two versions, to specify them, and answer no good purpose.

It hence became apparent that if this great tragedy was to be ex-humed from its comparative obscurity, by representation on the stage, all the characters must be made consistent with themselves, and all the events proper to them – all the parts must be made coherent – and all this be built with direct relationship to the whole, and direct tendency to the final results. Yet, amidst all this the great scenes must be religi-ously preserved, or I should do worse than nothing, and produce a weak and sacrilegious deformity. What I have, therefore, sought to do, is as though a grand old abbey – haunted, and falling into decay – stood before me, and I had undertaken to re-construct it anew with as much of its own materials as I could use – asking pardon for the rest – but preserving almost entire its majestic halls and archways, its loftiest turrets, its most secret and solemn chambers, where the soul, in its hours of agony, uplifted its voice to God.

Writing this Preface the night before performance, when no one can have certain knowledge of the effect of tragic scenes so awful, and others so new to the stage, I am anxious to record that I do not doubt but this tragedy of Webster's will be worthily acted at Sadler's Wells, not only by Mr Phelps, Miss Glyn, and Mr Bennett, but by all princi-pals and seconds in the performance. Be the result what it may, my cordial acknowledgments are due to the careful assiduity, the un-wearied energy, and watchfulness with which a tragedy, so long highly honoured in dramatic literature, has been placed by Mr Phelps upon the stage – to the pains taken by each performer in the rehearsals – and though I name Mr T. L. Greenwood last, he stands foremost in his appreciation of the present version of *The Duchess of Malfi*.

In this edition, printed from the prompter's copy, most of the acting directions are allowed to remain, with a view to render the numerous stage difficulties less onerous to future managers.

R. H. Horne

Prologue to *The Duchess of Malfi*   1850

The sun himself, his planets and his peers,
Circling some vaster centre of all spheres:
All *these* again in harmony combine –
Moving for ever, somewhere – by design!

The tree that hath no hope can bear no fruit:
Must stars come down to teach the oak its root?
Show how eternal nature in the earth
From light and air claims a perennial birth;
That while the heart of man remains the same,
The Drama bears within a constant flame,
Ready to light our progress, onward ever,
When *truth* and *power* combine in that endeavour;
Ready to re-illume its ancient stories,
And weave its brow with *new* and lasting glories!

In our fresh period vigourous life requires
More solid food for its exalting fires;
Great passions – doings – sufferings, great hopes still,
To urge us up the steep and thorny hill,
Where genius, science, liberty, combined,
Give lasting empire to the advancing mind.
Wherefore, tonight, we bring the inspiring themes
Of great, old Webster, – clad in whose strong beams
We venture forth on the uplifted sea
Of his invention's high-wrought poesy,
Steering to reach the storm-rent beacon tower,
Trusting his hand – and with full faith in power.

Charles Kingsley

[Webster's Weaknesses] from 'Plays and Puritans', *North British Review*, vol. 25   1856

Look, then, at Webster's two masterpieces, *Vittoria Corombona* and *The Duchess of Malfi*. A few words spent on them will surely not be wasted; for they are pretty generally agreed to be the best tragedies written since Shakespeare's time.

The whole story of *Vittoria Corombona* is one of sin and horror. The subject-matter of the play is altogether made up of the fiercest and the basest passions. But the play is not a study of those passions from which we may gain a great insight into human nature. There is no trace – nor is there, again, in *The Duchess of Malfi* – of that development of human souls for good or evil, which is Shakespeare's especial power – the power which, far more than any accidental 'beauties', makes his plays, to this day, the delight alike of the simple and the wise, while his contemporaries are all but forgotten. The highest aim of dramatic art is to exhibit the development of the human soul; to construct dramas in which the conclusion shall depend, not on the events, but on the characters; and in which the characters shall not be mere embodiments of a certain passion, or a certain 'humour': but persons, each unlike all others; each having a destiny of his own by virtue of his own peculiarities, and of his own will; and each proceeding toward that destiny as he shall conquer, or yield to, circumstances; unfolding his own strength and weakness before the eyes of the audience: and that in such a way, that, after his first introduction, they should be able (in proportion to their knowledge of human nature) to predict his conduct under those circumstances. This is indeed 'high art': but we find no more of it in Webster than in the rest. His characters, be they old or young, come on the stage ready-made, full grown, and stereotyped; and therefore, in general, they are not characters at all, but mere passions or humours in human form. Now and then he essays to draw a character: but it is analytically, by description, not synthetically and dramatically, by letting the man exhibit himself in action; and in *The Duchess of Malfi* he falls into the great mistake of telling, by Antonio's mouth, more about the Duke and the Cardinal than he afterwards makes them act. Very different is Shakespeare's method of giving, at the outset, some single delicate hint about his personages, which will serve as a clue to their whole future conduct; thus 'showing the whole in each part', and stamping each man with a personality, to a degree which no other dramatist has ever approached.

But the truth is, the study of human nature is not Webster's aim. He has to arouse terror and pity, not thought, and he does it in his own way, by blood and fury, madmen and screech-owls, not without a rugged power. There are scenes of his, certainly, like that of Vittoria's trial, which have been praised for their delineation of character: but it is one thing to solve the problem, which Shakespeare has so handled in *Lear*, *Othello*, and *Richard III* – 'Given a mixed character, to show how he may become criminal', and to solve Webster's 'Given a ready-made criminal, to show how he commits his crimes'. To us the knowledge of character shown in Vittoria's trial scene is not an insight into Vittoria's essential heart and brain, but a general acquaintance with the conduct of all bold bad women when brought to bay. Poor Elia, who knew the world from books, and human nature principally from his own loving and gentle heart, talks of Vittoria's 'innocence-resembling boldness'[1] and 'seeming to see that matchless beauty of her face, which inspires such gay confidence in her', and so forth.

Perfectly just and true, not of Vittoria merely, but of the average of bad young women in the presence of a police magistrate: yet amounting in all merely to this, that the strength of Webster's confest master-scene lies simply in intimate acquaintance with vicious nature in general. We will say no more on this matter; save to ask, *Cui bono?* Was the art of which this was the highest manifestation likely to be of much use to mankind, much less able to excuse its palpably disgusting and injurious accompaniments?

The Duchess of Malfi is certainly in a purer and loftier strain: but in spite of the praise which has been lavished on her, we must take the liberty to doubt whether the poor Duchess is a 'person' at all. General goodness and beauty, intense though pure affection for a man below her in rank, and a will to carry out her purpose at all hazards, are not enough to distinguish her from thousands of other women: but Webster has no such purpose. What he was thinking and writing of

1 C. Lamb, *Specimens of English Dramatic Poets*, p. 229. From which specimens, be it remembered, he has had to expunge not only all the comic scenes, but generally the greater part of the plot itself, to make the book at all tolerable.

was, not truth, but effect; not the Duchess, but her story; not her brothers, but their rage; not Antonio, her major-domo and husband, but his good and bad fortunes; and thus he has made Antonio merely insipid, the brothers merely unnatural, and the Duchess (in the critical moment of the play) merely forward. That curious scene, in which she acquaints Antonio with her love for him, and makes him marry her, is, on the whole, painful. Webster himself seems to have felt that it was so; and, dreading lest he had gone too far, to have tried to redeem the Duchess at the end by making her break down in two exquisite lines of loving shame: but he has utterly forgotten to explain or justify her love, by giving to Antonio (as Shakespeare would probably have done) such strong specialties of character as would compel, and therefore excuse, his mistress's affection. He has plenty of time to do this in the first scenes – time which he wastes on irrelevant matter; and all that we gather from them is that Antonio is a worthy and thoughtful person. If he gives promise of being more, he utterly disappoints that promise afterwards. In the scene in which the Duchess tells her love, he is far smaller, rather than greater, than the Antonio of the opening scene: though (as there) altogether passive. He hears his mistress's declaration just as any other respectable youth might; is exceedingly astonished, and a good deal frightened; has to be talked out of his fears till one naturally expects a revulsion on the Duchess's part into something like scorn or shame (which might have given a good opportunity for calling out sudden strength in Antonio): but so busy is Webster with his business of drawing mere blind love, that he leaves Antonio to be a mere puppet, whose worthiness we are to believe in only from the Duchess's assurance to him that he is the perfection of all that a man should be; which, as all lovers are of the same opinion the day before the wedding, is not of much importance.

Neither in his subsequent misfortunes does Antonio make the least struggle to prove himself worthy of his mistress's affection. He is very resigned, and loving, and so forth. To win renown by great deeds, and so prove his wife in the right to her brothers and all the world, never crosses his imagination. His highest aim (and that only at last) is slavishly to entreat pardon from his brothers-in-law, for the mere offence of marrying their sister; and he dies by an improbable accident, the same pious and respectable insipidity which he has lived – 'ne valant pas la peine qui se donne pour lui'. The prison-scenes between the Duchess and her tormentors are painful enough, if to give pain be a dramatic virtue; and she appears in them really noble; and might have appeared far more so, had Webster taken half as much pains with her as he has with the madmen, ruffians, ghosts, and screech-owls in which his heart really delights. The only character really worked out, so as to live and grow under his hand, is Bosola, who, of course, is the villain of the piece, and being a rough fabric, is easily manufactured with rough tools. Still, Webster has his wonderful touches here and there –

CARIOLA: Hence, villains, tyrants, murderers! alas!
What will you do with my lady? call for help!
DUCHESS: To whom? to our next neighbours? they are mad folk . . .
Farewell, Cariola . . .
I pray thee, look thou giv'st my little boy
Some syrup for his cold, and let the girl
Say her prayers ere she sleep. – Now, what you please –
What death?
                                        (IV ii 196–206)

And so the play ends, as does *Vittoria Corombona*, with half-a-dozen murders *coram populo*, howls, despair, bedlam and the shambles; putting the reader marvellously in mind of that well-known old book of the same era, Reynold's *God's Revenge*, in which, with all due pious horror and bombastic sermonizing, the national appetite for abominations is duly fed with some fifty unreadable Spanish histories, French histories, Italian histories, and so forth, one or two of which, of course, are known to have furnished subjects for the playwrights of the day.
                                        (48–53)

George Daniel (anonymously)

Preface to '*The Duchess of Malfi*', *a Tragedy in Five Acts, Adapted from John Webster* ?1860

The present adaptation of *The Duchess of Malfi* for the stage is performed with a due respect for the genius of the author. The moral of the play is sterling and sound: on that score, therefore, it required not to be interfered with. Scenes too long for representation have been shortened and exuberances pruned. The occasional dross (even Shakespeare has his naps on Parnassus and good old Homer sometimes nods) has been expunged; but every grain of gold is carefully preserved and the action remains integral and undisturbed ... For one hundred and forty-three years *The Duchess of Malfi* has unaccountably been consigned to the shelf ... on 20 November 1850 this play was revived at the Theatre Royal, Sadler's Wells, and received by a numerous and judicious audience with honour due. All that classical taste could suggest and decorative and pictorial art supply was called into requisition. The spectator was left nothing to imagine much less to desire. The scene in this respect was perfect. The acting deserves high praise. Mr Phelps in the haughty Ferdinand portrayed with eminent skill the ingenious untiring and unrelenting vengeance of a vainglorious noble rendered heartless by disappointed ambition and family pride. His deep remorse and sorrow in the sequel was a natural and finely-marked transition. Bosola may rank among Mr George Bennett's most vigorous and finished performances. The incarnate villain and spy could not have been entrusted to abler hands. The sarcastic devilry of the character was admirable ... The passions that distract and tear the august and suffering heroine are so various and complicated and her miseries so intolerable and intense that truly to represent them requires tragic powers of a very superior order. Miss Glyn acted the Duchess, and the public for many a long day have not beheld a performance of more intellectual energy, of higher mental and physical [power] than that which we now record. The delicate and difficult parts of the character (more difficult from their peculiar delicacy) were exquisitely true to nature. Her denunciations were withering and her dying exclamation 'Mercy' beautiful and affecting.

A. C. Swinburne

John Webster from *Sonnets on the Elizabethan Poets*   1882

Thunder: the flesh quails, and the soul bows down.
   Night: east, west, south, and northward, very night.

Star upon struggling star strives into sight,
Star after shuddering star the deep storms drown.
The very throne of night, her very crown,
    A man lays hand on, and usurps her right,
    Song from the highest of heaven's imperious height
Shoots, as a fire to smite some towering town.
Rage, anguish, harrowing fear, heart-crazing crime,
Make monstrous all the murderous face of Time
    Shown in the spheral orbit of a glass
Revolving. Earth cries out from all her graves,
Frail, on frail rafts, across wide-wallowing waves,
    Shapes here and there of child and mother pass.

A. C. Swinburne

[Chance and Terror in Webster] from 'John Webster', *Nineteenth Century*, vol. 19, no. 112   1886

Aeschylus is above all things the poet of righteousness. 'But in any wise, I say unto thee, revere thou the altar of righteousness': this is the crowning admonition of his doctrine, as its crowning prospect is the reconciliation or atonement of the principle of retribution with the principle of redemption, of the powers of the mystery of darkness with the coeternal forces of the spirit of wisdom, of the lord of inspiration and of light. The doctrine of Shakespeare, where it is not vaguer, is darker in its implication of injustice, in its acceptance of accident, than the impression of the doctrine of Aeschylus. Fate, irreversible and inscrutable, is the only force of which we feel the impact, of which we trace the sign, in the upshot of *Othello* or *King Lear*. The last step into the darkness remained to be taken by 'the most tragic' of all English poets. With Shakespeare – and assuredly not with Aeschylus – righteousness itself seems subject and subordinate to the masterdom of fate: but fate itself, in the tragic world of Webster, seems merely the servant or the synonym of chance. The two chief agents in his two great tragedies pass away – the phrase was, perhaps, unconsciously repeated – 'in a mist': perplexed, indomitable, defiant of hope and fear; bitter and sceptical and bloody in penitence or impenitence alike.

And the mist which encompasses the departing spirits of these moody and mocking men of blood seems equally to involve the lives of their chastisers and their victims. Blind accident and blundering mishap – 'such a mistake', says one of the criminals, 'as I have often seen in a play' – are the steersmen of their fortunes and the doomsmen of their deeds. The effect of this method or the result of this view, whether adopted for dramatic objects or ingrained in the writer's temperament, is equally fit for pure tragedy and unfit for any form of drama not purely tragic in evolution and event. In *The Devil's Law-Case* it is offensive, because the upshot is incongruous and insufficient: in *The White Devil* and *The Duchess of Malfi* it is admirable, because the results are adequate and coherent. But in all these three plays alike, and in these three plays only, the peculiar tone of Webster's genius, the peculiar force of his imagination, is distinct and absolute in its fullness of effect. The author of *Appius and Virginia* would have earned an honourable and enduring place in the history of English letters as a worthy member – one among many – of a great school in poetry, a deserving representative of a great epoch in literature: but the author of these three plays has a solitary station, an indisputable distinction of his own. The greatest poets of all time are not more mutually independent than this one – a lesser poet only than those greatest – is essentially independent of them all.

The first quality which all readers recognize, and which may strike a superficial reader as the exclusive or excessive note of his genius and his work, is of course his command of terror. Except in Aeschylus, in Dante, and in Shakespeare, I at least know not where to seek for passages which in sheer force of tragic and noble horror – to the vulgar shock of ignoble or brutal horror he never condescends to submit his reader or subdue his inspiration – may be set against the subtlest, the deepest, the sublimest passages of Webster. Other gifts he had as great in themselves, as precious and as necessary to the poet: but on this side he is incomparable and unique. Neither Marlowe nor Shakespeare had so fine, so accurate, so infallible a sense of the delicate line of demarcation which divides the impressive and the terrible from the horrible and the loathsome – Victor Hugo and Honoré de Balzac from Eugène Sue and Émile Zola. On his theatre we find no presentation of old men with their beards torn off and their eyes gouged out, of young men imprisoned in reeking cesspools and impaled with red-hot spits.

Again and again his passionate and daring genius attains the utmost
limit and rounds the final goal of tragedy; never once does it break
the bounds of pure poetic instinct. If ever for a moment it may seem
to graze that goal too closely, to brush too sharply by those bounds,
the very next moment finds it clear of any such risk and remote from
any such temptation as sometimes entrapped or seduced the foremost
of its forerunners in the field. And yet this is the field in which its
paces are most superbly shown. No name among all the names of
great poets will recur so soon as Webster's to the reader who knows
what it signifies, as he reads or repeats the verses in which a greater[1]
than this great poet – a greater than all since Shakespeare – has expressed the latent mystery of terror which lurks in all the highest
poetry or beauty, and distinguishes it inexplicably and inevitably
from all that is but a little lower than the highest. . . .

(868–9)

The immeasurable superiority of Aeschylus to his successors in this
quality of instinctive righteousness . . . is shared no less by Webster than
by Shakespeare . . . as there is no poet morally nobler than Webster so
there is no poet ignobler in the moral sense than Euripides : while as a
dramatic artist – an artist in character, action and emotion – the de-
generate tragedian of Athens, compared to the second tragic dramatist
of England, is as a mutilated monkey to a well-made man. . . . In the
deepest and highest and purest qualities of tragic poetry Webster
stands nearer to Shakespeare than any other English poet stands to
Webster; and so much nearer as to be a good second; while it is at
least questionable whether even Shelley can reasonably be accepted as
a good third. Not one among the predecessors, contemporaries, or
successors of Shakespeare and Webster has given proof of this double
faculty – this coequal mastery of terror and pity, undiscoloured and
undistorted, but vivified and glorified, by the splendour of immediate and infallible imagination. The most grovelling realism could
scarcely be so impudent in stupidity as to pretend an aim at a more
perfect presentation of truth : the most fervent fancy, the most sensitive taste, could hardly dream of a desire for more exquisite expression of natural passion in a form of utterance more naturally exalted
and refined.

1 Victor Hugo. [Ed.]

In all the vast and voluminous records of critical error there can be discovered no falsehood more foolish or more flagrant than the vulgar tradition which represents this high-souled and gentle-hearted poet as one morbidly fascinated by a fantastic attraction towards the 'violent delights' of horror and the nervous or sensational excitements of criminal detail: nor can there be conceived a more perverse or futile misapprehension than that which represents John Webster as one whose instinct led him by some obscure and oblique propensity to darken the darkness of southern crime or vice by an infusion of northern seriousness, of introspective cynicism and reflective intensity in wrongdoing, into the easy levity and infantine simplicity of spontaneous wickedness which distinguished the moral and social corruption of renascent Italy. . . . The great if not incomparable power displayed in Webster's delineation of such criminals as Flamineo and Bosola – Bonapartes in the bud, Napoleons in a nutshell, Caesars who have missed their Rubicon and collapse into the likeness of a Catiline – is a sign rather of his noble English loathing for the traditions associated with such names as Caesar and Medici and Borgia, Catiline and Iscariot and Napoleon, than of any sympathetic interest in such incarnations of historic crime. Flamineo especially, the ardent pimp, the enthusiastic pandar, who prostitutes his sister and assassinates his brother with such earnest and single-hearted devotion to his own straightforward self-interest, has in him a sublime fervour of rascality.

(870–71; 875)

John Addington Symonds

'Webster and Tourneur', from the Introduction to his edition of plays by Webster and Tourneur   1888

It is just this power of blending tenderness and pity with the exhibition of acute moral anguish by which Webster is so superior to Tourneur as a dramatist.

Both playwrights have this point in common, that their forte lies not in the construction of plots, or in the creation of characters, so much as in an acute sense for dramatic situations. Their plots are involved and stippled in with slender touches; they lack breadth, and

do not rightly hang together. Their characters, though forcibly conceived, tend to monotony, and move mechanically. But when it is
needful to develop a poignant, a passionate, or a delicate situation,
Tourneur and Webster show themselves to be masters of their art.
They find inevitable words, the right utterance, not indeed always for
their specific personages, but for generic humanity, under the *peine
forte et dure* of intense emotional pressure. Webster, being the larger,
nobler, deeper in his touch on nature, offers a greater variety of situations which reveal the struggles of the human soul with sin and fate.
He is also better able to sustain these situations at a high dramatic
pitch – as in the scene of Vittoria before her judges, and the scene of
the Duchess of Malfi's assassination. Still Tourneur can display a few
such moments by apocalyptic flashes – notably in the scenes where
Vendice deals with his mother and sister.

Both playwrights indulge the late Elizabethan predilection for con-
ceits. Webster, here as elsewhere, proves himself the finer artist. He
inserts Vittoria's dream, Antonio's dialogue with Echo, Bosola's
Masque of Madmen, accidentally and subserviently to action. Tourneur
enlarges needlessly, but with lurid rhetorical effect, upon the grisly
humours suggested by the skull of Vendice's dead mistress. Using
similar materials, the one asserts his claim to be called the nobler poet
by more steady observance of the Greek precept 'Nothing over-
much'. Words to the same effect might be written about their several
employment of blank verse and prose. Both follow Shakespeare's
distribution of these forms, while both run verse into prose as Shakespeare never did. Yet I think we may detect a subtler discriminative
quality in Webster's most chaotic periods than we can in Tourneur's;
and what upon this point deserves notice is that Webster, of the two,
alone shows lyrical faculty. His three dirges are of exquisite melodic
rhythm, in a rich low minor key; much of his blank verse has the ring
of music; and even his prose suggests the colour of song by its cadence.
This cannot be said of the sinister and arid Muse of Tourneur …
[Webster] is not a poet to be dealt with by any summary method; for
he touches the depths of human nature in ways that need the subtlest
analysis for their proper explanation. I am, however, loth to close
without a word or two concerning the peculiarities of Webster's
dramatic style. Owing to condensation of thought and compression of
language, his plays offer considerable difficulties to readers who ap-

proach them for the first time. So many fantastic incidents are crowded into a single action, and the dialogue is burdened with so much profoundly studied matter, that the general impression is apt to be blurred. We rise from the perusal of his Italian tragedies with a deep sense of the poet's power and personality, an ineffaceable recollection of one or two resplendent scenes, and a clear conception of the leading characters. Meanwhile the outlines of the fable, the structure of the drama as a complete work of art, seem to elude our grasp. The persons, who have played their part upon the stage of our imagination, stand apart from one another, like figures in a *tableau vivant*. *Appius and Virginia*, indeed, proves that Webster understood the value of a simple plot, and that he was able to work one out with conscientious firmness. But in *Vittoria Corombona* and *The Duchess of Malfi*, each part is etched with equal effort after luminous effect upon a murky background; and the whole play is a mosaic of these parts. It lacks the breadth which comes from concentration on a master-motive. We feel that the author had a certain depth of tone and intricacy of design in view, combining sensational effect and sententious pregnancy of diction in works of laboured art. It is probable that able representation upon the public stage of an Elizabethan theatre gave them the coherence, the animation, and the movement which a chamber-student misses. When familiarity has brought us acquainted with Webster's way of working, we perceive that he treats terrible and striking subjects with a concentrated vigour special to his genius. Each word and trait of character has been studied for a particular effect. Brief lightning flashes of astute self-revelation illuminate the midnight darkness of the lost souls he has painted. Flowers of the purest and most human pathos, like Giovanni de Medici's dialogue with his uncle in *Vittoria Corombona*, bloom by the charnel-house on which the poet's fancy loved to dwell. The culmination of these tragedies, setting like stormy suns in blood-red clouds, is prepared by gradual approaches and degrees of horror. No dramatist showed more consummate ability in heightening terrific effects, in laying bare the inner mysteries of crime, remorse, and pain combined to make men miserable. He seems to have had a natural bias toward the dreadful stuff with which he deals so powerfully. He was drawn to comprehend and reproduce abnormal elements of spiritual anguish. The materials with which he builds are sought for in the ruined places of abandoned lives, in the agonies of madness and

despair, in the sarcasms of reckless atheism, in slow tortures, griefs
beyond endurance, the tempests of sin-haunted conscience, the spasms
of fratricidal bloodshed, the deaths of frantic hope-deserted criminals.
He is often melodramatic in the means employed to bring these psychological elements of tragedy home to our imagination. He makes
free use of poisoned engines, daggers, pistols, disguised murderers,
masques, and nightmares. Yet his firm grasp upon the essential qualities of diseased and guilty human nature, his profound pity for the
innocent who suffer shipwreck in the storm of evil passions not their
own, save him, even at his gloomiest and wildest, from the unrealities
and extravagances into which less potent artists – Tourneur, for example – blundered. That the tendency to brood on what is ghastly
belonged to Webster's idiosyncrasy appears in his use of metaphor. He
cannot say the simplest thing without giving it a sinister turn – as thus:

>   you speak as if a man
> Should know what fowl is *coffin'd* in a bak'd meat,
> Afore you cut it up.[1]
>
> > (*The White Devil*, IV ii 19–21)

When knaves come to preferment, they rise *as gallowses are raised*
i' th' Low Countries, one upon another's shoulders.

> (*The White Devil*, II i 320–22)

> Pleasure of life! what is't? only the *good hours*
> *Of an ague.*
>
> > (*The Duchess of Malfi*, v iv 67–8)

I would sooner *eat a dead pigeon taken from the soles of the feet of one
sick of the plague*, than kiss one of you fasting.

> (*The Duchess of Malfi*, II i 38–40)

In his dialogue, people bandy phrases like – 'O you screech-owl!' and
'Thou foul black cloud!' A sister warns her brother to think twice
before committing suicide, with this weird admonition:

>   I prithee yet remember,
> Millions are now in graves, which at last day
> Like mandrakes shall rise shrieking.
>
> > (*The White Devil*, v vi 65–7)

---

1 'Coffin' is, in fact, the normal Elizabethan word for a pastry case; and is
used in contexts as little sinister as cook-books. [Ed.]

But enough has now been said about these peculiarities of Webster's dramatic style. It is needful to become acclimatized to his specific mannerism, both in the way of working and the tone of thinking before we can appreciate his real greatness as a dramatic poet and moralist. Then we recognize the truth of what has recently been written of him by an acute and sympathetic critic[1]: 'There is no poet morally nobler than Webster.'

(xii–xiii; xix–xxiii)

A. C. Swinburne

Letter to William Poel   27 October 1892

I must send you a word of thanks for the honour done to me as a Websterian by your gift of a box on the 25th and for the great pleasure I had in seeing that transcendent masterpiece of tragedy restored to the stage under such favourable auspices. How great that pleasure was you may judge when I tell you that I was just twelve years old when I first read so much of *The Duchess* as is given in Campbell's *Specimens*, and was as much entranced and fascinated at that not very mature age as I am now and have been ever since by its unique beauty and power.

I must congratulate you most cordially on the benefits you have conferred upon all lovers of English dramatic poetry at its best and highest – in other words, upon all lovers of what is best and highest in the literature, or rather in the creative work of all countries and all ages. And I most earnestly hope that you may see your way to doing as much for other great works of the same great age – especially, I need not say, of the same great hand. I think I must have been the only person present on Tuesday who had brought with him a copy of the Author's edition '1623'. I wish I had had the privilege of showing you the beautiful little quarto which I had slipped into an inside breast pocket. But I hope you may be kind enough to allow me an opportunity of showing you my little collection of such rarities. It

1 Swinburne (see above, p. 68). [Ed.]

would be no sort of return for your kindness, but it would be a great pleasure for me, and might, I think, be of some interest to you.

Believe me, in the meantime,

Yours very gratefully,

A. C. Swinburne

William Archer

'Webster, Lamb and Swinburne', *New Review*, vol. 8, no. 44 1893

The recent performance of Webster's *The Duchess of Malfi* at the Independent Theatre must have done one good service if no other. It must have brought home to many of the audience the need for a careful scrutiny of what may be called the Lamb tradition with respect to the Elizabethan dramatists. To say so is to take your life in your hands, for never had critical tradition devouter or more puissant champions. I myself, in making the suggestion, am conscious of a feeling of impiety. To the most fanatical worshipper of Charles Lamb I would say, 'Nay, an thou'lt mouth I'll rant as well as thou', were it not that the motion with which one thinks of that exquisite spirit is so intimate and personal as to seem almost profane by utterance. In the love of Lamb, I take it, all literary sects and parties are at one. Not to love him is to place yourself without the pale of literature, almost of humanity. Nor do I for a moment deny that the discovery, the illumination, the revivifying of the Elizabethan drama is one of his chief claims upon our gratitude. In the dark treasure-cave where jewels and dross had long lain indistinguishable, he said, 'Let there be light', and there was light. The gems shone forth, a possession for ever: and if the discoverer's eyes were a little bit dazzled, if he now and then mistook the superficial glitter of the dross for the inborn glow of the jewel, shall that be held to detract from the value and the renown of his discovery? It is, after all, his humanity that we love in Lamb: and humanity is not infallible.

I see, on second thoughts, that I have used a misleading image. My point is not that Lamb mistook dross for jewels, but that he now and then mistook the value of the dramatic setting in which he found his poetic jewels enchased. He regarded the Elizabethan drama too much in the light of absolute literature, making it a law unto itself. He took too little account of the historic influences, the material conditions, under which it was produced; and in this the inheritors and expounders of his doctrine have faithfully followed his lead. Poetry – pure beauty, force, dignity, perfection of utterance – is in reality one and eternal. What is well said is well said, whether it be addressed to Ionian villagers or to Roman courtiers, to the populace of sixteenth-century London, or to the exquisites of seventeenth-century Versailles. And that which seems well said because of its consonance with a temporary fashion, is in reality ill said. Fine style is fine style – and poetry is the fine flower of fine style – in virtue of its harmony with primal instincts, with universal laws of perception and association, with fundamental conditions of intellectual, emotional, and sensuous life. It appeals to no conventions, to no ephemeral modes of thought; wherefore it may be studied and appraised as a thing in itself, apart from all historical or sociological knowledge. Drama, on the other hand, is a thing of convention, of fashion. The drama of any given period (in so far as it is a natural, not a merely imitative, product) is strictly a part of its manners and customs, and must be studied as a social institution. Its merits and defects must be read in the light of the material and intellectual circumstances which gave it birth, and the conventions of one period must not be mistaken for everlasting canons of art. Lamb and his disciples, as it seems to me, are subject to this illusion. Their knowledge of the Elizabethan period is imperfect on the historical side, and on the literary side so intimate as to be uncritical. Is this a paradox? Surely not. Is it not rather a truism that if we stand too near a given object we cannot see it in its true relations and proportions? Lamb read himself into the literature of the period until he himself became an Elizabethan in spirit. His moral and aesthetic perceptions, and especially his notions of dramatic effect, became wholly Elizabethanized. 'Elia hath not so fixed his nativity', he declared in one of his most whimsical papers, 'but that, if he seeth occasion, he will be born again in whatever place, and at whatever period, shall seem good unto him.' By way of preparation for his study of the Elizabethans, he seems to throw back his nativity from 1775 to 1575. This makes his criticism delightful, but inconclusive. Prince Posterity must not abdicate the privileges, which are also the duties, of his heirship to the ages.

In dealing with an art so absolutely conditioned by time and place as the drama, we must not sublimate into an ideal and practice, even the noblest practice, of one particular period, and that, so far as its theatrical audiences were concerned, a semi-barbarous one. By all means let us be capable, on occasion, of taking the Elizabethan point of view; but let us not therefore abandon for ever the point of view of universal art, or, in other words, of right reason. Lamb's estimate of the pure poetry contained in the Elizabethan drama will always be valid, for excellence of style, as aforesaid, is one and eternal. Whoso has eyes to see it at all is always at the right point of view. But in drama, even under what may be called the poetical convention, pure beauty of expression is a subordinate and inessential quality; and Lamb, I submit, was not at the right point of view for estimating the Elizabethan drama *as* drama, in its relation to other dramatic literatures and to the ideal of dramatic creation. His disciples, too, partly by reason of their discipleship, have failed to place themselves at the just point of view. They have, if anything, exaggerated his tendency to make the Elizabethan drama a law unto itself. Therefore, I repeat, it is high time that the whole Lamb tradition should be subjected to careful scrutiny.

I have neither the learning, the leisure, nor the skill for such a task. For the present, at any rate, I can only attempt, in a few desultory remarks on *The Duchess of Malfi*, to indicate to better qualified critics the line of thought which, as it seems to me, they ought to follow. Onlookers, we know, see most of the game, and an outsider may sometimes attain to a clearer and saner vision of things than is possible for an adept. Specialist criticism, if I may call it so, has in Mr Swinburne an illustrious and redoubtable champion. In learning, insight, sympathy, eloquence, he stands alone. Were I to measure myself against him in all or any of these qualities, my presumption would be such as it would tax even his rhetoric to characterize. My will, like Orlando's, hath in it a more modest working. Far from presuming to rival him as an expert, I claim no advantage save that of *in*expertness, detachment of mind, comparative aloofness of standpoint. Erudition will not always guide a critic to the best point of view. Intensity of vision may even be deceptive if the object be not approached at the proper angle.

Let me in the first place clear the ground, and refresh the reader's memory, by means of a brief synopsis of *The Duchess of Malfi*.

Webster found in Bandello the bare incident of a marriage between a Duchess of Malfi and her major-domo, both of whom are killed at the instigation of her brother, the Cardinal of Arragon. Bandello casually mentions 'Bosolo' as the name of the man who shot Antonio; and there is also a vague reference to an unnamed brother of the Cardinal's. To all intents and purposes, however, the play, both as regards character and incident, is of Webster's own invention. He borrowed scarcely a single detail from the Italian novel.

In the first act, at Malfi, Ferdinand, Duke of Calabria, and his brother, the Cardinal of Arragon, in parting from their sister, the widowed Duchess of Malfi, warn her, in threatening terms, not to think of marrying again. They set one Bosola to spy upon her actions. No sooner are their backs turned than the Duchess summons her major-domo, Antonio Bologna, proposes marriage to him, and marries him (*per verba* [*de*] *presenti*, as she puts it) on the spot. In the second act, Bosola suspects that the Duchess is pregnant, and lays a trap to make her reveal her condition. This hastens her delivery, and Bosola's suspicion is converted into certainty when he picks up a paper in which Antonio has cast the nativity of the new-born child. It never occurs to him that Antonio may be the father; but he posts off to Rome to inform his employers of his discovery. Bosola's intelligence annoys the Cardinal, and throws Ferdinand into a foul-mouthed frenzy of rage, which brings the act to a close. Ferdinand's frenzy, however, is not a *furor brevis*. He is so patient in his wrath that before the third act opens, his sister, living in undisturbed conjugal felicity, has had two more children. Bosola is still spying upon her and eager to discover her paramour, but does not even now suspect Antonio. Ferdinand, by means of a secret door, enters his sister's chamber and upbraids her savagely, professing as his motive an extreme concern for her lost virtue. Seeing that they are on the brink of discovery, she accuses Antonio of embezzlement and pretends to dismiss him from her service, promising to follow him to Ancona, where he is to take refuge. Bosola, by affecting sympathy with the disgraced Antonio, worms her secret out of her, and of course makes known the truth to his employers. The action now wanders to Loretto, where Antonio and the Duchess are separated. Antonio takes refuge in Milan, and the Duchess, captured by Bosola, is led back to Malfi.

We now come to what Mr Swinburne calls 'the overwhelming

terrors and the overpowering beauties of that unique and marvellous fourth act, in which the genius of this poet spreads its fullest and its darkest wing for the longest and the strongest of its flights'. The scene is the room in her palace in which the Duchess is imprisoned. Ferdinand, entering in the dark, pretends to be reconciled with her, and gives her, instead of his own hand, that of a dead man, leading her to believe that it is Antonio's. Then a curtain is drawn back, and (in an alcove, I suppose) are revealed waxen images representing the dead bodies of Antonio and their children. The Duchess does not suspect the trick which is being played upon her, and (oddly enough) makes no attempt to approach or touch the supposed corpses. A grief-stricken woman might be expected to kiss her dead children, and so discover the fraud; but the Duchess is too much taken up (as Lamb puts it) with 'speaking the dialect of despair', and saying things that have 'a snatch of Tartarus and the souls in bale', to think of any such simple and natural proceeding. Then Ferdinand releases the mad-folk from 'the common hospital', and sets them 'to sing and dance and act their gambols to the full o' the moon' around her chamber. Presently they enter, singing:

O, let us howl, some heavy note,
  Some deadly dogged howl,
Sounding as from the threat'ning throat
  Of beasts, and fatal fowl!

(IV ii 61-4)

They indulge in ribald ravings, dance a dance 'with music answerable thereto', and then go off again as Bosola enters, disguised as an old man. He announces himself as a tomb-maker, introduces 'executioners, with a coffin, cords, and a bell', and proceeds to speak 'the living person's dirge' in order 'to bring her by degrees to mortification'. Then the Duchess is strangled, her children are strangled,[1] and her maid, Cariola, is strangled, all on the open stage. Ferdinand goes mad at sight of this slaughter-house, and Bosola, suddenly penitent, sets off for Milan to carry the news to Antonio. In the fifth act, at Milan, the Cardinal's mistress, Julia, is poisoned; Bosola kills Antonio, mistaking him for the Cardinal; then he kills the Cardinal's servant, the Cardinal himself, and Ferdinand, who, by the way, is still raving

1 This error is derived from Dyce's edition. [Ed.]

mad; and Ferdinand, before he dies, kills Bosola. Antonio's friend, Delio, and one of the children are left alive.

In this tragedy, then, five men, three women, and two children come to violent ends, the children and two of the women being strangled on the open stage; yet, says Mr Swinburne,

in all the vast and voluminous records of critical error there can be discovered no falsehood more foolish or more flagrant than the vulgar tradition which represents this high-souled and gentle-hearted poet as one morbidly fascinated by a fantastic attraction towards the 'violent delights' of horror, and the nervous or sensational excitements of criminal detail.

'What', [says Lamb] 'are "Luke's iron crown", the brazen bull of Perillus, Procrustes' bed, to the waxen images which counterfeit death, to the wild masque of madmen, the tomb-maker, the bell-man, the living person's dirge, the mortification by degrees! To move a horror skilfully, to touch a soul to the quick, to lay upon fear as much as it can bear, to wean and weary a life till it is ready to drop, and then step in with mortal instruments to take its last forfeit; this only a Webster can do. Writers of an inferior genius may "upon horror's head horrors accumulate", but they cannot do this. They mistake quantity for quality, they "terrify babes with painted devils", but they know not how a soul is capable of being moved; their terrors want dignity, their affrightments are without decorum.'

Well, well! We are to understand, then, that the hideous and dragged-in antics of insanity constitute a decorous affrightment, and that the public strangling of two little children is not a 'violent delight'!

When we thus find great critics putting forth judgements which read like extravagant and wanton paradoxes, must we not suspect an illusion somewhere? Their expressions are, on the face of it, in flagrant contradiction with the facts (which the reader may verify for himself) set forth in my account of the play. But from such an account, from a bald narrative of facts, what element is necessarily excluded? Clearly that of style, of verbal felicity, of what Mr Swinburne calls 'literary power, poetic beauty, charm of passionate or pathetic fancy'. Now in these qualities – qualities of which Lamb and Mr Swinburne are judges

beyond all appeal – Webster undoubtedly stands very high. In spite of
a metrical laxity which Mr Swinburne himself deplores, this play contains many passages of great inherent beauty, and a still greater number of speeches of a quaint and, so to speak, unexpected dramatic
force and appropriateness. Take for instance Antonio's speech when
the Duchess feigns to dismiss him from her household:

> O, the inconstant
> And rotten ground of service! – you may see
> 'Tis ev'n like him, that in a winter night
> Takes a long slumber o'er a dying fire,
> As loth to part from't; yet parts thence as cold
> As when he first sat down.
>
> (III ii 198–203)

Here, again, is an often-quoted speech of the Duchess to Cariola
while the madmen are howling round her apartment:

> I'll tell thee a miracle –
> I am not mad yet, to my cause of sorrow.
> Th' heaven o'er my head seems made of molten brass,
> The earth of flaming sulphur, yet I am not mad:
> I am acquainted with sad misery,
> As the tann'd galley-slave is with his oar;
> Necessity makes me suffer constantly,
> And custom makes it easy . . .
>
> (IV ii 23–30)

I could fill page after page with passages of the like imaginative
beauty and vitality, but must content myself with reminding the
reader of the immortal dirge, and quoting these four lines from it:

> *Of what is't fools make such vain keeping?*
> *Sin their conception, their birth weeping;*
> *Their life a general mist of error,*
> *Their death a hideous storm of terror.*
>
> (IV ii 186–9)

The man who wrote this was in truth a poet, and Mr Swinburne
may, if he is so disposed, class him as 'a lesser poet only than the
greatest'. It must be remembered, indeed, that he was one of 'the

early risers of literature' who 'found language with the dew upon it' – in other words, he lived at a period when comparatively small men had the knack of writing astonishingly great verse. But that is a side consideration, and nothing to the present purpose. What is certain is that the writings of Webster are full of 'literary power, poetic beauty, and charm of passionate and pathetic fancy'. Is it not possible that these qualities, to which they are so keenly sensitive, may have misled Lamb and Mr Swinburne? Receiving great delight from a work in dramatic form, may they not have concluded too hastily that their pleasure was due to its dramatic merits, and transferred to the characters and the fable admiration which belongs by right to the language and the imagery? In a word, may they not have mistaken a low form of drama for a high, and even the highest, because they found it robed in regal purple of pure poetry?

Whatever may have been Webster's personal tastes, there cannot be the smallest doubt that the average Elizabethan audience was avid of 'the "violent delights" of horror, and the nervous or sensational excitements of criminal detail'. It is futile to pretend that either the gallants and masked fair ones in the 'rooms', or the citizens and 'prentices in the 'yard' did not love bloodshed and physical horror in action, reckless crudity, and even deliberate lewdness, in speech. No playwright of the period failed to minister to these tastes, for in Elizabeth's time, no less than in our own, the drama's laws the drama's patrons gave. The stage was not only the vehicle for the highest poetry and philosophy of the time; it was also its *Punch* and its *Pick-Me-Up*, its *London Journal*, its *Police News* and its *Penny Dreadful*. In respect of physical horror, at any rate, Shakespeare pandered less to the mob than almost any of his contemporaries, and in nothing did he show more clearly that he was not of an age but for all time. Nor can we doubt that several even of the choicest spirits of the age, found the less difficulty in gratifying the popular taste for gruesomeness and gore, because their own imagination was haunted in a strange uncanny fashion by the legendary crimes of the Italian Renaissance. Was not this pre-eminently the case of Webster? When we find a playwright, in his two acknowledged masterpieces, drenching the stage with blood even beyond the wont of his contemporaries[1] and searching out

1 There are eight violent deaths in *The White Devil* and ten in *The Duchess of Malfi*.

every possible circumstance of horror – ghosts, maniacs, severed limbs and all the paraphernalia of the charnel-house and the tomb – with no conceivable purpose except just to make our flesh creep, may we not reasonably, or rather must we not inevitably, conclude that he either revelled in 'violent delights' for their own sake, or wantonly pandered to the popular craving for them? If Mr Swinburne accepts the latter alternative – if he would have us believe that the Webster of the tragedies is not the real Webster, but is playing an abhorrent part to ingratiate himself with the groundlings – then his position, if essentially unprovable, is also essentially incontrovertible. But I do not understand him to claim any private or peculiar knowledge of Webster's character. What he evidently means is that in these very tragedies we can discover the 'high soul' and 'gentle heart' of the poet, and can *not* discover any morbid predilection for 'violent delights'. High-souled and gentle-hearted he may possibly have been, for these qualities are not incompatible with the vilest perversions of the aesthetic sense. But to argue that Webster's aesthetic sense was refined and unperverted is simply to maintain that black is white and blood is rose-water.

'Webster does not deal in horrors for their own sake', we shall be told, 'but uses them as means towards the illustration and development of character'. Could he not have made clear to us the resignation and fortitude of the Duchess of Malfi without the ghastly mummery of the dead hand and the waxen corpses? To argue so is simply to deny his competence as a dramatic poet. I have heard it maintained that the strangling of Cariola is designed to contrast with that of the Duchess – the frantic terror of the maid serving to throw into relief the noble courage of the mistress. Who can fail to perceive that if this were the intention, the death of the maid must of necessity precede that of the mistress, not follow it, as in Webster? When an effect of contrast is aimed at, and the things to be contrasted cannot be displayed simultaneously, it is clear that the minor, so to speak, must precede the major, the darkness must precede the light. In other words, the background must be established before the object to be set off against it is presented to our view. And then the children! What effect of contrast is served by the massacre of the innocents? Whose character does it serve to illustrate? Their mother is already dead, or at least unconscious. Had they been strangled before her eyes, the effect would have been one of unparalleled, intolerable brutality, but it would, in a certain sense, have been dramatic. As it is, their death is a mere mechanical piling of horror upon horror. It does not even throw any new light on the character of Bosola; when a man is wading in blood, an inch more or less is no great matter. What it *does* throw light upon is the character, or at least the aesthetic sense, of Webster and his public. It is perfectly evident that Elizabethan audiences found a pleasurable excitement in the crude fact of seeing little children strangled on the stage, and that Webster, to say the least of it, had no insuperable objection to gratifying that taste.

Far be it from me to argue that horror has not its legitimate place in literature and in drama. 'To move a horror skilfully, to touch a soul to the quick' is neither an easy nor an unworthy task. My point is that in *The Duchess of Malfi* (and, to a minor degree, in *The White Devil*) the horrors are *un*skilfully moved – that they are frigid, mechanical, brutal. Literature is literature in virtue of the brain-power implicit in it; and there goes no more brain power to the invention of these massacres and monstrosities than to carving a turnip lantern and sticking it on a pole.

Much might be said, if space permitted, of Webster's construction and characterization. Of dramatic concentration he did not dream. Though a younger man than Shakespeare (whose 'right happy and copious industry' he bracketed with that of Dekker and Heywood, and postponed to the loftier talents of Chapman and Jonson), he reverted to a stage of literary development which Shakespeare had outgrown. In *The White Devil* and *The Duchess of Malfi* the differentiation between romance and drama is still incomplete. They are not constructed plays, but loose-strung, go-as-you-please romances in dialogue.[1] The motivation of *The Duchess of Malfi* is haphazard even beyond the Elizabethan average. No motive is assigned in the earlier part of the play for the brother's virulent and almost monomaniac opposition to the very idea of their sister's marrying again. After her death, Ferdinand explains that he hoped to gain 'an infinite mass of treasure' if she died unmarried, and we may presume that the Cardinal would have been his co-heir. But this motive, even when we are tardily informed of it, does not account for his epilepsies of rage and

1 *Appius and Virginia* is vastly superior to them in point of form, and contains, along with much admirable writing, some scenes of great dramatic power.

cruelty, which seem sometimes to spring from regard for the family honour, sometimes from a rabid enthusiasm for 'virtue' in the abstract. Perhaps we are to understand that all these motives combine to work up his fundamentally cruel nature to the pitch of madness. This might be a plausible theory enough, but we arrive at it only by conjecture. It is more than doubtful whether Webster himself was at all clear as to his characters' motives. In Ferdinand he provided Burbage with an effective part in which to 'tear a cat', and neither author, actor, nor audience inquired too curiously into the reasons for his frenzies and his cruelties. A similar difficulty confronts us in Bosola. This 'moody and mocking man of blood' is certainly not, like the ordinary melodramatic villain, hewn all of one piece. There is an appearance of subtlety in his character because it is full of contradictions. But there is no difficulty in making a character inconsistent; the task of the artist is to show an underlying harmony between the apparently conflicting attributes. Bosola seems sometimes to revel in his infamy, at others to be the unwilling instrument of a power he cannot resist. 'And though I loathed the evil,' he says to Ferdinand after the massacre, 'yet I loved you that did counsel it.' But this is the first and last we hear of any sentimental devotion on the spy's part towards his employers; nor can we discover the smallest ground for such a feeling. Mr Swinburne himself has a momentary misgiving as to 'the sudden vehemence of transformation, which seems to fall like fire from Heaven upon the two chief criminals who figure on the stage of murder'. But he quickly pulls himself together, explaining that 'the whole atmosphere of the action is so charged with thunder that this double and simultaneous shock of moral electricity rather thrills us with admiration and faith than chills us with repulsion and distrust'. On the whole, I am inclined to think that Webster came very near to creating in Bosola one of the most complex and most human villains in drama, a living illustration of that age-old but ever new paradox: 'Video meliora, proboque; deteriora sequor.'[1] But the fatal lack of clearness ruins everything. We cannot help feeling from time to time that the poet is writing for mere momentary effect, and has suffered the general scheme of the character to slip out of sight. All we can say with confidence is that, artistically, Bosola is worth a score of Flamineos. The way in which the action is suffered to straggle over quite

1 I see and approve better things, but follow worse.

unnecessary stretches of time and space bespeaks the romance rather than the drama. Ferdinand's fury becomes doubly incredible and ineffective when two years or more are suffered to elapse between his reception of Bosola's intelligence and his descent upon the Duchess. The only advantage of this delay is that but for it we should have to go without the massacre of the innocents. The relevance of the passage in which Delio makes love to the Cardinal's mistress utterly escapes me; indeed Julia is altogether a mere excrescence on the play. In shifting the scene to Loretto, Webster seems at first sight to have slavishly and mechanically followed Bandello; but his motive was probably to work in the dumb-show pageant of the Cardinal's military investiture. This to-ing and fro-ing, in any case, seriously enfeebles the action. The right, if need be, to jump not only from Amalfi to Ancona, but from China to Peru, is certainly one of the vital privileges of the romantic drama; but it is no less certain that changes of scene must be justified by some clear artistic advantage, else they merely injure the general effect. Wantonly to ignore the unities is no less an error than to sacrifice everything to their observance.

This is scarcely the place in which to consider Mr Swinburne's assertion that 'Webster is without exception the cleanliest writer of his time'. I think it must be based on some private interpretation of the term 'cleanly'; but I do not profess to have weighed grossness against grossness with any nicety. The point, at any rate, is quite inessential. The gist of my argument, so far as it can be summed up in a phrase, is this: that Webster was not, in the special sense of the word, a great dramatist, but was a great poet who wrote haphazard dramatic or melodramatic romances for an eagerly receptive but semi-barbarous public.

(96–106)

William Poel

'A New Criticism of Webster's *Duchess of Malfi*', a review of William Archer's 'Webster, Lamb and Swinburne', *Library Review*, vol. 2 1893

In a recent number of the *New Review* Mr Archer expresses the opinion that Webster was 'a great poet who wrote haphazard dramatic romances for an eagerly receptive but semi-barbarous public'; and adds that Webster excels in verbal felicity, and in writing beautiful language which is full of imagery and literary power. Of Webster's dramatic felicity and dramatic power Mr Archer is apparently incredulous. The play of *The Duchess of Malfi* is 'robed in regal purple of pure poetry', but the dramatic setting in which the poetic jewels are enchased is valueless. In other words, Webster's verse to be admired must be dissociated from the play for which it is written. But Webster's poetry, of all others, cannot be separated from its dramatic interest. The immortal dirge may be, as Mr Archer affirms, true poetry, but coming from the lips of Bosola at a moment when the suffering woman is facing her own grave, the words have an additional force and meaning. They become then convincing. Nor is it reasonable to ignore the dramatic instinct needed to conceive dialogue that gives point to the situation. Later on in the same scene Bosola says to Ferdinand

You have bloodily approv'd the ancient truth,
That kindred commonly do worse agree
Than remote strangers.

(IV ii 270–72)

and these words, in themselves pregnant with knowledge of human nature, are made doubly suggestive by the dramatist's skill in having them spoken at the moment when the action gives reality to them. In fact, Webster's most celebrated passages are not great simply because they are pre-eminent in beauty of idea and felicity of expression, but because they carry with them dramatic force by being appropriate to character and situation. 'The real object of the drama,' says Macaulay, 'is the exhibition of human character, and those situations which most signally develop character form the best plot.' Judged by this standard, a well-constructed play may be trifling, dull, and unnatural, while 'a haphazard dramatic romance' that has in it some scenes inferior in power and passion to nothing in the whole range of the drama, may entitle the author to the position of a great dramatist.

A difficulty in appreciating the actions and motives of Webster's characters may arise from that imperfect historical knowledge which we are told is the characteristic of Lamb's criticism. Webster wrote his play not for the purpose of dealing 'in horror for horror's sake', nor 'just to make the flesh creep', but with a desire to give vital embodiment to the manners and morals of the Italian Renaissance, as they appeared to the imagination of Englishmen. As Vernon Lee ably points out, it was the very strangeness and horror of Italian life, as compared with the dull decorum of English households, that constituted the attraction of Italian tragedy for Elizabethan playgoers. They were familiar with the saying that 'nothing in Italy was cheaper than human life'. Their own Ascham had written that he found in Italy, during a nine days' stay in one small city, more liberty to sin 'than ever he heard tell of in our noble citie of London in nine yeare'. No wonder, then, if the metaphysical judgement of the Puritan urged Elizabethan dramatists to show, by the action of their dramas, that there existed a higher power than the mere strength of those fiercer passions which occurred in Italy, the land of passion in the sixteenth century. Looked at from this point of view, much in the play that is unintelligible can be explained. Burckhardt, in his *Renaissance of Italy*, tells us that a warm imagination kept ever alive the memory of injuries, real or supposed; more especially in a country that allowed each man to take the law into his own hands. Not only a husband, but even a brother, in order to satisfy the family honour, would take upon himself the act of vengeance; nor would a father scruple to kill his own daughter, if the dignity of his house had been compromised by an unworthy marriage. Besides, an Italian's revenge was never a half-and-half affair. The Duchess's children are 'massacred' because the whole name and race of Antonio must be rooted out. Cariola, too, must die, because she helped to bring about the hated marriage. It is this desire for truth to Italian life that causes Webster to introduce Julia, and the pre-eminently Italian dialogue between Julia and Delio. Without Julia we do not get our typical Cardinal of the Italian Renaissance, a man experienced in simony, poisoning, and lust. There is even a higher motive for her appearance in the play. She is designed as a set-off to the Duchess; as an instance of unholy love in contrast to the chaste love of the Duchess. Bosola is a masterly study of the Italian 'familiar', who is at the same time a humanist. He is refined, subtle, indifferent, cynical. A criminal in action but not in constitution. A man forced by his position to know all the inward resources of his own nature, passing or permanent, and conscious of the possibility of a very brief period of power and influence. It is necessary, moreover, in judging of this play to take into consideration the restrictions put upon the dramatist by the novelist. Webster's audience was too familiar with the various incidents of the story to allow of the dramatist ignoring them. In one instance only does Webster depart from a statement of Bandello, and that is in making the Cardinal the younger and not the elder brother – an unaccountable oversight on the part ot Bandello – for Italian Cardinals were invariably the younger sons of noble houses.

Mr Robert Louis Stevenson says that to read a play is a knack: the fruit of much knowledge, and some imagination, comparable to that of reading score, 'the reader is apt to miss the proper point of view'. To see dramatic propriety and dramatic power in *The Duchess of Malfi*, there may be needed both critical and historical imagination.

(21–4)

Rupert Brooke

from 'Characteristics of Webster', *John Webster and the Elizabethan Drama* 1916

All these childishnesses and blunders in Webster's plays, soliloquies, asides, generalizations, couplets, and the rest, are due, no doubt, to carelessness and technical incapacity. His gifts were of a different kind. But the continual generalizations arise also from a particular bent of his mind, and a special need he felt. It is normal in the human mind, it was unusually strong in the Elizabethans, and it found its summit in Webster of all of that time – the desire to discover the general rule your particular instance illustrates, and the delight of enunciating it. Many people find their only intellectual pleasure in life, in the continued practice of this. But drama seems, or seemed, to demand it with especial hunger; most of all the poetic drama. The Greeks felt this, and in the form of drama they developed this was one of the chief intellectual functions of the chorus. I say 'intellectual', meaning that in their music and movement they appealed through other channels to the audience – though here, too, in part, to something the same taste in the audience, that is to say, the desire to feel a little disjunct from the individual case, and to view it against some sort of background. Metre itself has, psychologically, the same effect, a little. But the brain demands to be told τὸ μὴ φῦναι νικᾷ[1] or μίμνει δὲ μίμνοντος ἐν χρόνῳ Διὸς παθεῖν τὸν ἔρξαντα,[2] or any of the other deductions and rules.

The Greeks, then, received, to their satisfaction, the knowledge of other instances or of the general rule or moral, from the chorus. It is interesting to see the various ways of achieving the effects of a chorus that later drama has used. For to some extent the need is always felt, though not violently enough to overcome the dramatic disadvantages of an actual chorus. Sometimes one character in a play is put aside to serve the purpose, like the holy man in Maxim Gorki's *The Lower Depths*. Or the characters sit down and, a little unrealistically, argue out their moral, as in Mr Shaw's plays. Mr Shaw and a good many modern German, English, and Scandinavian writers, also depend on the spectator having picked up, from prefaces and elsewhere, the general body of the author's views against the background of which any particular play is to be performed. Ibsen had two devices. One was to sum up the matter in some prominent and startling remark near the end, like the famous 'People don't *do* such things!' The other was to have a half-mystical background, continually hinted at; the mountain-mines in *John Gabriel Borkman*, the heights in *When we Dead Awaken*, the sea in *The Lady from the Sea*, the wild duck. In certain catchwords these methods met; 'homes for men and women', 'ghosts', 'you don't mean it!' and the rest. The temptation to point a moral in the last words of a play is almost irresistible; and sometimes justified. A well-known modern play called *Waste* ends, 'The waste! the waste of it all!' The Elizabethans were very fond of doing this. They had the advantage that they could end with a rhymed couplet. But they were liable to do it at the end of any scene or episode. Webster was addicted to this practice. Towards their close his plays became a string of passionate generalities. Antonio and Vittoria both die uttering warnings against 'the courts of princes'. Other characters alternate human cries at their own distress with great generalizations about life and death. These give to the hearts of the spectators such comfort and such an outlet for their confused pity and grief as music and a chorus afford in other cases. But Webster also felt the need of

1 It is best not to have been born. (Version of Sophocles, *Oedipus Coloneus*, 1225). [Ed.]

2 So long as it is the fate of Zeus to rule it is the fate of man to pay for his actions. (Aeschylus, *Agamemnon*, 1563). [Ed.]

such broad moralizing in the middle of his tragedies. Sometimes he pours through the mouth of such characters as Bosola and Flamineo, generalization after dull generalization, without illuminating. Greek choruses have failed in the same way. But when a gnome that *is* successful comes, it is worth the pains. The solidity and immensity of Webster's mind behind the incidents is revealed. Flamineo fills this part at the death of Brachiano. But often he and Bosola are a different, and very Websterian, chorus. Their ceaseless comments of indecency and mockery are used in some scenes to throw up by contrast and enhance by interpretation the passions and sufferings of human beings. They provide a background for Prometheus; but a background of entrails and vultures, not the cliffs of the Caucasus. The horror of suffering is intensified by such means till it is unbearable. The crisis of her travail comes on the tormented body and mind of the Duchess (II i) to the swift accompaniment of Bosola's mockery. Brachiano's wooing, and his later recapture, of Vittoria, take on the sick dreadfulness of figures in a nightmare, whose shadows parody them with obscene caricature; because of the ceaseless ape-like comments of Flamineo, cold, itchy, filthily knowing. . . .

We are getting beyond the attitude, born of the industrial age and the childish enthusiasm for property as such, which condemns plagiarism, imitation, and borrowing. The Elizabethans had for the most part healthy and sensible views on the subject. They practised and encouraged the habit. When Langbaine, in his preface to *Momus Triumphans*, 'condemns Plagiaries' (though he is only thinking of plots, even then), it is a sign of the decadence towards stupidity. The poet and the dramatist work with words, ideas, and phrases. It is ridiculous, and shows a wild incomprehension of the principles of literature, to demand that each should only use his own; every man's brain is filled by thoughts and words of other people's. Webster wanted to make Bosola say fine things. He had many in his mind or his note-book: some were borrowed, some his own. He put them down, and they answer their purpose splendidly.

> I stand like one
> That long hath ta'en a sweet and golden dream:
> I am angry with myself, now that I wake.
>
> (IV ii 323–5)

That was, or may have been, of his own invention.

The weakest arm is strong enough, that strikes
With the sword of justice.

(v ii 344-5)

That he had found in Sidney. There is no difference. In any case the first, original, passage was probably in part due to his friends' influence; and the words he used were originally wholly 'plagiarized' from his mother or his nursemaid. 'Originality' is only plagiarizing from a great many.

So Webster reset other people's jewels and redoubled their lustre. 'The soul must be held fast with one's teeth . . .' he found Montaigne remarkably saying in a stoical passage. The phrase stuck. Bosola, on the point of death, cries:[1]

Yes, I hold my weary soul in my teeth,
'Tis ready to part from me.

(v v 75-6)

It is unforgettable.

Webster improved even Donne, in this way; in a passage of amazing, quiet, hopeless pathos, the parting of Antonio and the Duchess (*Duchess of Malfi*, III v), which is one long series of triumphant borrowings:

We seem ambitious God's whole work to undo;
Of nothing He made us, and we strive too
To bring ourselves to nothing back,

Donne writes in *An Anatomy of the World*,

Heaven fashion'd us of nothing; and we strive
To bring ourselves to nothing,

(III v 82-3)

are Antonio's moving words.

This last example illustrates one kind of the changes other than metrical Webster used to make. He generally altered a word or two,

---

1 It is only because there are scores of other certain borrowings of Webster from Montaigne that I accept this one. By itself it would not be a convincing plagiarism.

with an extraordinarily sure touch, which proves his genius for literature. He gave the passages life and vigour, always harmonious with
his own style. You see, by this chance side-light, the poet at work,
with great vividness. 'Fashion'd' for 'made' here, is not a great improvement; but it brings the sentence curiously into the key of the
rest of the scene. The metrical skill is astounding – the calm weight of
'fashion'd'; the slight tremble of 'Heaven' at the beginning of the
line; the adaptation from Donne's stiff heavy combative accent, the
line ending with 'and we strive too', to the simpler easier cadence
more suited to speech and to pathos, '. . .; and we strive'; and the
repetition of 'nothing' in the same place in the two lines.

The . . . borrowing from Sidney gives good instances of change,
among others the half-slangy vividness of

> Thou art a fool, then,
> To waste thy pity on a thing so wretched
> As cannot pity itself . . . ,
>
> (*The Duchess of Malfi*, IV i 89–90)

for Sidney's mannered, dim,

and therefore besought him not to cast his
love in so unfruitful a place as could not love itself.

But the same places in *The Duchess of Malfi* and the *Arcadia* have a
much finer example. The description of Queen Erona is transferred
to the Duchess again. Sidney says that in her sorrow, one could 'perceive the shape of loveliness more perfectly in woe than in joyfulness'.
Webster turned this, with a touch, to poetry in its sheerest beauty.

BOSOLA: You may discern the shape of loveliness
More perfect in her tears, than in her smiles.

(IV ii 7–8)

It is just this substitution of the concrete for the abstract – which is
the nearest one could get to a definition of the difference between a
thought in good prose and the same thought in good poetry – that
Webster excels in. . . .

The chief value of working through a note-book, from a literary
point of view, is this. A man tends to collect quotations, phrases, and
ideas, that particularly appeal to and fit in with his own personality.

If that personality is a strong one, and the point of his work is the pungency with which it is imbued with this strong taste, the not too injudicious agglutination of these external fragments will vastly enrich and heighten the total effect. And this is, on the whole, what happens with Webster. The heaping-up of images and phrases helps to confuse and impress the hearer, and gives body to a taste that might otherwise have been too thin to carry. Webster, in fine, belongs to the caddis-worm school of writers, who do not become their complete selves until they are incrusted with a thousand orts and chips and fragments from the world around.

It would be possible to go on for a long time classifying various characteristics of Webster, and discovering them in different passages or incidents in his plays. And it would be possible, too, to lay one's finger on several natural reactions and permanent associations in that brain. All have noticed his continual brooding over death. He was, more particularly, obsessed by the idea of the violence of the moment of death. Soul and body appeared to him so interlaced that he could not conceive of their separation without a struggle and pain. Again, his mind was always turning to metaphors of storms and bad weather, and especially the phenomenon of lightning. He is for ever speaking of men lightening to speech or action; he saw words as the flash from the thundercloud of wrath or passion.

But, after all, the chief characteristic of Webster's two plays and of many things in those plays, is that they are good; and the chief characteristic of Webster is that he is a good dramatist. The great thing about *The Duchess of Malfi* is that it is the material for a superb play; the great thing about the fine or noble things in it is not that they illustrate anything or belong to any class, but, in each case, the fine and noble thing itself. All one could do would be to print them out at length; and this is no place for that; it is easier to buy Webster's works (though, in this scandalous country, not very easy). The end of the matter is that Webster was a great writer; and the way in which one uses great writers is two-fold. There is the exhilarating way of reading their writing; and there is the essence of the whole man, or of the man's whole work, which you carry away and permanently keep with you. This essence generally presents itself more or less in the form of a view of the universe, recognizable rather by its emotional than by its logical content. The world called Webster is a peculiar one. It is inhabited by people driven, like animals, and perhaps like men, only by their instincts, but more blindly and ruinously. Life there seems to flow into its forms and shapes with an irregular abnormal and horrible volume. That is ultimately the most sickly, distressing feature of Webster's characters, their foul and indestructible vitality. It fills one with the repulsion one feels at the unending soulless energy that heaves and pulses through the lowest forms of life. They kill, love, torture one another blindly and without ceasing. A play of Webster's is full of the feverish and ghastly turmoil of a nest of maggots. Maggots are what the inhabitants of this universe most suggest and resemble. The sight of their fever is only alleviated by the permanent calm, unfriendly summits and darknesses of the background of death and doom. For that is equally a part of Webster's universe. Human beings are writhing grubs in an immense night. And the night is without stars or moon. But it has sometimes a certain quietude in its darkness; but not very much.

(136–58)

William Archer

from a review of the 1919 production of *The Duchess of Malfi*, *Nineteenth Century*, vol. 87, no. 515   January 1920

The long-delayed reaction against the cult of the lesser Elizabethans, initiated by Charles Lamb and caricatured by Swinburne, is being powerfully promoted by the activities of the Phoenix Society, which has recently been founded for the production of Elizabethan and Restoration plays. John Webster's *Duchess of Malfi*, revived last November at Hammersmith, had a very 'bad Press'. The privilege of listening to its occasional beauties of diction was felt to be dearly bought at the price of enduring three hours of coarse and sanguinary melodrama. But dramatic criticism in these days is so restricted in space that no one, so far as I have seen, has studied the structure of this famous 'masterpiece', and shown that, even apart from its embroidery of horrors, the play is a fundamentally bad one. It is true that technical standards are not absolute, but vary in relation to the material conditions of the stage for which a play is designed. But even under Elizabethan conditions, there was nothing, except his singular inexpertness, to prevent Webster from telling his story well. Massinger, or even Middleton, would have made a very different thing of it.

In the Second Act, we start a cumbersome underplot, concerned with the Cardinal's mistress, Julia, which serves no purpose except to provide us with a scene of lust and murder in the last Act. We presently find that the Duchess is about to give birth to a child, and that the lynx-eyed Bosola, though he suspects her condition, has no idea who is the father. We see him ferreting around the Duchess's apartments at the time of her lying-in; and his suspicions are confirmed when he picks up a calculation of the child's nativity which Antonio has casually dropped. What should we say of a modern dramatist who should bring about the revelation of a deadly secret through the inconceivable folly of a leading character, who first composes a compromising document, and then drops it in the actual presence of a man whom he knows to be a spy! . . .

And now comes a curious and characteristic point. In spite of the foaming fury of the Arragonians, they do nothing at all to avenge their precious 'honour', or to save it from further stains. They stand idly by for at least a couple of years, while the Duchess, at her leisure, bears two more children to Antonio! If there exists a common-sense principle so clear and compulsive that it may fairly be called a law, it is surely that a violent passion, once aroused, must 'ne'er feel retiring ebb, but keep due on ' till it has vented itself in destructive action. What should we say if a modern dramatist presented to us such a broken-backed play? It may be urged that Webster was only following his narrative source in giving the Duchess and Antonio three children. But he was under no obligation to follow it. His business was to compress the very prolix narrative, as it appears in Painter's *Palace of Pleasure*, into a good play. And in Painter there is no detective set to watch the Duchess. Bosola does not appear until the very end of the story, when he is hired to murder Antonio. What is so ridiculous in Webster is the position of this paid spy, who is a member of the Duchess's household for three years, and watches her producing a surreptitious family, without ever discovering who the father is. Can there be the least doubt that Webster ought to have made the brothers leave their sister unwatched until scandalous rumours reached them, that they should then have sent an agent to find out what was going on, and that, on his discovering the secret, the catastrophe should have followed like a thunder-clap? The part Webster assigns to Bosola is a glaring example of constructive inefficiency. . . .

We now come to the act – the Fourth – which has earned for Webster the reputation of a superb tragic poet. Antonio has escaped to Milan, and the Duchess is back in Amalfi, where Ferdinand favours her with a visit. Alleging that he has 'rashly made a solemn vow never to see her again', he begs her to receive him in the dark. Then, affecting to 'seal his peace with her', he thrusts upon her a dead man's hand. She at first receives it as his, remarking

> You are very cold.
> I fear you are not well after your travel:
>
> (IV i 51)

– and then cries 'Ha! lights! – O, horrible!' Is the invention of this ghastly practical joke – for it is Webster's: he did not find it in his original – is it a thing to be admired, and to earn its inventor a place only a little below Aeschylus and Shakespeare? I submit that any morbid-minded schoolboy could have conceived it, and that the humblest melodramatist of today would not dare to affront his transpontine audiences[1] by asking them to applaud such a grisly absurdity.

Next the ingenious Ferdinand draws a curtain, and shows the Duchess wax figures of Antonio and their son, apparently lying dead. It is manifestly impossible that Ferdinand can have secured portraits in wax of the man and child; yet the Duchess takes the figures for reality, and is duly horrified. It would have been infinitely easier, safer and more dramatic to have lied to her in words. This waxen lie is the device of a dramatist whose imagination works on the level of a Tussaud Chamber of Horrors. . . .

With the death of the Duchess, the interest of the play is over; for Antonio is admittedly a shadowy character as to whose fate we are very indifferent; and though we are willing enough to see Ferdinand, the Cardinal, and Bosola punished, we could quite well dispense with that gratification. Webster, however, is not the man to leave any of his *dramatis personae* alive if he can help it; so, as Rupert Brooke says, he kills off his criminals 'with various confusions and in various

1 The Americans, supposed to be particularly addicted to melodrama. [Ed.]

horror'. The Cardinal's irrelevant mistress, Julia, dies of kissing a poisoned book – a favourite incident with the Elizabethans. The Cardinal himself is killed by Bosola, his attendants disregarding his cries for help, because he has told them that he will very likely imitate the ravings of his mad brother, and no one must pay any attention – a piece of imbecile ingenuity such as tyros in playwriting are apt to plume themselves upon. Bosola kills Antonio by mistake, and Ferdinand and Bosola kill each other. There is scarcely room on the stage for all the corpses; which is perhaps the reason why, in the Phoenix revival, Ferdinand stands on his head to die, and waves his legs in the air.

All the editors of *The Duchess of Malfi* make a bald statement that Lope de Vega treated the same theme; but I have seen no comparison between Lope's play and Webster's. It is not one of his well-known works; but after some trouble I discovered it at the British Museum and read it. The Spanish and the English conventions are so very different that minute comparison is hardly possible. *El Mayordomo de la Duquesa de Amalfi* is not so much a play as an opera, full of brilliant bravura passages. But Lope's play is a much less barbarous product than Webster's; and I have no hesitation in saying that his catastrophe is immeasurably superior. It is highly concentrated, and, though rather too horrible for modern tastes, intensely dramatic. The Duchess and Antonio have parted, as in the original story. Then Ferdinand (here called Julio) succeeds in persuading them that he is reconciled to their union, and that Antonio has only to return to Amalfi for all to end happily. We see Antonio pass from one room into another in which he expects to find the Duchess; and then we see the Duchess hurrying to meet Antonio; but when the curtains are opened behind which she expects to find him, what she does find is a table set forth with three salvers on which are the heads of Antonio and their two children. This plunge from the height of joyful expectancy to the abyss of anguish and despair is incalculably more dramatic than Webster's laborious piling up of artificial horrors. After a pathetic outburst of lamentation, the Duchess, who has been poisoned, falls dead.

Lope's conclusion, too, is humanized by the fact that the Duke of Amalfi, the Duchess's legitimate son, whom Webster only mentions in passing, warmly espouses his mother's cause. I should be glad to know what the admirers of Webster's Duchess make of the fact that she never gives a word or a thought to the offspring of her first marriage.

This attempt to apply rational canons of dramatic construction to an Elizabethan 'masterpiece' will doubtless be regarded in many quarters as little less than sacrilegious. The time is surely approaching, however, when the criticism of the Elizabethans will no longer be left to scholars who know nothing of the theatre (Lamb's own plays show clearly how little he understood it), and who have not the elementary power of distinguishing between poetic and specifically dramatic merit.

(126–32)

Part Three Modern Views

Introduction

The most important single difference between the criticism of
Webster that came before the Great War and that which came after
is so obvious that it is easy to ignore and so ubiquitous that it is
hard to describe. In the later period literary criticism became a
professional (University-based) pursuit. This was a process that had,
of course, begun much earlier. E. E. Stoll's monograph, *John
Webster: the periods of his work determined by his relations to the drama
of his day* (1905) marked the absorption of Webster into the
machinery of German/American thesis-scholarship; and the machine
has been chewing him over ever since. Webster is read today far
more by those who have a duty to understand him than by those
who have a yearning to enjoy him; and the Webster industry
promotes this by tabulating, documenting, analysing, collating,
trying to bring into focus a work which is sought as objectively
'there', as it was in the beginning. Stoll's prime concern was with
the generic categories to which Webster's tragedies might be thought
to belong. He carefully analysed the plot elements, setting these in
the context of other 'revenge plays'; and so he explained their
imperfection of plot as failures to live up to an ideal generic model.
It is not unimportant to note that the model used has the virtues of
'well-made' nineteenth century plays – plays whose total coherence
can be judged in terms of the logic of a plot-summary.

Generic studies have remained, throughout the period, a
standard and useful means of organizing into significant patterns
the vast amount of material that literary-historical research has
uncovered. The danger is, of course, that the pattern will have a
factitious certainty which only conceals the complexity of the
literature. Webster's relation to the so-called revenge tradition is a
case in point. Some elements in Webster's tragedies (ghosts,
poisoning, madness) also appear in some plays self-consciously
concerned with revenge. It is not clear, however, that his dramatic
methods are best described as modifications of theirs. The historical
pattern that results is too simple to be very useful:

Webster, together with Fletcher, is the bridge between the older Elizabethans and the so-called decadent drama of Massinger and Ford.

It is probable that the organic model of growth-maturity-decline (naïvety-balance-decadence) is inescapable in literary history; but in combination with genre-study it is excessively simplifying. Harold Jenkins's essay in the revenge tradition (printed in part below, p. 263) has the advantage that only two plays are involved, so plot-summaries can be avoided. None the less the terms of the comparison are still established by the earlier play, and this seems a prejudging of Webster. For Webster's tragedies can only be justified, it would seem, in quite different terms from *Hamlet*.

It is clear that a scholarly method which tries to put *The White Devil* and *The Duchess of Malfi* into a context of other Jacobean tragedies does not, by itself, ensure much of a taste for them. The method is in fact very much at the mercy of the sensibility which selects similarities and differences, and applies such historical evidence as is said to be significant. One illustration of the necessary dependence of historical evidence on the judgement that deals with it appears in the controversy between F. W. Wadsworth (*Philological Quarterly*, 1956) and Clifford Leech (*Philological Quarterly*, 1958). This turns on the relation between Elizabethan ideas on remarriage and *The Duchess of Malfi*. It is clear that the Elizabethan evidence is mixed, and concerned primarily with practical details. Questions of the length of time between the death of a first husband and the marriage to a second, or about the 'worthiness' of the second, are either not to be answered from the play, or depend for their objective weight on our subjective interpretation of the nuance of the play.

The development of academic criticism has, in fact, in the period discussed, moved away from a passive reliance on the scientific handling of evidence as a road to objective truth. It has become

obvious that concealed subjective valuations are nearly always
present in these processes. Professional criticism, claiming its own
internal standards of truth, consistency and validation has come to
the centre of university 'English', though without much loss in the
strenuousness of historical research.

In this process, as it affects Webster – but Webster is not
untypical in this – the seminal mind is that of T. S. Eliot. Eliot's
introductory essay in *Four Elizabethan Dramatists* (1924) discusses the
nineteenth-century attitudes to the Elizabethans and remarks on the
essential similarity of Swinburne and Archer, in spite of their
apparent opposition:

No two critics of Elizabethan drama could appear to be more
opposed than Swinburne and Mr William Archer; yet their
assumptions are fundamentally the same, for the distinction between poetry and drama, which Mr Archer makes explicit, is
implicit in the view of Swinburne; Swinburne as well as Mr
Archer allows us to entertain the belief that the difference between modern drama and Elizabethan drama is represented by
a gain of dramatic technique and the loss of poetry.

Implicit in this comment is, of course, the assumption that both
Archer and Swinburne were wrong. Eliot was seeking throughout
this period for a new definition of poetic drama. His review of the
1919 production of *The Duchess of Malfi* (permission to reprint this
has been refused) is a good example of his important understanding
that the failure of Elizabethan classics on the modern stage is due less
to their inherent weakness than to the unfitness of modern actors
to represent their virtues: 'For poetry is something which the
actor cannot improve or "interpret" . . . poetry can only be
transmitted.' Eliot saw that a true poetic drama would have to be
sustained in terms neither of 'passage-worship' nor of plot-summary,
but on a 'pattern below the level of plot and character' (as he says

in his preface to G. Wilson Knight's *The Wheel of Fire*, 1930), on
the Symbolist basis of 'the figure in the carpet', giving coherence
and meaning to actions which may, on the surface, seem random and
arbitrary. In fact only the plays of Maeterlinck or Hofmansthal or
the Plays for Dancers of W. B. Yeats could hope to live up to this
ideal of tight aesthetic control; the Elizabethan drama certainly
cannot. Eliot points out that it is nearly all ruined by its appetite for
realism. The point that Archer and Swinburne are in basic agreement
with one another is well made; but it requires an addendum:
Archer and Eliot are also in basic agreement. For if Archer supposes
that the virtue of realism is ruined by the non-realism of Elizabethan
conventions, Eliot accepts the model and simply stands it on its
head. For him it is a case of the virtues of convention being
ruined by the hunger for realism. This is an unfortunate impasse
for critics of a drama that lived by combining realism and
convention.

The difficulty of imagining such a combination pervades the
whole period. It is nicely illustrated by the attitudes of various
critics to Webster's sententiae, those moralizing couplets with which
he punctuates the action, in seeming disregard of ordinary theatrical
proprieties. Tourneur seems to be acceptable here (for reasons to be
discussed below) where Webster is not. It is quite easy to see that
The Revenger's Tragedy is built on explicit moral assumptions, and
that the sententiae are part of this dehumanized morality structure.
Webster's sententiae seem to be more random; and it is often
alleged that they bear no relation to the rest of the play. Ian Jack
(1949) sees them as 'extraneous background of moral doctrine',
which 'has nothing to do with the action of the plays'; it is
'superimposed'. W. D. Boklund (1957) says that the world of
The White Devil is completely amoral; he thinks that the
'substitution of a flippant aestheticism for a system of moral
standards appears to be complete'. Commenting on Isabella,
Cornelia and Marcello he says,

The pat sententiousness with which the virtuous alternative is expressed makes the gulf between these accepted Christian tenets and the practice of those who ignore them yawn larger than ever. The futility of such virtue in the world of *The White Devil* is painfully obvious.

Robert Ornstein in *The Moral Vision of Jacobean Tragedy* (1960) examines both plays and finds the final moral lessons inadequate:

Although these sententious aphorisms are not irrelevant to what preceded them, they seem a bit like annotations by another hand – Christian glosses, as it were, on a pagan epic of courage and consuming passion. They do not suddenly crystallize a moral judgement embodied in Webster's portrayal of character, nor do they capture the essential significance of the lives on which they comment so weightily.

Clifford Leech in his *John Webster* (1951) says that the sententiae are not

... separated from the action or used for purposes of relief: they come in death scenes, in final utterances of major characters. The result is an effect of distancing when immediacy would be better.

The reader of the play may wonder why the critic does not examine the effect of distancing on himself rather than ask that the play should be limited to a nineteenth-century repertory of effects. In fact Professor Leech later (1963) writes positively of distancing techniques in *The Duchess of Malfi*. The change of view between 1951 and 1963 may be related to a general shift of theatrical taste, and the acceptance of a wider range of effects, in that period. Certainly, up to 1951 there was little evidence from the contemporary theatre that the dramaturgy of Shaw and Archer was other than immutable.

We must notice, however, that, though there is a theatrical impasse, not all attitudes to Webster are equally stationary. Webster's

poetical quality is very close to that which Eliot completely
refurbished. Dr Johnson's pejorative description of the
Metaphysicals as poets in whom 'the most heterogeneous ideas are
yoked by violence together' was turned by Eliot into a piece of
praise: the seventeenth-century sensibility could digest and fuse
disparate experiences into new-made wholes. The Metaphysical
poets became the favourite poets of a new generation. But the
'unity of sensibility' which may hold together the thirty lines or so
of a Donne lyric is not sufficient to unify a play eighty to a hundred
times that length. Drama as an imitation of life relates not simply to
hypothetical or metaphorical existences (as in the brilliantly successful
dramatic monologues of the Eliot school) but to actual people
responding to actual societies. And even among dramatists Webster
is difficult in this respect; for he clearly wished to make his people
real to the audience, both by including actual historical events (e.g. the
annunciation of a new Pope) and by underlining the domestic details
of individual relationships. From Eliot's point of view this could only
be a betrayal of the pure art of poetic drama, an early symptom of
that debilitating fever which appeared in English art some time in
the seventeenth century and left the patient permanently enfeebled.
Webster the metaphysical poet had to be praised; but Webster the
playwright has to be explained away rather than explained. His
immense poetic potential was wasted by the current of theatrical
decadence in which he moved. As far as Webster is concerned the
Swinburne/Archer dichotomy seems to have reasserted itself.

Eliot did not find Webster congenial enough to warrant a
complete essay; but the stray remarks he makes about him can often
be seen to be the seeds of much subsequent writing. He calls him
'a very great literary and dramatic genius directed towards chaos',
and this formed a point of departure for the Cambridge critics of
the thirties, L. G. Salingar, W. A. Edwards, M. C. Bradbrook and
L. C. Knights. Professor Bradbrook's *Themes and Conventions of
Elizabethan Tragedy* (1935) is the most sustained interpretation of the

whole field. Like Eliot and Salingar she prefers the more schematic
plays, *The Revenger's Tragedy* and Middleton's *The Changeling*,
which the new methods were bringing into high esteem. In
comparison to Tourneur, Webster seems to her, as he had seemed
to earlier critics, in only uncertain control of his material. Professor
Bradbrook sees the 'double nature' of Webster's characters, for
example, as being in two halves, 'not alternating', 'but blurred and
run together'. She observes what she takes to be a desire for
naturalism; and no one, of course, has ever seen naturalism as a
possible unifying factor in Webster's work. 'As a result,' she says,
'there is no pattern of characters, nor is there any structure of
themes as in Tourneur's plays.'

L. G. Salingar is more concerned with the placing of Webster in a
historical scheme, which clearly derives from Eliot's 'dissociation of
sensibility' line on the seventeenth century, and L. C. Knights's
development of this in *Drama and Society in the Age of Jonson* (1937).
Salingar (writing in *Scrutiny* in 1938) attributes the satisfyingly
schematic nature of *The Revenger's Tragedy* to the survival of the
Morality tradition from the Middle Ages, and sees what follows the
death of this tradition as a trend towards 'semi- or pseudo-naturalism'.
Only Shakespeare succeeds with naturalism; Webster, in the
absence of any morally sustaining convention, can only seem a
failed Shakespeare, stumbling from one muddled expedient
to another:

His picture of society resembles Tourneur's; but the Morality
elements, which had represented for the latter the dramatic
equivalents for a central core of judgements and feelings have
disappeared; and Webster, unable to come to rest on any attitude from which to value his people, more stable or more
penetrating than a pose of stoical bravado, could not write
coherent drama at all. Where they are not simply melodrama,
his plays depend on exploiting immediate sensations disjointed

from their dramatic contexts; and this applies not only to his stagecraft, but to his verse, which works by analogous means, and which gains, as Tourneur loses, from quotation in short passages.

Ian Jack (*Scrutiny*, 1949) makes the same moral strictures on Webster as man and artist (see below, p. 157). Webster was 'denied insight into any virtue other than stoical courage'; he could have looked to the morality tradition for inspiration had he wished, but perversely chose the 'philosophical poverty' of the revenge tradition.

The proximity of Webster's methods to Shakespeare's seems almost fatal to the attempt to give him a status of his own. Salinger, like Edwards and Bradbrook, assumes that if Webster had been more able he would have been more like Shakespeare. Edwards (*Scrutiny*, 1933) compares Flamineo and Bosola with Hamlet,

whose bitterness about women's painting springs out of the immediate situation and in turn affects it. Flamineo and Bosola are like bores who imagine themselves raconteurs. Why need Bosola swoop down on an old woman to unload his notes on cosmetics, for instance?

Not being as un-Shakespearian as Tourneur 'poor Webster' (as Archer calls him) has to be seen as a failed or decadent Shakespeare.

Later work in the same tradition pounds away at the same points. T. B. Tomlinson's *Elizabethan and Jacobean Tragedy* (1964), C. O. MacDonald's *The Rhetoric of Tragedy* (1966) and D. L. Frost's *The School of Shakespeare* (1968) seem to show that the vein is virtually exhausted, and that new insight into Webster is not likely to be derived from these premises.

Another line of criticism that the twentieth century has applied to Webster can be seen, like the foregoing, to descend from Eliot; but in this case it comes to Webster only by way of Shakespeare. Myth-symbol-image criticism proved highly successful with Shakespeare's plays; it can be said to have become a dominant mode of Shakespeare criticism by the fifties. It acquired a technique and a vocabulary of its own, first of all, perhaps, in G. Wilson Knight's *The Wheel of Fire* (1930), to which T. S. Eliot contributed an important preface. Wilson Knight's 'spatial' criticism found meaning in Shakespeare's plays through their symbolism of music, tempests, royalty, etc., through 'manifold correspondences of imaginative quality extending throughout the whole play'. The reader responded first of all to these general forms, and only secondarily to plot and character.

Una Ellis-Fermor (*The Jacobean Drama*, 1936) was the first to attempt a direct application of 'spatial' methods to Webster. But her outline of the possible application of these methods in an introductory chapter is hardly answered when she comes to detail. The imagery of Webster is in fact rather resistant to Knight's kind of interpretation. It cannot be expanded into the same suggestive generalizations as Shakespeare's. The emphasis is far more on circumscribed local and satiric effects, and attention is drawn away from the content of the image to the obliquity of its organization. In the only full-scale analysis of Webster's imagery (1955), Hereward T. Price has to stress the ironic relationship of the parts rather than the grandeur of their generality (see below, p. 176). Moody E. Prior (1947) shows in other ways the difficulties of analysing Webster's imagery. C. W. Davies ('The structure of *The Duchess of Malfi*: an approach', *English*, 1958–9) writes well on Webster's characters as creations of the world of imagery in which they are involved. It is this focus which makes them vivid and 'real' and supports the fragmentary verisimilitude they possess. As we read through these critics it becomes obvious that Webster's structures are too deliberate, too intellectual, too much a mosaic made out of his own reading, to be properly susceptible of 'spatial' analysis.

An increasingly common view among the most recent critics of Webster is that his tragedies are not to be described in terms of any single model; since they involve two separate kinds of motivation simultaneously present, they require of the audience two separate modes of judgement. It follows that the effect aimed at can only be described as a species of counterpoint. Eliot may be thought to have fathered this type of criticism also. He says that Webster

in his greatest tragedies has a kind of pity for *all* his characters, an attitude to good and bad alike which helps to unify the Webster pattern.

The earliest plea that the reader of Webster should hold two ideas in his head at one time comes from James Smith writing in *Scrutiny* in December 1939 – a remarkably independent and pioneering piece of work. Commenting on the 'broken' quality of the opening of *The White Devil*, Smith says: 'The spectator is required to judge not so much between statements, as to base a judgement on a group of them.' Speaking of the dialogues he says that they are 'concerted pieces and nothing can be abstracted'; and he draws attention to the 'diversity of aspect and function' of some of the speeches without drawing the conclusion which has seemed logical to many critics, that if more than one effect or purpose is observable at one time, Webster must have been confused himself. In her essay on fate and chance in *The Duchess of Malfi* (1947), printed below (p. 132), Professor Bradbrook makes a point which is relevant here; between the alternative explanations of life provided by fate and chance, 'the astounding and gratifying thing is that he should have been able to resist the temptation to state a case'.

The most extended case for Webster as a uniquely successful master of counterpoint is Travis Bogard's *The Tragic Satire of John Webster* (1955) (see below, p. 174). Bogard does not think Archer's case can be said to be satisfactorily answered until it can be shown that Webster's 'dramaturgy' is 'determined not by play-making formulas but by that shaping vision of experience without which no play can be more than melodrama'. He says that Webster is a great dramatist because 'seeing the world with both pity and contempt he remained faithful to his vision by blending two almost incompatible genres – tragedy and satire'. Whether or not one finishes Bogard's book feeling that his formal explanation of Webster's excellences is wholly satisfactory, the excellence of his own illuminations of many aspects of the plays is undeniable. The 'double action' of the plays is traced in terms of 'satiric counterpoint to the tragic action'. He shows convincingly how the prevailing imagery fits into this pattern by establishing a tone which 'runs counter to the dominant action of the scene'. He joins the comparison-with-Shakespeare debate with a view which puts Webster on positive ground of his own:

If Shakespeare's tragedy is a vortex – centering the moral universe in the suffering soul of an individual, then Webster's may be likened to a framed general action like a stage panorama which makes its most significant revelations through the presentation of man's relations to man.

I.-S. Ekeblad (p. 202) and J. L. Calderwood (p. 266) make use of another framework. They suggest that Webster's effects in *The Duchess of Malfi* are held together by the use of rituals, which imply valuations without embodying them in character. Webster's patterns override the complexity of the material contained in the plays, the naturalism, the fantasy, the abstraction, as in a masque rather than a play (as normally defined). Miss Ekeblad and Mr Calderwood both concentrate on the scenes of the Duchess's torment. Miss Ekeblad's subtle and persuasive treatment of these episodes is the most convincing answer yet written to Eliot's charge that convention is ruined by realism. But we still await an extension of this answer to cover the whole structure of the plays.

Professor J. R. Brown, in the critical introduction to his edition of *The White Devil* (printed below, p. 235), draws on many of the same assumptions as Miss Ekeblad. He speaks of the 'Gothic aggregation' of the structure, its multiplicity of effect, its counterpointing of highlighted individual moments against a generalized framework of sententious comment; in these and other ways he is able to describe effectively the play we respond to. It is hard not to feel that these critics are sympathetically in touch with far more of the plays than was available to the sympathy of earlier critics. But something is still lacking. This might be described as a simplification of the truths already known. We ought to be able to formulate a 'general law' which will describe all the instances in their basic terms. When this is written it may then be possible to return to the question of Webster's relation to Shakespeare and his other contemporaries without seeing him too simply as either decadent or aberrant.

T. S. Eliot

Whispers of Immortality from *Poems*   1919

Webster was much possessed by death
And saw the skull beneath the skin;
And breastless creatures under ground
Leaned backward with a lipless grin.

Daffodil bulbs instead of balls
Stared from the sockets of the eyes!
He knew that thought clings round dead limbs
Tightening its lusts and luxuries.

Donne, I suppose, was such another
Who found no substitute for sense,
To seize and clutch and penetrate;
Expert beyond experience,

He knew the anguish of the marrow
The ague of the skeleton;
No contact possible to flesh
Allayed the fever of the bone.

Grishkin is nice: her Russian eye
Is underlined for emphasis;
Uncorseted, her friendly bust
Gives promise of pneumatic bliss.

The couched Brazilian jaguar
Compels the scampering marmoset
With subtle effluence of cat;
Grishkin has a maisonnette;

The sleek Brazilian jaguar
Does not in its arboreal gloom
Distil so rank a feline smell
As Grishkin in a drawing-room.

And even the Abstract Entities
Circumambulate her charm;
But our lot crawls between dry ribs
To keep our metaphysics warm.

W. A. Edwards

[Webster and Character-Writing] from 'Revaluations: John Webster', *Scrutiny*, vol. 2 1933

The style of the conceited character-writer has obvious defects when it comes to dramatic writing. It is the style of an objective, rather cynical observer, commenting and reflecting upon men and actions, and constantly invites admiration for the elegance of its manner. It tends towards epigram and maxim, and uses simile rather than metaphor – Bacon's Essays represent it at its best. For dramatic utterance such a style of writing is too formal, too far from speech-idiom. We need only contrast the Cardinal's character of a whore with Ulysses' reaction towards Cressida. The Cardinal's definitions are neat and apt; they delight us by their ingenuity; but his sketch is a series of disconnected observations. We are left thinking of the last epigram and trying vainly to recollect the others. At the end of his speech we lack any clear conception of the whore, and are conscious only of an admiration for the Cardinal's talent as a wit.

In the phrase and in the single image Webster is often superb, yet he scarcely ever succeeds in writing a successful *passage* of verse, still less a whole scene. As in Bacon, we meet with the same short-windedness everywhere, the full stop of the aphorism, the suggestion of a penny-in-the-slot machine. He assembles three or four images in a passage and they remain discrete components, do not enforce or modify each other:

>   . . . pray observe me.
> We see that undermining more prevails
> Than doth the cannon. Bear your wrongs conceal'd,
> And, patient as the tortoise, let this camel
> Stalk o'er your back unbruis'd: sleep with the lion

And let this brood of secure foolish mice
Play with your nostrils, till the time be ripe
For the bloody audit and the fatal gripe:
Aim like a cunning fowler, close one eye
That you the better may your game espy.

(*The White Devil*, IV i 12–21)

In more than one particular this passage suggests Lyly – the same
bestiary comparisons, the same non-progressive circling round a single
idea, and the same undramatic interest, one feels, in finding still
another analogy. Compare it with this paragraph from *Euphues*:

Couldst thou Euphues, for the love of a fruitless pleasure, violate
the league of faithful friendship? If thou didst determine with thyself
at the first to be false why didst thou swear to be true. If to be true,
why art thou false? . . . Dost thou not know that a perfect friend
should be like a glow-worm, which shinest most bright in the
dark? or like the pure frankincense, which smelleth more sweet
when it is in the fire? or at the least not unlike the damask rose
which is sweeter in the still than on the stalk? But thou Euphues
dost rather resemble the swallow, which in the summer creepeth
under the eaves of every house, and in the winter leaveth nothing
but dirt behind, or the bumble-bee, which having sucked honey out
of the fair flower doth leave it and loathe it, or the spider, which
in the finest web doth hang the fairest fly.

Webster's inability to write a sustained passage of verse finds its
counterpart in his incompetent plotting. On the plane of action neither
tragedy is worth much consideration. They could be taken as an
illustration of Bosola's summing-up of life:

Their life a general mist of error
Their death a hideous storm of terror

(IV ii 188–9)

(and the terror largely of the wax-works type). Mr Lucas is willing to
blame Webster's public for his melodramatic interests and effects:

For the men who crowded the Phoenix and the Red Bull lived
both in the theatre and outside it far more in the moment for the

moment's sake than the cultured classes of today; accordingly it was a succession of great moments they wanted on the stage, not a well-made play. They did not at each instant look forward to what was coming or what had been. If a dramatist gave them great situations, ablaze with passion and poetry, it would have seemed to them a chilly sort of pedantry that peered too closely into the machinery by which they were produced. They did not want their fire-works analysed. They were in fact very like a modern cinema audience, with the vast difference that they had also an appetite for poetry.

But this is a poor explanation. The same public was equipped in the main with a grammar-school education which concentrated on a training in the use of language; it listened to speeches and sermons which today can be read only with difficulty; and it applauded plays as close-knit as *The Alchemist* and *Volpone*, and plays which made demands on its capacity to appreciate poetry and the patterns and symbols used in poetic drama – the tragedies of Shakespeare, for instance.

A far more plausible suggestion is that Webster wrote melodrama because he had a taste for it, and that in writing his tragedies he was concerned as a popular play-wright to turn out plays which would please every kind of play-goer. He starts from a story packed with incidents well suited to melodrama, and alters it very little. At times one suspects he wrote with his tongue in his cheek; Flamineo's interview with the Ghost of Brachiano, at least, suggests this. The Ghost is a genuine ghost – Flamineo the sceptic is hardly the man to suffer from 'vain imaginings', and it carries a flower-pot – not even a harassed man would imagine a flower-pot. Flamineo seems his normal self – the curious observer, the investigator, the busy prying mind. Like a good journalist he keeps his head and interviews: Brachiano's views on the other world, the truth of churchmen's theories about communication with the dead, the best religion to die in, how long he may expect to live. After the Ghost has gone Flamineo runs over the events of the day, methodically listing his misfortunes:

> the disgrace
The prince threw on me; next the piteous sight
Of my dead brother: and my mother's dotage;
And last this terrible vision.   (v v 146–9)

That word 'terrible' rouses our suspicions. Flamineo seems to have been not in the least upset, but we see that the audience ought to have been thrilled, and are told so.

(17–19)

U. Ellis-Fermor

[Form in Jacobean Drama], *The Jacobean Drama*   1936

In examining the form of Jacobean tragedy – for it is mainly in tragedy that the question arises – we notice two things. First that each of the major dramatists, if he reach maturity of work at all, tends to make for himself a form which mirrors his thought, his comment upon events or people and their relations, rather than to select primarily a chronological sequence of events to make a pattern; thus, Webster's notorious neglect of events in *The Duchess of Malfi* (a neglect which does not even trouble to make the action plausible by readjusting a few confusing references) is balanced by the surprising shapeliness which appears when we look at the play as a two-dimensional map of moods and personalities in their relations to each other rather than as a single-dimensional line of progression from event to event. Second, that, while these plays may seem to have little relation to the forms which other dramatists or groups of dramatists have chosen for their expression, their formal excellence sometimes becomes much clearer when we compare it with that developed by artists working in other mediums; thus there are sometimes clearer resemblances in fundamental form between the structure of Ben Jonson or Ford or Webster and a painting or a musical composition of similar magnitude than there are between these artists and other dramatists. It has, of course, been pointed out[1] that the Jacobean audience, and apparently the dramatist, preferred to experience a succession of striking situations and to carry away a number of such separate images, rather than the memory of a unified and integrated aesthetic experience – that it had, in short, neither use nor capacity for the Aristotelian 'whole'. This is probably true of the audience and consequently of the dramatists as men of business. But the artist, particularly the Jacobean artist, is notoriously good at serving two masters provided one be the public and the other his own instinct. He sometimes serves the first in the apparent form, the chronological sequence of events, and the second in the real, underlying form which maps the territory as an area of human experience. The omission of a few essential links in what we like to call the 'plot' of The Duchess of Malfi is thus seen to offer no difficulty in either world.

(30–31)

James Smith

'The Tragedy of Blood', Scrutiny, vol. 8   1939

Webster, like many or perhaps most of the Elizabethans, has been over-praised; more certainly and more dangerously he has been praised for the wrong reasons. In consequence there has developed a tendency either to praise him not at all, or to under-praise; and conflicts have arisen, mistaken, I think, on both sides, by which possibly right reasons for praise have been obscured.

For example, both his detractors and his admirers agree that he lacks constructive ability. His poetry, say the latter, is a poetry of flashes, of fragments; such a poetry, reply the former, is not poetry at all – or at any rate it is not dramatic poetry. Both I would say repose a very generous trust in general principles of criticism; whereas the matter of literature is of such variety that, unless general principles are continually tested and supplemented, they are as likely as not to mislead. Before allowing that Webster cannot construct, his admirers should

1 In recent criticism we may recall the comments of Mr F. L. Lucas on the structure of Webster's tragedies. (See especially the Introduction to his edition, vol. 1, pp. 17–22.)

perhaps consider whether the type of construction in which obviously he fails – in which dramatic tension is gradually increased through a number of acts, then decreased more swiftly but still gradually – whether this type of construction, though common, is the only type possible; and whether it is a type which, in *The White Devil*, he even attempted. And on the other hand the detractors should perhaps ask themselves whether, whatever the precision and homogeneity to be predicted of an ideal drama or poem – in which no word would be superfluous, and no phrase in the slightest degree either above or below its context – human imbecility allows this precision to be realized in a work of any length. If not, then in Webster's work it is important to consider not the fact that, but the degree to which, it contains inequalities. For this may not be so great as to prevent it being effective as an artistic – a poetic, a dramatic – whole.

Whether or not it is so can of course be decided only by reading it. In the rest of this paper I shall endeavour to explain why, after reading *The White Devil*, I think that it is so. Or at least that is what I shall try to do in part: for I shall be able to treat only the first of the above questions, about the play's construction. In any case this is what needs to be considered first: to those who, neglecting it, hasten (as is quite likely) to decide that defects outweigh excellencies in Webster's verse I can only say that the excellencies are undoubtedly great; and perhaps more easily under-estimated than the defects are ignored.

The opening of the play has often been noted for its abruptness; but has, I think, other qualities worthy of attention. Lodovico is announcing that he has been banished, Antonelli and Gasparo are condoling with him:

LODOVICO: Banish'd?
ANTONELLI: It griev'd me much to hear the sentence.
LODOVICO: Ha, ha, O Democritus thy Gods
That govern the whole world! – Courtly reward,
And punishment. Fortune's a right whore.
If she give aught, she deals it in small parcels,
That she may take away all at one swoop.
This 'tis to have great enemies, God quite them:
Your wolf no longer seems to be a wolf
Than when she's hungry.   (i i 1–9)

Lodovico is moved: so much is obvious from the substance of his sentences. But also their brevity, and an emphasis which they acquire either by straddling the pentameter or by filling it to the point, suggest that this emotion is not beyond control and will lead to action. To what kind of action? for Lodovico contradicts himself. He pours scorn on the gods while at the same time he invokes their aid; his enemy he considers to be now Fortune which is capricious, now great men who are malevolent; the latter he hints are both hungry and satiate; contemptible by nature (for they are wolves), but enviable for what they have been able to achieve. The contradictions are the more obvious because conjunctions are few; and the sentences – this is an unusual connexion or lack of connexion between them – seem not so much to follow and resume, as to qualify or comment on one another as they lie side by side. It must I think be allowed that they do so; and the speech in consequence taken not so much as an account of Lodovico as a piece of acting or material for such an account. This the reader must draft for himself, as it is not supplied from the stage.

What then is the account to be? As Lodovico appears both to believe and to disbelieve in order, whether human or divine, it is tempting to dismiss him as merely incoherent. But if he were so, he would be incapable of [action and speech]; and of these the first is unlikely to be true, the second impossible. It may, I think, be nearer the truth that he realizes only faintly the nature and consequences of action, speech, or belief; and that, for the sake of saying or doing something, he is willing to adopt, not insincerely but ignorantly, any and any number of scraps of beliefs. His mind is disorderly, while at the same time it is decisive, and this is perhaps what his manner of speech is intended to convey: as the separate sentences fall on the ear they are decisive, they appear disorderly as they seek to fit into a whole.

Qualities of this kind are at any rate of sufficient importance for Webster to bring them into prominence by a contrast. The dialogue between Antonelli and Gasparo which immediately follows is so orderly as at first sight to appear mechanical; and so feeble as to be bathetic at what, again at first sight, appears its climax:

ANTONELLI: Come my Lord,
You are justly doom'd; look but a little back

Into your former life: you have in three years
Ruin'd the noblest earldom –
GASPARO: Your followers
Have swallowed you like mummia, and being sick
With such unnatural and horrid physic
Vomit you up i'th' kennel –
ANTONELLI: All the damnable degrees
Of drinkings have you stagger'd through – one citizen
Is lord of two fair manors call'd you master,
Only for caviare.
GASPARO: Those noblemen
Which were invited to your prodigal feasts,
Wherein the phoenix scarce could scape your throats,
Laught at your misery . . .
                              Worse than these,
You have acted certain murders here in Rome,
Bloody and full of horror.
                        (1 i 12–32)

The speeches begin and end in the middle of a line, and a seesaw-like
balance is immediately obvious about them. The lines about murder
could hardly be more perfunctory.

The dialogue has however positive qualities, and its function is not
merely to be a foil to Lodovico. It would, I think, be as true to say that
the latter's speech is foil to the dialogue: for as do the sentences within
the speech, the two lie side by side commenting upon and qualifying
one another. Once again the spectator is required to judge not so much
between statements, as to base a judgement upon a group of them.

Antonelli and Gasparo speak of justice, which is a principle of order.
Their justice is however of a peculiar kind, according to which extravagance and gluttony are less serious than murder. As has been said,
murder is mentioned only perfunctorily; it is also last in the dialogue;
while extravagance and gluttony which precede it are, on the other
hand, not inadequately described. That Antonelli and Gasparo believe
in a justice of this kind should not perhaps be suspected, even for a
moment; but if so, it is necessary only to glance at their descriptions.
If these hint at any feeling at all – and I think they do – it is at approval
of what they professedly condemn. Behind imitations of a drunkard's
voice and gait,

> All the damnable degrees
> Of drinkings have you stagger'd through ...

it is difficult not to be aware of complacency; behind the verse about

> prodigal feasts
> Wherein the phoenix scarce could scape your throats ...

of envy and admiration. Gasparo's and Antonelli's parade of the word justice, it seems clear, is mere hypocrisy.

They are mocking rather than rebuking Lodovico; or if they rebuke him at all, it is for not being sufficiently hypocritical as they are. To be sure of future indulgence, vice needs to take account both of public opinion and of its own resources. The former cannot be persistently outraged; the latter, by a man in Lodovico's station, need to be husbanded. As he has indulged too early and too often, he is rightly a subject to 'jest upon'. The dialogue is an artifice – hence its artificial structure; and by it the speakers intend that artifice shall be recommended. It shall be so by veiled precept, but still more by open example.

Lodovico however will not learn. His eyes, unaccustomed to the future, do not seize any of the benefits in the way of licence likely to flow from present constraint. The latter appears not prudence but affectation; and in an aside to the audience he ridicules Gasparo and Antonelli's way of speaking:

> This well goes with two buckets, I must tend
> The pouring out of either. (I i 29–30)

Later, when the affectation reaches its height in the lines about murder:

> You have acted certain murders here in Rome
> Bloody and full of horror,

his ridicule comes into the open. ''Las,' he replies, 'they were flea-bitings', presenting Antonelli and Gasparo with a more adequate expression of their common views.

But he is not, I think, rebuking them for hypocrisy, any more than they have rebuked him. If he is the more sympathetic as he is the simpler character, he is not the more virtuous; and any attempt to sympathize with him wholly or even to a marked degree would be to

misread the scene. The mystifications and accommodations paraded
by Antonelli and Gasparo get in his way as a man of action; they discredit action on which he has been engaged in the past: impatiently
therefore – but no more than impatiently; certainly not in the interests
of virtue – he brushes them aside.

I hope it will not appear I am refining too much on a small part of a
comparatively unimportant scene. A tradition of some strength has to
be broken: if it cannot be said that the scene and the play as a whole
has received insufficient, it has received the wrong kind of attention.
On the one hand, the romantically inclined have read into it admiration for Lodovico's precipitancy, which accordingly they have called
courage or heroism; the post-romantics on the other, rightly rejecting
these as of no value, have concluded that there is no reference whatever to values in the play. Nor indeed in the whole of Webster; whose
work therefore is negligible. Whereas the truth, I am suggesting,
would seem to be that here at any rate by opposing two negative
values in such a way that neither dominates nor obscures the other;
that, like the sentences and the speeches we have considered, they continue side by side; a pointed reference to positives is made. Antonelli
and Gasparo rebuke Lodovico for his brutish lack of prudence; he
them, for their diabolic cunning. And thus, by something it would not
be improper to call construction, standards are introduced into the
picture of a world of evil; though as yet there is no one in it who
illustrates them by his actions or his words.

These deductions based on a few opening lines might I think be
confirmed from other parts of the play. Throughout Lodovico shows
himself to be a creature of impulses; clear-headed enough for these to
be followed with success, not for them to be compared one against the
other and if need be suppressed.

Instruction to thee,

says Monticelso,

Comes like sweet showers to over-hard'ned ground;
They wet, but pierce not deep. (IV iii 122–4)

He falls in love with the Duchess, or rather 'pursues her with hot
lust'; if Webster gives no warning of this, that I think is due not to his

oversight, but to the nature of his theme. Upon the Duchess's death Lodovico swears to avenge her. And if Monticelso's refusal of support causes him for a moment to hesitate, a single sign of approval, or what he takes for such, precipitates him upon his course once again. Francisco easily makes him a devoted tool; and at the end of the play the sight of his vengeance so fills him that he can admit the possibility of no other sensation:

The rack, the gallows, and the torturing wheel
Shall be but sound sleeps to me, – here's my rest –
I limb'd this night-piece and it was my best.
                    (v vi 295–7)

Here there is both intellectual and physical insensibility; not as in a hero or martyr a triumph of intellect or morals over sense. Antonelli and Gasparo on the other hand are deemed worthy to be Francisco's accomplices, Antonelli at least saving his skin. But the clearest confirmation of what I have been trying to say is perhaps to be found in that part of the first scene not yet dealt with.

Its function, let me premise, is to prepare the background against which, during the second scene, the principal characters are to appear. To use a common metaphor, the atmosphere is to be created in which they breathe. And if what has been said is at all true, this is done rather by actions than by words: Lodovico first executes a movement, then Antonelli and Gasparo – the reader being left to a very large extent to draw his own conclusions. In the opening lines the movements are comparatively sober, as if to establish that they are possible or likely in men. Webster wishes it to be clear that the subject he is portraying and criticizing is humanity. Afterwards it is open to him to make clearer what his criticism is to be. The movements are exaggerated, approaching near to caricature; or, to keep within terms of the drama, to what Mr Eliot in writing of *The Jew of Malta* called farce. After gossip which reveals to the audience that Brachiano pursues 'by close panderism . . . the honour of Vittoria Corombona' Antonelli continues:

Have a full man within you, –
We see that trees bear no such pleasant fruit
There where they grew first, as where they are new set:

Perfumes the more they are chaf'd the more they render
Their pleasing scents, and so affliction
Expresseth virtue, fully, whether true
Or else adulterate.
                                    (I i 45–51)

This note is familiar from other plays: it is that of 'For though the Camomile, the more it is trodden on, the faster it grows . . .'. But whereas Falstaff does not expect to be taken seriously when he talks in this way, Antonelli and Gasparo are unprepared for Lodovico's gibe:

                    Leave your painted comforts, –
I'll make Italian cut-works in their guts
If ever I return.
                                    (I i 51–3)

Their sole rejoinder is however an 'O sir!'; it is their manners rather than their morals which Lodovico has outraged.

As the two sets of rogues leave the stage, Lodovico hopes for a quick death, advising Antonelli and Gasparo to make ready against a similar necessity. But they are so far from fearing it that they offer aid for his future plans. Thus they part, in spite of divergence in evil, expressing mutual esteem; but, as has been said, this divergence and esteem are intended to rouse the audience to their common condemnation.

In Scene ii the principles of construction suggested by Scene i are employed for the ordering and presentation of far more important matter. The great Duke of Brachiano, of whom passing mention has already been made, is introduced in person, and with him the principal characters.

He is surrounded by the paraphernalia of greatness – coaches, train, and lights. But he has no sooner summoned his confidant and, out of the midst of these, seized opportunity to whisper:

BRACHIANO: Flamineo.
FLAMINEO: My lord.
BRACHIANO: Quite lost, Flamineo.
                                    (I ii 3)

than they are dismissed. In the play he is to sacrifice greatness to his passion.

The dialogue which follows is of the kind now familiar. The two speakers, in far from perfect sympathy one with another, are as far from perfect communication; neither gives himself a fair account of the other, and both need therefore to be read with equal attention. Only in that way is it possible to know what Webster thought of them, and what he intended the reader to think. On the one hand Brachiano continues the train of reflections, imprecise on the whole but in so far as it is otherwise by no means discreditable, suggested by his 'Quite lost'. This exclamation was one rather of love, if unlawful love, than of lust; of self-abandonment to another, than of self-assertion at another's expense. Accordingly, to Flamineo's news that Vittoria awaits him, Brachiano replies:

Are we so happy?

(I ii 10)

and again, a few minutes later,

We are happy above thought, because 'bove merit.

(I ii 16)

Then prudence or conscience begins to disturb him:

O but her jealous husband.

(I ii 26)

Finally this reminder of obstacles in the way of his passion rouses the fear that it may not be satisfied:

O should she fail to come, –

(I ii 38)

While at the same time Flamineo pours forth a torrent of reflections on the lasciviousness of women, the imbecility of husbands, the vanity of love.

It has been objected to both Webster and Flamineo that the reflections are not new. This is true, but not therefore a fault. For Brachiano's incipient passion is a difficult problem: in so far as it inclines to vice and lust Flamineo welcomes it, as it promises a hold upon Brachiano; love and virtue on the other hand must loosen that hold perhaps even remove it if conscience, as it has begun, continues stirring. So he has to encourage the passion, and at the same time to degrade it. One way, the most obvious and perhaps the only way, is by assimilating it to the subjects of commonplace conversation, indecent and otherwise: things sanctioned or commanded by custom, but rendered at the same time sordid and contemptible.

The dialogue at cross-purposes, Flamineo deliberately ignoring the possibly higher purposes of Brachiano, thus serves to indicate a judgement on Flamineo; but Brachiano is also judged, in that he sees nothing incongruous in choosing Flamineo as confidant. The indecent commonplaces do not startle him into attention; they would not seem new to him – what is new is his passion, so new that he does not know how to handle it. He would be the predestined victim of Flamineo were not Vittoria – who is however another evil – at hand.

If we pause for a moment to look ahead, it will, I think, be seen that throughout the play Brachiano is characterized either by hesitancy and hebetude, as now, or by what naturally succeeds them in a mind, blindness and obstinacy. It is Vittoria who operates the change. When at length introduced into her presence, his first speech is a confession of inarticulacy:

Let me into your bosom happy lady,
Pour out instead of eloquence my vows . . .
(I ii 205–6)

She replies with mockery that is scarcely veiled:

      Sir in the way of pity
I wish you heart-whole . . .
Sure sir a loathed cruelty in ladies
Is as to doctors many funerals:
It takes away their credit.
(I ii 208–12)

Nevertheless her answer has assured him that he is articulate to some degree; she has acknowledged his passion, given him confidence in himself; he is overwhelmed with gratitude, he is hers from that moment. He can be jealous of her, as a possible object of another man's veneration; but that there is anything about her which should not be venerated, he obstinately refuses to admit. Though he has

shared her crimes, for him she remains a 'good woman' to the end.
He shares her shame in the public court, for her sake he defies Grand
Duke and Pope. He begins to defy even Flamineo; but that is too late,
when a common ruin is enveloping them all.

Vittoria herself is partly defined by the above and similar answers
to Brachiano – confident, condescending, even impertinent; at the
same time well-judged and effective: more clearly by her share in a
concerted piece which is the central, as it is the most remarkable, passage in this scene. I call it concerted because, like the dialogues considered hitherto, all its parts are of equal importance and must be
considered at once; but also, by a device of eavesdropping and asides,
they are made so to speak to sound at once. The writing almost ceases
to be writing and to be dramatic; it becomes operatic and almost a
score.

Vittoria and Flamineo are in the centre of the stage, conversing both
openly, and in undertones. The open conversation is intended for
Camillo, Vittoria's husband, who is listening off. He has been promised that, if he would retire, Flamineo would woo Vittoria for him,
to receive him back into her graces. Every public compliment to
Camillo however is cancelled by a whispered slight:

Shall a gentleman so well descended as Camillo (a lousy
slave that within this twenty years rode . . . 'mongst spits and
dripping-pans).

(I ii 130–33)

Thus two parts are already sounding at once, affecting and enriching
each other. For it is as impossible for the audience to take the whisper-
ings as it [is] to take the shoutings at the value they would have in
isolation. Camillo has already been exhibited – not an impressive person, but one who has shown signs of good feeling and good sense (he
has, for example, refused to believe either that Brachiano's designs
are a figment of his imagination, or that Vittoria is licentious because
she is denied liberty); further he has confided his interests to Flamineo,
who is therefore not only abusing him, but abusing him grossly;
finally Camillo's very weakness and insignificance render the whispered detraction as unnecessary, as the public encomia are absurd. All
this is, I think, kept before the hearer's mind by the contrast between
the two; who is in consequence moved not so much to laughter by

Flamineo's buffoonery, as to distaste. Flamineo is playing the fool not primarily for the audience, but for himself. The task he has undertaken degrades himself as well as Brachiano; as it deprives him of self-respect he can continue with it only by procuring continual diversion – as in this uproarious way.

At the same time a third part is sounding – Vittoria's. It consists chiefly of rests. To Flamineo's first representation that her husband is discontented she replies disingenuously that she has paid him marks of public respect: 'I did nothing to displease him; I carved to him at supper.' After that, though her desire to be rid of Camillo is as urgent as Flamineo's, she is silent; and that she gives no sign of approval to his buffoonery must, I think, be taken to mean that she disapproves. She has of course no need of it to continue in her task; which if evil, is not so evil as Flamineo's. She seeks, not to obtain a blackmailer's hold on Brachiano, but to reign publicly as his duchess; to commit adultery, to procure murder – but not to forfeit all claims to her own or her fellow's esteem. She seeks indeed the very opposite, though by mistaken means. And so her silence at this point performs, like almost everything else, at least a double function: it is a criticism of Flamineo, strengthening the criticism already formed by the audience; at the same time it is a criticism on herself, for what she does not approve of she must nevertheless endure. Though she despises Flamineo, he is a valuable ally whom as yet she dare not offend; it is some time before, though sick at the baiting of Camillo, she ventures to suggest that it be cut short: 'How shall's rid him hence?'

The passage is complicated to a yet further degree. For not only Camillo, but Brachiano, is listening[1]; is listening too for a purpose very similar to Camillo's. To him, as to Camillo, Flamineo has promised that he will woo Vittoria. So that everything Flamineo says openly has not only a double sense, in so far as it is or is not understood to be qualified by what at the same time he is whispering; it has also a third and a fourth sense, in so far as it is understood to apply to Camillo or to Brachiano. Each of course applies it to himself, but Vittoria and the audience apply it to both. And for the audience there results a final sense, compounded of all the rest; if indeed it can be called a single sense, when it is rich and complicated. It is rather a

1 No editor gives this in a stage-direction; but it seems to me obvious that it is happening.

harmony or a *fugato*, to return to the metaphor of a concert which I have already used; which can be heard only by reading the play, which cannot be reproduced in a single train of words, but glossed only, now from one aspect, now from another.

In dealing with simpler dialogues, I have suggested that both parts to them should be considered together; and that neither can be taken as, in isolation, summing up the dialogue and therefore capable of standing alone. This is much more obviously true of passages from a piece of writing like the above. Abstracted from their context they can give rise only to obviously unsatisfactory and therefore widely divergent opinions. The following adjuration of Flamineo's has for example been accepted, according to the predilections of the critics, now as a 'flash' of genuine poetry, now as a piece of fustian:

Thou shalt lie in a bed stuff'd with turtles' feathers, swoon in perfumed linen like the fellow was smothered in roses, – so perfect shall be thy happiness, that as men at sea think land and trees and ships go that way they go, so both heaven and earth shall seem to go your voyage. Shalt meet him, 'tis fix'd with nails of diamonds to inevitable necessity.

(I ii 154–60)

But the passage is neither the one nor the other; rather it has aspects of both, being a fragment of close and careful dramatic writing. Now it directs the reader's attention to Brachiano, now to Camillo, of both of whom it is spoken; now to Flamineo who speaks it. This diversity of aspect and function would, it might be thought, be apparent from the fragment itself; from the otherwise inexplicable transition from the loose 'swoon in perfumed linen . . .' to the restrained 'So perfect shall be thy happiness . . .'; and again from the latter to the extravagant ''tis fix'd with nails of diamonds . . .'. But still more is it apparent from the fragment in its context; where it is followed immediately by Vittoria's impatient and business-like 'How shall's rid him hence?' This should discredit at least any attempt to deal with it as a flash of poetry.

I am sorry I have had to descend into such detail. Perhaps however it has served to make clear to some extent how I think the play should be read. All the play, I believe, should be read in a like manner. For the remaining part of Act I, for example, the concerted piece is carried

on with Brachiano and Vittoria in the centre of the stage, Flamineo
and Zanche on one side as a satyric chorus, and Cornelia behind. For
the first time in the play she is a representative of virtue. Her presence
is, to the audience, a running comment on the speeches of all the other
characters; especially upon Brachiano's to Vittoria:

You are lodged within his arms who shall protect you,
From all the fevers of a jealous husband,
From the poor envy of our phlegmatic duchess, –
(I ii 260–62)

In appearance it is an offer of chivalrous protection; when in reality –
as Vittoria knows, as Flamineo knows, as Brachiano would know if
he would think – it is an undertaking to commit a double murder.
Cornelia by her interruption tries to make him think; but it is too
late. And so Act II is not a succession of scenes between Isabella and
the Grand Duke, the Grand Duke and Brachiano, Brachiano and
Isabella, then between all three; rather the scenes interpenetrate one
another, are to be thought of, so to speak, as existing side by side.
Isabella asks her brother the Grand Duke to intercede with her husband, Brachiano; he promises to do so but does not, preferring to talk
politics; the dukes quarrel but, recognizing their need of each other,
are reconciled; Isabella is then sacrificed to Brachiano – or rather
would be, if she did not seize the occasion for sacrificing herself. In
Act III the Cardinal's denunciation of Vittoria should not be thought
of as singularly weak, as it is general in its terms; but weighed along
with his confession to the Grand Duke that, against Vittoria, they
have no case. If this is done, it will not appear necessary to exalt Vittoria
at the expense of her opponents; though shameless, she can show to
advantage against those who apparently believe they 'have their salvation by patent'. Or in the last Act, Flamineo's final attempt to despoil
Vittoria is but one with the attempts he has been making on Brachiano,
and would have continued to make had he not been forestalled by
death. Taking advantage of widowhood she is seeking to be rid of the
past, to set herself up at last as a great lady, even as a *dévote*; by that
past Flamineo compels her, giving her the opportunity, to seek his
murder. He is about to take revenge for this and for consistent betrayal
when Lodovico appears, prepared to be rid of him; then the young
Duke appears, determined to be rid of them all.

This sort of connexion I am suggesting exists between sentences within certain speeches, between the speeches in certain scenes, and between the majority of scenes themselves, exists, I believe, between all the acts. They are to be thought of not so much as following one another, but as existing side by side. They come of course in chronological succession, but Webster's interest is so little in this that either he does not suggest it (thereby laying himself open to the charge of not knowing how to construct): or he does so by undistinguished means – such as a dumb-shows, or soliloquies like Francisco's. This is not a soliloquy in the accepted meaning of the term, but the speech of a prolocutor. The acts as a whole do not show the development of different stages of the same story, perhaps their main purpose is not even to show the different stages. Rather I think they show different aspects of the same theme – the workings of evil which, though among the same people, must vary indefinitely. For it cannot rest until it is extinguished.

To read a play in this way is of course more difficult than to read it in the normal way. But perhaps we are becoming accustomed to the difficulty. With the disappearance of the Victorian notion of character, and in particular of developing character, as the most important element in drama, the latter's complexity as a pattern of elements all of which must be envisaged at once is becoming apparent to us. We no longer look at the play of *Hamlet* as or through the character of Hamlet; somewhat similarly, I am suggesting there is no character in the White Devil – neither Vittoria nor Flamineo nor Cornelia – through which the play can be looked at.

This is however a simplification. To some extent we can look at the play through Hamlet because to some extent it is possible and we are indeed invited to sympathize with him. There would not seem to be any character in *The White Devil* with whom we are invited to sympathize to any extent that matters – not even Cornelia, the representative of virtue. She is rather a point of reference than a character – a point from which we can take our moral bearings when, amid the amount and variety of vice, they are in danger of being obscured.

Two questions immediately suggest themselves: whether it is possible to write a play totally deprived of a sympathetic character, and whether if possible it is worth doing? The first question is academic, since obviously the play has been written; so is the second at least for me who hold the play to be successful. Both are however worth raising, since they make clear the cost at which any success of this kind must be purchased. There can be no character on the stage who can dominate the whole action; or – to make a possibly more modest demand – whose summing up and account of the action the spectator – even temporarily – can trust. A powerful influence for unity is thus absent.

I have already said how I think this disadvantage is overcome in *The White Devil*. I have repeated that no single party to a dialogue, that no single sentence in a speech can be taken as completely representative; both parties, all sentences, must be considered, and as far as possible impartially. And I have suggested that if they are so considered it will be seen how one serves to define the other, how a reference to a common standard in both of them becomes clear, how in consequence – though it may have no character as agent – an important moral unity is imposed.

Let me then proceed to the second question – is this worth doing? And the answer must depend on the purpose for which it is done. It will be in the affirmative if there is a purpose which is of value, and which can be achieved in no other way.

There is, I think, one such, and I have already hinted what it is. It is the portrayal of a world of evil – not wholly evil of course, for such a world could not be conceived; but one in which evil preponderates, and which therefore is working out its own destruction. This could not be presented as comprehended wholly or even largely by a single character; for of its essence it is incomprehensible. Yet its existence at various times in history is undoubted.

Here I return to the large theme suggested in my title; but only to touch upon it. The Tragedy of Blood seems to me to be the attempt of a succession of dramatists to deal with a world of evil, the existence of which was borne in upon them in late Elizabethan, early Jacobean times. Most of them attempted to do so by showing it, so to speak, from outside – by its effects on a comparatively virtuous person, not a member of itself. Such a person goes mad or is destroyed: the first example I suppose is Hieronimo, the most celebrated Lear. And the world of evil survives them – from outside it seems perfectly comprehensible, there is no reason why it should not go on. In Webster, however, or at least in *The White Devil*, the evil world is presented from within: it seems confusion, pointless activity; in the mind of the spectator alone there is awakened the notion of order; he desires vehemently to see it transferred to the stage and so his attention is held until the close of the fifth act. With the arrival of a new ruler, a new generation, the whole evil world is destroyed.

(265–80)

M. C. Bradbrook

'Fate and Chance in *The Duchess of Malfi*', *Modern Language Review*, vol. 42   1947

In the second prison scene of *The Duchess of Malfi* there is a significant echo of the most terrible chapter in the Pentateuch, which seems hitherto not to have been recognized:

> I'll tell thee a miracle –
> I am not mad yet, to my cause of sorrow.
> Th' heaven o'er my head seems made of molten brass,
> The earth of flaming sulphur, yet I am not mad:
>> (IV ii 25–8)

But it shall come to pass, if thou wilt not harken unto the voice of the Lord thy God, to observe to do all his commandments and his statutes which command thee this day; that all these curses shall come upon thee and overtake thee.

Cursed shalt thou be in the city and cursed shalt thou be in the field.
Cursed shall be thy basket and thy store.
Cursed shall be the fruit of thy body and the fruit of thy land. . . .
And the heaven that is over thy head shall be brass, and the earth that is under thee shall be iron. . . .
So that thou shalt be mad for the sight of thine eyes which thou shalt see.

(Book of Deuteronomy, xxviii 15–18,
23, 34)[1]

1 From the Authorized Version (1611) which appeared some two years before the play.

The Duchess both compares and distinguishes her plight from that depicted in the curse of Mount Ebal: the earth under her feet is not iron but the flaming sulphur of hell; nor is she granted the oblivion of madness. But the original context is not irrelevant, as it is in so many of Webster's borrowings.

The power of a curse, though it may be related to a coherent belief, is more usually superstitious, i.e. it involves the supernatural as part of the free energy, the undirected power of the universe. The horror of Webster's play depends upon a powerful sense of the supernatural combined with a scepticism far deeper than that of professed rebels like Marlowe. An intense capacity for feeling and suffering, within a clueless intellectual maze, springs from the deepened insight into character which was Webster's greatest strength as a dramatist.[1] Fear of the unseen and unapprehended encompasses all his characters: the world to come is even darker than the midnight in which all his greater scenes are laid.[2]

In what a shadow, or deep pit of darkness,
Doth womanish and fearful mankind live.
(v v 101-2)

The curse which falls upon the Duchess of Malfi is potent but undefinable, like the whole atmosphere of the supernatural in this play. The malice of her brothers is the immediate cause of her sufferings but even as the hidden vindictiveness of the Cardinal surpasses the savagery of Ferdinand, it is a power beyond these two which the Duchess curses first and foremost: no less than the 'stars' themselves, which include in themselves or by their influence the whole material universe, the frame of things entire.

I could curse the stars . . .
And those three smiling seasons of the year
Into a Russian winter, nay the world
To its first chaos.
(iv i 96-100)

1 Cf. Professor Hardin Craig, *The Enchanted Glass* (O.U.P., 1936), pp. 226-7.
2 The bedroom scene, the two prison scenes and the final scene are all night scenes. Cf. that chapter of Job which Bosola quotes elsewhere, 'the land of darkness and the shadow of death, A land of darkness, as darkness itself, and of the shadow of death, without any order, and where the light is as darkness' (The Book of Job, x 21-2). See below, p. 149.

To which Bosola, the instrument of Fate, opposes an implacable calm:

Look you, the stars shine still.   (IV i 100)

The Duchess's reply, though in itself a bitter jest, implies the contagious nature of a curse: 'Oh, but you must remember, my curse hath a great way to go' and runs on without a stop into the curse of the plague itself which she wishes on her brothers.

There are roughly five types of curse[1]: curses upon wrongdoers, either by the sufferer (imprecation) or the Church (excommunication); curses as adjunct to an oath; malignant cursing of the innocent by witches and sorcerers; hereditary curses (blights) upon a family – usually an extension of cursing in the first sense; and general curses upon specific acts, by whomsoever committed, which are a form of primitive legislation and of which the Jewish curse pronounced by the Levites from Mount Ebal is a powerful example.

The curse which the Duchess lays on her brothers invokes the powers of God and is a religious imprecation. Such a curse is the last weapon left to the helpless and oppressed, and was frequently used in Elizabethan tragedy, notably by Titus in *Titus Andronicus*, by Anne and other victims in *Richard III*, by Constance in *King John*, and pre-eminently by Timon and Lear. The power of such a curse was greatest in a parent or king, in whose outraged authority God saw an image of His own. Cornelia, therefore, when she utters her twofold curse upon Vittoria and Brachiano, is armed with this double power of authority and wrong.[2]

In the earlier scene where she first recognizes the doom which is upon her, the Duchess realizes that the hereditary curse lies upon her children, and says

1 This classification is my own. I have been unable to find any systematic study of the variety of curse beyond Ernest Crawley's little book, *Oath, Curse and Blessing* (Watts, 1934).
2 *The White Devil*, I ii 295–300. Cornelia kneels to utter this curse, as was commonly done. In the first Act of *The Devil's Law-Case*, the mother kneels and curses her daughter in the same way: and the daughter is aghast (I ii 112–14).

... I intend, since they were born accurs'd;
Curses shall be their first language.

(III v 115–16)

Indeed a curse, irrespective of the guilt or innocence of the individual, may well be hereditary in 'the royal blood of *Arragon*, and *Castile*' to which the Duchess and her brothers belong, the physical tie which twinned her with Ferdinand and which is the only cause of the tragedy.

Damn her that body of hers,
While that my blood ran pure in't, was more worth
Than that which thou wouldst comfort, call'd a soul –

(IV i 121–3)

he cries to Bosola, but the pure blood of her royal descent which it is her crime to have contaminated carried, as all would know, the curse of that madness which later overtook Ferdinand himself.[1]

The curses which Ferdinand so freely vents are spoken in a transport of rage, but the solemn act of banishment performed by the Cardinal and the States of Ancona, which must have been spectacularly one of the high lights of the play,[2] has the full weight of civil and ecclesiastical authority behind it. That this is misused authority the pilgrims who act as chorus to the scene bear witness; but the splendours of the shrine of Our Lady of Loretto had been used previously in drama as a background to Machiavellian 'policy'.[3]

In his earlier play Webster had used a good deal of merely furious cursing: Vittoria, Brachiano, and Isabella (in her play-acting) are more violent than deadly,[4] the politicians do not curse, and Cornelia herself at the end says to Flamineo:

The God of heaven forgive thee. Dost not wonder
I pray for thee? I'll tell thee what's the reason, –

1 The story of Juana the Mad, sister of Katherine of Aragon, must have been known to the audience, and that of the children of Philip II.
2 It was described by an Italian traveller in 1618 (E. E. Stoll, *John Webster*, Boston, 1905, p. 29).
3 By Chapman, *Byron's Tragedy*, I ii 78–82.
4 Vittoria, *The White Devil*, III ii 276–80, IV ii 105–26; Brachiano, II i 190–95, IV ii 41–7; Isabella, II i 246–55. Primitive curses often depend on a formula, and on being spoken in due posture, at a favourable hour of day.

I have scarce breath to number twenty minutes;
I'd not spend that in cursing.

(The White Devil, v ii 52–5)

In *The Duchess of Malfi* the most potent curses are 'not loud but deep'. A vow spoken with imprecation may constitute a curse: such is Brachiano's vow 'by his wedding ring' not to lie with Isabella, which she calls a 'cursed vow'. Ferdinand's vow never to see his sister more, which he makes the opportunity for a cruel deception, rebounds upon himself – as an unjust vow was likely to do – for it is the sight of her supposed dead face which unnerves him and awakes the madness in him.

It is Ferdinand who refers most frequently to the practices of the Black Art. Thrice does he accuse the Duchess herself of witchcraft,[1] but when Bosola suggests that she is the victim of sorcery, he scorns the idea:

> . . . do you think that herbs or charms
> Can force the will? Some trials have been made
> In this foolish practice; but the ingredients
> Were lenitive poisons, such as are of force
> To make the patient mad. . . .
> The witchcraft lies in her rank blood.[2]

(III i 72–8)

Nevertheless, part of her torment was that she was watched, i.e. prevented from sleeping, a recognized method of dealing with those who were themselves witches. In presenting the wax figures of Antonio and his children 'appearing as if they were dead', Ferdinand practices directly upon her life by a method analogous, as the Duchess herself recognizes, to the most famous and deadly of charms.

> . . . it wastes me more,
> Than were't my picture, fashion'd out of wax,
> Stuck with a magical needle, and then buried
> In some foul dunghill. . . .

(IV i 62–5)

1 I i 309–11, III i 78, III ii 139–41.
2 When Byron says that he has been bewitched by La Fin into committing treason, his accusers point out that witchcraft cannot affect the will, which, being one of the faculties of the rational soul – the others were reason and memory – could not be enforced.

At the same time Ferdinand leaves with her a dead man's hand bearing a ring, with the words 'Bury the print of it in your heart'. The Duchess, discovering it, cries:

What witchcraft doth he practise, that he hath left
A dead man's hand here?

(IV i 54–5)

This is a powerful charm which was also used in the cure of madness,[1] but which as the 'Hand of Glory' or *main de gloire* was an essential ingredient in the more deadly practices of the Black Art. The ring, which the Duchess is meant to see as Antonio's, is her own wedding ring which the Cardinal had violently torn from her before the shrine of Our Lady of Loretto: and a wedding ring was itself a sacred object possessed of virtuous powers.[2]

These horrible properties do in fact so benumb the Duchess that she feels to live is 'the greatest torture souls feel in hell' (IV i 70) and the servant who wishes her long life has pronounced a most 'horrible curse' upon her (IV i 93). The executioners 'pull down heaven upon' her (IV ii 231), and hell opens before her murderers, both Bosola (IV ii 269) and Ferdinand. The curse of her blood lies upon them and cries for vengeance.[3] The sight of her dead face enacts her silent revenge upon them. It was generally believed that in the presence of a murderer the wounds of a corpse would bleed, the eyes might open and fix him with a blighting look, or the dead hand might point to him in denunciation. The effect on Ferdinand is to awake remorse: he denounces the murder and his tool Bosola, saying that the deed is registered in hell (IV ii 303). This is perhaps an echo of Othello to the dead Desdemona: 'That look of thine will hurl my soul from heaven. . . .'

The form of madness which overtakes him, lycanthropy, was recognized as a diabolic possession:

The devil, knowing the constitution of men, and the particular diseases whereunto they are inclined, takes the vantage of some and

---

1 G. L. Kittredge, *Witchcraft in Old and New England* (Harvard, 1929), p. 142.
2 The duchess had proffered it to Antonio as sovereign for the eyesight, and Antonio had seen a saucy and ambitious devil dancing in the circle (I i 404–12).
3 A subject full y treated by writers on Revenge tragedy.

secondeth the nature of the disease by the concurrence of his own
delusion, thereby corrupting the imagination and working in the
mind a strong persuasion that they are become that which in
truth they are not. This is apparent in that disease, which is termed
Lycanthropia, where some, having their brains distempered with
melancholy, have verily thought themselves to be wolves and so
have behaved themselves. . . . For God in his just judgement may
suffer men to be bewitched by the devil, that to their conceit
they may seem to be like brute beasts, though in a deed they
remain the true men still.

> (William Perkins, *A Discourse of
> the Dammed art of Witchcraft* . . .
> *Works*, 1618, III, 611)[1]

In the last act Bosola and Antonio are haunted by the Duchess,
whilst Ferdinand and the Cardinal are haunted by devils, and death
overtakes all four.[2] The curse which has involved the whole family is
worked out.

> These wretched eminent things
> Leave no more fame behind 'em than should one
> Fall in a frost, and leave his print in snow;
> As soon as the sun shines, it ever melts,
> Both form, and matter: (v v 113–7)

The influence of the stars is the divine method of governing the world
as Sir Kenelm Digby points out in a passage which, though some
twenty years later than the date of *The Duchess of Malfi*, may be cited
as a typical statement of the general belief:

. . . no accident can be so bad in this life but that the celestial bodies
have power to change it to good . . . not chance but the heavens
and stars govern the world which are the only books of fate: whose

1 It is perhaps fair to add that King James in *Daemonologie* denied the supernatural origin of this disease. Bodin, *Demonomanie* (1580), accepts it.
2 Bosola, v ii 345–6; Antonio, v iii; Ferdinand, v ii 31–6, v iv 20–21; Cardinal,
v iv 27–8, v v 1–7. The origin of this last is indicated in T. B[ramhall], *A
Treatise of Spectres* . . . 1658, p. 37: 'A stubborn obstinate fellow a little before
he died (as report goes) said that looking into a Pond he saw a shadow in the
water which with a drawn sword threatened death to him. Sabellicus, lib. 1,
cap. 4.'

secret characters and influences but few, divinely inspired, can read in the true sense that their Creator gave them.

This in no way impugns the doctrine of free will, for God having framed the world upon the strife and counterpoise of contraries, such as hot and cold, poisons and antidotes, summer and winter, to human souls, His highest work, He gave

an entire liberty together with a constrained necessity which no way hinder or impeach each other.

The highest faculty of knowledge is the contemplation of the Creator and this the human soul is free to accept or reject, subject only to God's unconstraining foreknowledge. This inner freedom being granted, in the course of the outer world God governs not by direct and miraculous intervention, but arranges that

inferiors should be subaltern to and guided by their superiors: the heavens then and stars, being so in respect of us, not only in place but in dignity, duration, in quantity, in quality and in purity of substance . . . must of necessity be allowed by us to be the causes of all contingent accidents and the authors of our fortunes and actions whereby the liberty of the will doth not immediately and expressly repugn and wrestle against the disposition of the heavens. . . . since to meaner lights we by daily experience attribute the ominous presages of the deaths of kings, of revolutions and of empires, wars, pestilence, famine, dearths, and such other effects, let us without difficulty acknowledge a nobler operation in these glorious bodies that are the efficient causes of the other: and having admitted them for causes, you will grant that who hath the knowledge of their natures may, by calculating their motions for time to come, prognosticate their effects.[1]

By their foreknowledge, prognosticators could attempt to avert evil influences, and strengthen good ones – to rule the stars. This, however, was considered impious,[2] and although the casting of

1 *Private Memoirs of Sir Kenelm Digby*, ed. Sir N. H. Nicholas (1827), pp. 127–32.
2 Cf. Professor Hardin Craig, op. cit. p. 6. He quotes *Paradise Lost*, VIII, 83–4: 'Heaven is for thee too high | To know what passes there. Be lowly wise.' G. Cardano cast the horoscope of Christ.

horoscopes was common enough, Antonio's one attempt to read the stars brings disaster. The *Life* of Cardano makes plain the real discomforts of star-readers. Bosola, it would appear, does not believe in the power of the prognosticators; though he does not go so far, with Shakespeare's Edmund, as to deny the power of the stars themselves[1]:

BOSOLA: 'Tis rumour'd she hath had three bastards, but
By whom, we may go read i' th' stars.
FERDINAND: Why some
Hold opinion, all things are written there.
BOSOLA: Yes, if we could find spectacles to read them –
       (III i 59–62)

The most extensive statement of this doctrine comes in the central scene of Chapman's *Conspiracy of Byron*, a play to which *The Duchess of Malfi* shows particular indebtedness. The astrologer himself begins by foreseeing some danger to himself, which he feels unable to avert:

O the strange difference 'twixt us and the stars;
They work with inclinations strong and fatal,
And nothing know; and we know all their working
And nought can do, or nothing can prevent![2]
       (III iii 6–8)

When he has read the fatal horoscope of Byron in which a Caput Algol prognosticates that the Duke is to lose his head, Byron curses him, and defies the stars, because as a rational soul he is of nobler substance than they.

I am a nobler substance than the stars,
And shall the baser overrule the better? . . .
I have a will and faculties of choice
To do, or not to do: and reason why
I do, or not do this: the stars have none:
They know not why they shine, more than this taper,

1 D'Amville, in Tourneur's *Atheist's Tragedy*, denies 'him they call the Supreme of the Stars' (II iv 158), and consequently the influence of the stars also. In a later scene (v i) he identifies his gold as the 'Stars whose operations make | The fortunes and the destinies of men' (v i 22–3).
2 Cf. *The Duchess of Malfi*, III ii 77–9: 'O most imperfect light of human reason, | That makes us so unhappy, to foresee | What we can least prevent.'

Nor how they work, nor what: I'll change my course,
I'll piecemeal pull the frame of all my thoughts,
And cast my will into another mould. . . .
[I'll] kick at fate. Be free, all worthy spirits,
And stretch yourselves for greatness and for height,
Untruss your slaveries: you have height enough
Beneath this steep heaven to use all your reaches;
Tis too far off to let you, or respect you.

> (III iii 109–18, 130–34)

However, like other tragic heroes the Duke rushes on his ruin, disregarding all the omens and warnings which he receives, and in the end, his friends can only pray that he

. . . ope his breast and arms,
To all the storms Necessity can breathe,
And burst them all with his embraced death

> (*Byron's Tragedy*, v iii 212–14)

which he does in that fine image which is also echoed by the Duchess that the body is

A slave bound face to face with Death till death.[1]

> (v vi 38)

But Byron's triumphant defiance of death is no stoic acceptance of its pangs. He succeeds finally, in facing it – only that, and no more. He accepts the fact that a life as passionate and heroic as his own must be extinguished, but he cannot tolerate the circumstances: he, a single man, defies the 'kingdom's doom' (v iv 217), and his death, like his life, is a clash of opposites, 'vice and virtue, corruption, and eternesse' mixed (v iv 190–91). In this he is a true microcosm or little world of warring elements.

He cites, only to reject them, the conventional Stoic maxims, not because he does not believe them, but because he will not accept them as platitudes from the lips of the bishop who attends him.

---

1 Cf. *The Duchess of Malfi*, IV i 65–9: 'yon's an excellent property | For a tyrant, which I would account mercy – . . . If they would bind me to that lifeless trunk, | And let me freeze to death.' These particular lines of Byron are also printed separately by Chapman in *Euthymiae Raptus* (*Poems*, ed. P. B. Barrett, O.U.P. 1941, p. 195).

> Talk of knowledge!
> It serves for inward use.
>
> (v iv 50–51)

Chapman's perfect stoics, Clermont D'Ambois and Cato, whose tempers are so settled that no calamity can disturb them, are something less heroic, as well as less human. Though they claim to accept their fate 'freely', 'with a man's applause', the impression they give is rather one of indifference.[1] The Duchess, who submits to the chastisement of Heaven, though the instruments are tyrannous (III v 76–8), has a natural courage and nobility of spirit that rises at the scent of danger. When she turns, expecting to see her husband, and sees her brother behind her, her first words are:

> 'Tis welcome
>
> (III ii 69)

And again when she sees the troop of armed men making towards her across country:

> O, they are very welcome:
>
> (III v 95)

Bosola says that she seems 'rather to welcome the end of misery' than shun it (IV i 5–6), and at the very nadir of her hopes, when she has reached the calm at the centre of the whirlpool, the Duchess, equating herself, like Edgar, with the 'lowest and most dejected thing' of nature, discovers the anaesthesia that lies beyond.

> I am acquainted with sad misery,
> As the tann'd galley slave is with his oar,
> Necessity makes me suffer constantly,
> And custom makes it easy.
>
> (IV ii 27–30)

Her misery is *sad* because it is settled and established, because it is adult and mature, and because it is massive and heavy, like the oar, a physical burden.[2] *Necessity* may stand either for the situation or for the stern goddess, *saeva Necessitas*, who has created it: and *constantly*

---

1 *Revenge of Bussy D'Ambois*, III iv 70, IV i 149; cf. I iv 132, IV v 6.
2 For these various meanings of *sad*, *necessity*, and *constantly*, see *N.E.D.* s.v.

means both continuously, or incessantly, or steadfastly and heroically (which is the older sense). There are thus two meanings combined in this passage: the Duchess is inured to the pain which she cannot escape, but she has also learnt to suffer, and acquired strength from her sufferings. The first meaning is supported by the image of the galley slave: yet after all, it was only the strongest who could survive in the galleys.[1]

When, finally, Bosola brings in the coffin with the words 'may it arrive welcome . . .' the Duchess turns to face the last present of her Princely brothers with the words:

> I have so much obedience, in my blood,
> I wish it in their veins, to do them good.
>
> (IV ii 169-70)

This does not of course mean that she is obediently accepting death, but that her blood (i.e. her passions, all that Ferdinand meant by 'her rank blood') is now entirely obedient to her will, and therefore she is not physically terrified, or transported with physical rage as was Byron: she wishes that the choleric blood of her brothers were as obedient as hers. She is Duchess of Malfi still.

To doubt the power of the stars was perhaps atheistic and impious,[2] but on the other hand, to accept it would seem to leave Man, for all practical purposes, dependent on these second causes, and his fate to be, in Bosola's phrase, the star's tennis balls. This phrase was used also, however, with a significant variant – Fortune's tennis.[3] Fortune, or 'blind chance' was one of the commonest figures in Elizabethan pageantry, emblem books, and devices. With her wheel, upon which humanity was bound, 'her rolling restless stone'[4] and her blinded eyes, she might be presented in a favourable aspect as Chance or Opportunity, in which case she had a long forelock, to be seized by

---

1 In *Believe as You List*, a play which once or twice echoes Webster, the deposed King Antiochus, whose stoic fortitude defies imprisonment and torture, is literally sent to the galleys, and appears as a galley slave in Act v.
2 Lipsius, *De Constantia*, lib. 4, restated the classic argument for reconciling stellar influence and man's freewill, originally popularized in Boethius.
3 'The stars' tennis-balls', v iv 54. *Fortune's Tennis* was the title of a play by Dekker, now lost : and also of an anonymous fragment dated c. 1600 (Chambers, *Elizabethan Stage*, IV 14).
4 Fluellen's description of Fortune, *Henry V*, III vi 20 ff.

the active and aspiring man; but more frequently she personified the 'turning and inconstant and mutability and variation' of unregulated accident, which calls attention to itself only when the accident is unfavourable. It is in this aspect that Kent defies her when he is set in the stocks by Regan:

> Fortune, goodnight,
> Smile, once more turn thy wheel.
>
> *(King Lear*, II ii 179–80)[1]

Blind Fortune plays so large a role in *The Duchess of Malfi* that her influence may almost be thought to challenge that of the stars. It is the name under which the Duchess gives herself to Antonio, perhaps in recollection of the courtly habit by which ladies assumed such allegorical roles.[2] Later Delio, fearing that he [Antonio] is betrayed cries

> How fearfully
> Shows his ambition now! unfortunate Fortune!
>
> (II iv 80–81)

And if the dreadful horoscope which does in fact betray Antonio illustrates the malignancy of the stars, the accident which makes him drop it in Bosola's path is a freak of chance. This accident has often been censured as undramatic, a flaw in Webster's construction; it is on the contrary, eminently dramatic, as the recent production of this play made clear: it is precisely the kind of odd, unpredictable coincidence which, when events are wrought up to a sufficiently high pitch, almost be counted on to occur. In the late war, half the casualties resulted from some such accident – and half the miraculous escapes. Some one just happened to be called away before the bomb fell, or just happened to have gone into the cellar. It is of course only in times of violence that such accidents mean the difference between life and death.

The Duchess greets those who have come to apprehend her with a defiance of Fortune:

---

1 And – how typically – Cordelia: 'For thee, oppressed King, I am cast down,| Myself could else outfrown false Fortune's frown' (v iii 5–6).

2 e.g. in *Cynthia's Revels*, II i, Hedon says that he calls Lady Philautia, his Honour: and she calls him, her Ambition.

> O, they are very welcome;
> When Fortune's wheel is overcharg'd with princes,
> The weight makes it move swift. I would have my ruin
> Be sudden.
>
> (III v 95–8)

And in prison she thinks that her tragedy is terrible enough to un-muffle blind Fortune (IV ii 34–6). Antonio goes to his fatal interview with the same contempt of what Fortune can do:

> Though in our miseries Fortune have a part,
> Yet in our noble suff'rings, she hath none –
> Contempt of pain, that we may call our own.
>
> (v iii 56–8)

In the last act of *The Duchess of Malfi* mere ill-fortune directs the 'mistakes' by which Bosola and Antonio are killed: yet the Echo had bid Antonio fly his *Fate* (v iii 35), and when Delio begs him not to go to the Cardinal's that night, he replies with a bitter punning jest that suggests a stronger power than blind Chance at work:

> Necessity compels me[1]
>
> (v iii 32)

The play is filled with little omens, such as the Duchess's dream that her coronet of diamonds was changed to pearls, Antonio's name being drowned in blood, the tangling of the Duchess's hair,[2] and as the Pilgrim says, on witnessing their banishment:

> Fortune makes this conclusion general,
> *All things do help th' unhappy man to fall.*
>
> (III iv 43–4)

The alternative views that Fate or Chance rule the world are never set in open opposition to each other, and the omens might be interpreted as the work either of the one or the other. It is precisely this uncertainty at the heart of the play which is the heart of its darkness: either explanation, if it could be accepted as an explanation, would

1 Necessity in the sense of *poverty*, and necessity in the sense of *fate*. For another vital play upon this word, see the words of the Duchess quoted above, p. 142.
2 III v 13–15, II iii 41–5, III ii 53. Antonio says of the second, that the superstitious would call it ominous, but he believes it chance, 'mere accident'.

give some relief. But the opposition of Fate and Chance was in fact a familiar one;[1] the problem would be obvious to Webster's audience, without any formal antithesis being propounded. The astounding and gratifying thing is that he should have been able to resist the temptation to state a case; it is a renunciation of which few Elizabethans were capable, and least of all perhaps his friend Chapman.[2] The spectator, like the Duchess, goes into a wilderness where there is neither path nor friendly clue to be his guide. The Cardinal and Ferdinand may die acknowledging the justice of their ends in the highly sententious manner which was expected at the end of a Revenge play, but Bosola, to the end of his final couplet adds four mysterious words which come from a state far on the other side of despair.

Let worthy minds ne'er stagger in distrust
To suffer death, or shame for what is just –
Mine is another voyage.

(v v 103–5)

This blank feeling of Lucretian chaos is as far removed from the Deistic 'atheism' of Marlowe as from the determinist stoicism of Ford. Bosola, the conscience-struck and bewildered slave of greatness, so dominates any presentation of the play that the loves and crimes of the House of Arragon seem but a background to his tragedy.[3]

1 Perhaps the best example of this commonplace is the frontispiece of R. Recorde, *The Castell of Knowledge*, 1556, which shows a castle with Astrology on the top: on the left, Knowledge upholding the Sphere of Destiny, and on the right, blindfold Ignorance holds the cord of a crank which turns the Wheel of Fortune inscribed *Quomodo scandit, corruet statim*. The Motto runs: 'Though spiteful Fortune turned her wheel, | To stay the sphere of Uranye, | Yet doth this sphere resist that wheel | And fleeth all fortune's villainy. | Though earth do honour Fortune's ball | And bytells [? beetles] blind her wheel advance, | The heavens to Fortune are not thrall, | These spheres surmount all Fortune's chance.'

2 Compare, for example, these lines from a work much quoted by Webster in this play: 'It argues more power willingly to yield | To what by no repulse can be repelled | Than to be victor of the greatest state | We can with any fortune subjugate.' *Petrarch's Seven Penitential Psalms* (*Poems*, ed. P. B. Barrett, O.U.P. 1941, p. 294).

3 He is far more frequently present than any other figure: he unites the two groups, and he is the first character to exhibit the symptoms of melancholy which afterwards appear in the Duchess, Antonio, and the Cardinal, and which seem to emanate from him.

Ferdinand, the Cardinal, and the Duchess are born to rule: their imperious tempers are innate. Ferdinand draws his dagger before his sister, even when he has no reason to suspect her of a second marriage:

> This was my father's poniard: do you see?
> I'd be loth to see't look rusty, 'cause 'twas his.
>
> (1 i 331–2)

The Duchess turns away, and almost her next words are:

> If all my royal kindred
> Lay in my way unto this marriage:
> I'd make them my low footsteps.
>
> (1 i 341–3)

Bosola, a silent figure, listens to these high words from the Prince to whom he has already sold himself in what he recognizes as a diabolical bargain.[1] His sympathy for the Duchess in the discovery scene is far more deeply felt than the momentary flash of compunction which Brachiano's betrayers feel: and the shock of his final comment:

> What rests, but I reveal
> All to my Lord?
>
> (III ii 326–7)

is only deepened by his self-contempt. After her capture he essays to comfort the Duchess[2] without ever being able to defy Ferdinand who observes contemptuously:

> Thy pity is nothing of kin to thee
>
> (IV i 138)

The word echoes through the latter half of the play: pity, 'the miracle

---

1 'It seems you would create me | One of your familiars. . . . Take your Devils | Which hell calls angels; these curs'd gifts would make | You a corruptor, me an impudent traitor, | And should I take these they'd take me to hell' (1 i 257–66).

2 IV i 18, 86, 92, 137. *Pity*: III v 110–12; IV i 88–90, 95; IV ii 34, 273, 297, 347; v ii 281, 330–31; v iv 52. The word is almost always used ironically. Lipsius, op. cit., lib. I, dismisses pity as a weakness of the mind, distinguishing it from mercy, or the impulse to give active help, as a passive, self-indulgent and unfruitful affection.

of pity', and having carried out the murder, Bosola retorts the word upon his master:

But here begin your pity

(IV ii 257)

Remorse works in Ferdinand as madness: the Hell which he had fore-seen when he accepted Ferdinand's gold engulfs Bosola, and wakens in him the same vengeful love which in the earlier play Lodovico had felt for the wronged Duchess Isabella. It is Bosola, not Antonio, who speaks the most passionate lines in the play:

Return, fair soul, from darkness, and lead mine
Out of this sensible hell: – she's warm, she breathes: –
Upon thy pale lips I will melt my heart
To store them with fresh colour.

(IV ii 342–5)

He weeps (IV ii 362) and later he is haunted by the memory of the scene:

    ... still methinks the duchess
Haunts me: there, there! –
'Tis nothing but my melancholy.

(V ii 345–7)

It is as the embodiment of that blind and bewildered pity which, striking with his bitterness, occasionally rises into a general disillusion, that Bosola dominates the play. His great speech on the vanity of life, addressed to the captive Duchess in preparation for her death, recalls in its function the great speech of the Duke to the captive and con-demned Claudio in *Measure for Measure*, but its immediate source is the Book of Job. This speech, more than any other, epitomizes what the play is really concerned with.

Thou art a box of worm-seed, at best, but a salvatory of green mummy: – what's this flesh? a little crudded milk, fantastical puff-paste; our bodies are weaker then those paper prisons boys use to keep flies in; more contemptible, since ours is to preserve earth-worms. Didst thou ever see a lark in a cage? such is the soul in the body: this world is like her little turf of grass, and

the heaven o'er our heads, like her looking-glass, only gives us a
miserable knowledge of the small compass of our prison.[1]

(IV ii 124–33)

Webster had a delicate balance to maintain between the theatrical
and the doctrinal in this scene. There is no doubt that the 'scene of
suffering' in a Senecal play included physical atrocities of a kind which
could not be paralleled in Webster:[2] and that in the plays of the Machiavellian villain parricide was a necessary ingredient. It was therefore
necessary, if his subject were to be brought home to his audience, that
the action should be violent. In such a case the natural compensating
impulse of the Elizabethan dramatist was to indulge in extended
monologue, such as Constance's apostrophe to Death in *King John*,
the 'passions' of Marston's characters, or the great set speeches of
Chapman's tragic heroes. But Webster successfully steers between this
Scylla and Charybdis. The pageantry of madness and death, the waxen
figures, the disguises of Bosola all suggest that the events are inadequate to express the nature of the sorrow in which the Duchess is en-
folded. The quality of her endurance is as far removed from the stoic
insensibility of the 'Senecal man' – Feliche, Clermont, or Charlemont
– as it is from the hysteric passions of Marston's Antonio. Her insensibility is the natural insensibility of extreme shock, and it passes.
Through her 'sensible hell' she moves as a human figure, whose delicate gradations of mood show that even at the end, it is life, vulnerable
but unquenchable, which dazzles the eyes of Ferdinand and which he
(and we) mistake for death.

(281–91)

---

1 'Remember, I beseech thee, that thou hast made me as the clay; and wilt
thou bring me into dust again? Hast thou not poured me out as milk and
curdled me like cheese? Thou hast clothed me with skin and flesh, and hast
fenced me with bones and sinews. . . . Hast thou with him spread out the sky,
which is strong and as a molten looking glass?' (The Book of Job, x 9–11,
xxxvii 18.) The rest of chapter x is all highly relevant, e.g. the verses quoted on
p. 133, n. 2, and also ix 22–4. The verse directly used here by Webster seems
also to be behind one of the sonnets of G. M. Hopkins: 'Bones built in me,
flesh filled, blood brimmed the curse' (*Poems*, no. 45).
2 e.g. in *Tancred and Gismunda* the father murders his daughter's lover, sends
her his heart in a golden goblet, and when she poisons herself her father blinds
himself on the stage and then kills himself. The date of this play is 1599.
Massinger's *Virgin Martyr*, perhaps the most revolting of all Elizabethan plays,
has even a larger variety of tortures.

Edmund Wilson

[*The Duchess of Malfi* in London, 1947] from 'Notes on London at the End of the War', *Europe without Baedeker*   1967

Unlikely though it may appear, the Elizabethan *Duchess of Malfi*, not professionally performed in many years, is probably the most fascinating show to be seen on the stage in London. It seems to me, in fact, one of the best productions that I have ever seen of anything anywhere. You would think that this old tragedy of blood, with its grotesque horrors and highly-wrought poetry, is the kind of thing of which a revival would be sure to turn out boring or comic; but this production by the poet George Rylands is so immensely imaginative and skilful and the acting at the same time so dynamic and so disciplined that it holds you from beginning to end. You might have thought that Webster's style was too precious for the stage, but every speech has its force and its point. And they somehow get the emotions of wartime into both *Richard II* and the *Duchess*: the speeding up of crime and horror, the cumulative obsession with grievance and revenge. No: *The Duchess of Malfi* is not funny. You understand what Gertrude Stein means when she says that she reread, during the war, in France, Shakespeare's tragedies and historical plays and realized for the first time that human life could be like that. One sees the fall of Richard II just as Hitler is staggering to defeat; and, in *The Duchess of Malfi*, the scene where her doom is announced to the Duchess amidst the drivellings of the liberated madmen, at the moment of the exposé of the German concentration camps.

(12)

David Cecil

[Webster's View of Life] from 'John Webster', *Poets and Story-Tellers* 1949

And such then is Webster's tragic vision of the world: a fallen place in which suffering outweighs happiness and all activities are tainted with sin; where evil is the controlling force, and good – just because it is good – is inevitably quietest; hoping, at best and with luck, to slip through the tempest of existence, unnoticed. Yet it is also a place where the moral law cannot be thwarted indefinitely. So that finally evil destroys itself, justice is vindicated.

Let guilty men remember their black deeds
Do lean on crutches, made of slender reeds.

In this, the final couplet of *The White Devil*, Webster states the moral truth which the whole preceding drama has been designed to illustrate. The last lines of *The Duchess of Malfi* propound the converse truth:

Integrity of life is fame's best friend,
Which nobly, beyond death, shall crown the end.

Heaven is just, for all the apparent horror of man's life. In the end virtue is glorified; but only beyond death.

Let us examine how this view of life exhibits itself in the action of each play. The key figure therefore is always a villain; one of Webster's deliberate intellectual sinners. For since Webster was primarily a man of intellect concerned with ideas, it is the intellectual sinner who interests him most. What happens to a man who directs his life, consciously and calculatedly in defiance of the Divine Law? This is the question that absorbs Webster. He studies it in two diverse examples. In *The White Devil* the deliberate sinner is Flamineo. He is the typical Machiavellian Italian adventurer, as he appeared to an English Protestant eye, ruthless, cynical, consciously anti-moral, living only to advance his fortunes. He sees the best chance of doing this, by making use of the adulterous passion which the Duke Brachiano has conceived for his beautiful sister. He plots to bring them together, and is led by his plots to commit one crime after another, each worse than the last. First he instigates their adultery, then he arranges the murder of Brachiano's wife and Vittoria's husband. Horror at his crimes provokes the wrath of Marcello, his virtuous brother; he kills Marcello in a rage; Cornelia their mother goes mad with grief. Flamineo is thus responsible for his mother's madness as well as his brother's murder. Up to this point his schemes have been successful. Now, however, Divine justice begins to operate to bring punishment on to the sinner. Brachiano is killed in revenge for his wife's death. It

looks as if a similar vengeance will soon fall upon Vittoria and
Flamineo. Flamineo realizes this, he is filled with gloomy apprehen-
sions as to his future; and these are further darkened by spiritual
terrors. With the decline of his fortune a profound melancholy, shot
through with agonizing shafts of guilty fear, fills his breast; incarnat-
ing itself in superstitious premonitions of misfortune, and shuddering
conjectures as to the ultimate fate of his soul. Brachiano's ghost
appears before him:

What a mockery hath death made thee? (cries Flamineo) Thou
    look'st sad.
In what place art thou? in yon starry gallery?
Or in the cursed dungeon? No? not speak?
Pray, sir, resolve me, what religion's best
For a man to die in? or is it in your knowledge
To answer me how long I have to live?
                                    (v iv 125-31)

Desperately he tries to put his fears by; and concentrates on devising
some scheme to save him from his enemies. In order to discover
whether he can trust his sister to stand by him, he concocts a fantastic
hoax, which involves her agreeing to kill herself with him in a suicide
pact. It reveals that he cannot trust her; she is ready to kill him but not
herself. The evil-doer has no friends, even among his fellow criminals.
What right has he to expect loyalty, when his own actions are founded
on a considered repudiation of all but self-interested motives? At this
point the avengers arrive to kill him. His last speeches disclose
Flamineo's final state of mind. He is not repentant. By now he has
become a damned soul, and, as such, incapable of repentance. To the
last he speaks with a defiant mocking courage. But it masks an absolute despair. Though no longer capable of appreciating the value of
good, he yet realizes that evil-doing is also profitless. Like Macbeth,
Shakespeare's parallel study of a soul's damnation, he has come to
think that life is a tale told by an idiot, signifying nothing, and falls
back on a complete nihilism.

                        I do not look
Who went before, nor who shall follow me;
No, at myself I will begin and end ...

This busy trade of life appears most vain,
Since rest breeds rest, where all seek pain by pain.

(v vi 256–74)

In *The Duchess of Malfi* the development is different. For here the intellectual villain Bosola is not wholly given up to the devil. There is a strain of good in him; and in the end this strain of good leads him not to damnation but to repentance. From the first his amorality is shown to be the result largely of harsh circumstances, and as such more excusable. He is a middle-aged soldier of fortune, so embittered by poverty, ingratitude, and bad luck, that he is ready to yield to any temptation that comes his way. Why be scrupulous in a wholly unscrupulous world? Ferdinand and the Cardinal take advantage of his desperate mood and make him their creature in their plots against their sister, the Duchess. Under their pressure, he proceeds, like Flamineo, from crime to crime. For he spies on the Duchess, who trusts him; then he betrays her secret; then when the brothers begin to wreak vengeance on her, he becomes first her torturer, afterwards her murderer. But he has never liked his task from the beginning. As it gets more odious, he recoils more and more, receives the brothers' orders with a kind of bitter detachment, praises her courage to them, talks to her, even while he is engineering her torments, with a strange melancholy irony. Finally in the magnificent scene when he stands with the Duke Ferdinand by her dead body, he finds himself unable any longer to shut his ears to the clamour of conscience. The spectacle of his victim, dead, innocent, and beautiful, brings home to him the full horror of what he has done:

I stand like one
That long hath ta'en a sweet and golden dream:
I am angry with myself now that I wake . . .
I would not change my peace of conscience
For all the wealth of Europe.

(IV ii 323–5, 340–41)

In the last section of the play he tries to make amends for his sins, seeks out Antonio, the Duchess's husband, to tell him the truth and offer him assistance in bringing justice on her brothers. But only with partial success; the brothers are killed, it is true, but so is Antonio. And, by a wonderful stroke of dramatic irony, he falls by Bosola's hand: in the darkness Bosola has mistaken him for the Cardinal. For, so Webster seems to say, the moral law is inexorable. We cannot undo the evil we have committed. Indeed God may punish us by making our efforts the unwitting cause of further evil.

This last section of *The Duchess of Malfi*, it may be noted in passing, illustrates how little Webster has been properly understood even by his admirers. Because the play is called *The Duchess of Malfi*, she has been looked on as its key figure; and her creator has been censured for continuing the play for another act after her death. But though she is the heroine in the sense that she is the chief object of our sympathies, she does not provide the chief motive force in the action; nor is it, in her relation to that action, that the theme of the play is to be found. This theme, as always with Webster, is the act of sin and its consequences. Till these consequences are followed out to their final conclusion, the dramatist's intention is not made plain. Moreover the central figure, as far as that action is concerned, is the man who murders her; the man who has elected, against the promptings of his better self, to be the devil's agent in the drama.

Webster, then, was not so wrong about himself as might at first sight be supposed. So far from being a mere flamboyant sensation-monger, an unthinking composer of eloquent melodramas, he is a stern moral teacher whose plays are carefully designed to enforce the philosophy of human conduct in which he believes. This in itself, however, does not prove the popular view wrong. A hostile critic might say that whatever Webster's intention, the impression they make is all the same, extravagant, irrational, and melodramatic, crammed with irrelevancies and horrors that offend alike against taste and probability. The fact that his aims are so serious, make these faults more flagrant: good Grand Guignol is bad tragedy. Once again such a criticism shows a failure to grasp the nature of Webster's art. To incarnate his spiritual drama with the full intensity which it demands he must use symbols: the battle of heaven and hell cannot be convincingly conveyed in a mode of humdrum everyday realism. And Webster's interpretation of this spiritual battle can only appropriately be expressed in the most extravagant symbols. The wild and bloody conventions of Elizabethan melodrama provided a most appropriate vehicle for conveying his hell-haunted vision of human existence. Perhaps Lodovico and Duke Ferdinand do lack rational motive for their terrific crimes. But in Webster's view people commit crimes, not from rational motives, but because they are corrupted by that original sin with which all mortal flesh is tainted, because they succumb to the promptings of that devil who is always whispering in human ears suggestions to obey his diabolical will. We, who live in an unreligious society, are always asking that the actions of a criminal should be accounted for to us by some rational and human cause; poverty, bad upbringing, psychological maladjustment. The Elizabethans, members of society soaked in the Christian tradition, took for granted that the soul of every human being is continually the battleground between the forces of spiritual evil and spiritual good. Superficially a man may commit a sin for a practical motive; but the practical motive is merely the means by which the devil has persuaded him to yield to that inherent inclination to evil implanted in him from birth. The Elizabethans could believe in Ferdinand and Iago and Goneril and the rest of them without having to be told exactly why they were wicked: everyone has the disposition to be wicked if he chooses to give in to it.

Again Webster's horrors – his ghosts and torturers – are not, as with his lesser contemporaries, mere theatrical devices to awaken a pleasing shudder. They are symbolic incarnations of that spiritual terror and diabolical delight in suffering, which are, to him, central features of the human drama. Duke Ferdinand and the Cardinal are creatures of hell: the prison in which they confine the Duchess, made hideous by the clamour of lunatics and the ghastly images of murdered children, exhibit to us, in visible form, the hell on earth, which it is their nature to create. Even Webster's irrelevant scenes of pageantry, little though they have to do with the plot, contribute essential features to his picture of human life. Here, moving before us, are those ceremonies of worldly dignity, of whose superficial seductive splendour Webster is acutely aware, and whose fundamental hollowness he is concerned to expose.

Further, the fact that Webster does not write in a realistic convention allows his imagination full play: and thus enables him to make sermons into works of art. Realistically treated, the stories of *The White Devil* and *The Duchess of Malfi* would be merely painful and repulsive. But strangely enough in Webster's hands they become beautiful; they are alight with a dark gleaming Rembrandt-like splen-

dour. For every episode, every thought in them comes to us irradiated
by the unearthly leaping flame of their author's creative vision. Consider the scene in which Vittoria, lying in Brachiano's arms, suggests
to him that he should murder his wife and her husband:

VITTORIA: To pass away the time I'll tell your grace
A dream I had last night.
BRACHIANO: Most wishedly.
VITTORIA: A foolish idle dream, –
Methought I walk'd about the mid of night
Into a church-yard, where a goodly yew-tree
Spread her large root in ground, – under that yew,
As I sat sadly leaning on a grave,
Chequered with cross-sticks, there came stealing in
Your duchess and my husband, one of them
A pick-axe bore, th' other a rusty spade,
And in rough terms they gan to challenge me,
About this yew.
BRACHIANO: That tree.
VITTORIA: This harmless yew.
They told me my intent was to root up
That well-grown yew, and plant i'th'stead of it
A withered blackthorn; and for that they vow'd
To bury me alive: my husband straight
With pick-axe gan to dig, and your fell duchess
With shovel, like a Fury, voided out
The earth, and scatter'd bones, – Lord how methought,
I trembled, and yet for all this terror
I could not pray. . . .
When to my rescue there arose methought
A whirlwind, which let fall a massy arm
From that strong plant,
And both were struck dead by that sacred yew,
In that base shallow grave that was their due.
FLAMINEO: Excellent devil.
She hath taught him in a dream
To make away his duchess and her husband.
                              (I ii 229-58)

In real life, even in Elizabethan real life, people do not instigate murders by relating weird dreams. But Webster, by conceiving his scene thus, turns an ugly episode of lust and treachery and assassination into a thing of sinister magnificence. The strange precise images set the fancy mysteriously and sublimely astir: the ear thrills to the subtle muted music of the versification.

Yet though he beautifies the horror of his scene, Webster does not soften it. It is here that the fact he was an Elizabethan was so lucky for him. The Elizabethan poetic imagination did not shrink from the grotesque and the horrible. On the contrary, fantastic and full-blooded, it craved such food and grew strong on it. Vittoria's dream clothes her evil suggestion with imaginative splendour; it also brings out much more clearly than a realistic treatment would do, the true nature of the act she is promoting; its spiritual wickedness, its relation to the supernatural forces of sin and death, of which it is the offspring. Less ugly than a realist's version of the same incident, Webster's is also far more penetrating.

Indeed, Webster is a true tragic poet: one who, facing the most dreadful and baffling facts of human experience in all their unmitigated horror, yet transmutes them by the depth and grandeur of his vision into a thing of glory. This is the rarest sort of poet – and the greatest. Certainly Webster deserves his growing fame.

(34-43)

Ian Jack

'The Case of John Webster', *Scrutiny*, vol. 16   1949

Disintegration characterizes the view of life which inspired Webster's best-known plays. It is perfectly true, as Dr Tillyard remarks,[1] that Webster, like the rest of his age, inherited 'the Elizabethan world-picture'; but in his work we see that world-picture falling in ruins. When Dr Tillyard goes on to say that Webster's characters belong 'to a world of violent crime and violent change, of sin, blood and repentance, yet to a world loyal to a theological scheme', and adds:

1 *The Elizabethan World Picture*, pp. 17-18.

'indeed all the violence of Elizabethan drama has nothing to do with a dissolution of moral standards: on the contrary, it can afford to indulge itself just because those standards were so powerful', he is overlooking the highly significant differences between Elizabethan drama and Jacobean drama, and uttering a dangerous half-truth. No doubt there is a definite 'theological scheme' behind Webster, in the sense that it was familiar to his audience and himself, and could therefore be drawn on for imagery; but *The White Devil* and *The Duchess of Malfi* are our best evidence that the Elizabethan theological scheme could no longer hold together.

Henry James pointed out that the ultimate source of a novel's value is the quality of the mind which produced it;[1] and the same is true of drama. Great tragedy can be written only by a man who has achieved – at least for the period of composition – a profound *and balanced* insight into life. Webster – his plays are our evidence – did not achieve such an insight. The imagery, verse-texture, themes, and 'philosophy' of his plays all point to a fundamental flaw, which is ultimately a moral flaw.

If one reads through *The White Devil* and *The Duchess of Malfi*, noting down the *sententiae* and moralizing asides of the various characters, one finds oneself in possession of a definite attempt at a 'philosophy', a moral to the tale:

Integrity of life, is fame's best friend,
Which nobly, beyond Death, shall crown the end.

(*The Duchess of Malfi*, V v 120–21)

This philosophy is Stoical and Senecan, with a Roman emphasis on the responsibilities of Princes:

The lives of princes should like dials move,
Whose regular example is so strong,
They make the times by them go right or wrong.

(*The White Devil*, I ii 287–9)

But this background of moral doctrine has nothing to do with the action of the plays: so far from growing out of the action, it bears all the marks of having been superimposed by the poet in a cooler, less creative mood, than that in which the Duchess and Flamineo had

1 *The Art of Fiction.*

their birth.[1] There is no correspondence between the axioms and the life represented in the drama. This dissociation is the fundamental flaw in Webster.

What was wrong, apparently, was that there was available no philosophy of life which kindled Webster's imagination as certain aspects of Hell, or Chaos, kindled it. No moral order represented itself to his imagination as real. Consequently his plays contain brilliant passages of poetry – they appear whenever he touches on the small area which acted as his inspiration – but lack imaginative coherence. They have indeed a unity, the unity for which the 'mist' is a symbol; but one mood, isolated and out of focus, cannot be the basis of a profound tragic vision. Webster himself seems to have understood this better than some of his more enthusiastic critics; but this attempt to shore up chaos with a sententious philosophy is a flagrant artistic insincerity. Webster fails to realize his Senecan philosophy as he realizes his glimpses of Hell.

We might say that Webster suffered from the poverty – the philosophical poverty – of the tradition in which he worked; but the fact that he chose to write in the Revenge tradition at all is itself evidence of a lack of harmony in his own mind. For other traditions were available, notably the tradition of the Morality, to which Shakespeare's great tragedies owe more than has even yet been understood.[2] Webster's choice of the Revenge tradition, his failure to give life to his Senecan moralizings, and (we may add) the fact that his work contains no convincing statement of the *positive* aspect of the doctrine of Degree, are all related: Degree and Order – as we come to see – were not real enough to Webster to stir his imagination. A lower concept of the Universe, and of Man's place in it, was all that he could compass.

This explains the fascination which the 'Machiavellian' had for Webster. To the conservative Elizabethan the Machiavellian doctrine seemed merely the denial of that Order and Degree which held the

1 The fact that Webster used commonplace books supports this diagnosis.
2 *Hamlet* owes more to the Revenge tradition, and less to the tradition of the Morality, than any other of Shakespeare's great tragedies; and while it contains passages of brilliant poetry, *Hamlet* lacks the unity and the tremendous moral force of *King Lear* and *Macbeth*. It is with the Shakespeare of *Hamlet* that Webster has something in common.

Universe together: Machiavellianism was anarchism. It is not surprising that a mind as unbalanced as Webster's should have allowed
the Machiavellian ideal to usurp the place in his thought which a more
conservative poet would have reserved for Degree. As a consequence
there are a remarkable number of 'politicians' in his two plays.

Flamineo in *The White Devil* is a good example. He acts as pander
to his sister Vittoria, contrives her husband's death, and treats his
mother with a cold, sub-human ferocity:

> I pray will you go to bed then,
> Lest you be blasted?
>
> (I ii 273-4)

He treacherously murders his brother in his mother's presence, and
proclaims that nothing but a limitation of his natural ability prevents
him from double-crossing his master, Brachiano: 'I had as good a
will to cozen him, as e'er an officer of them all. But I had not cunning
enough to do it' (v iii 57-9). He tries to corrupt even Giovanni with
cynical advice. It is only when he is listening to the 'superstitious
howling' (v iv 65) of his mother over the brother whom he has
killed that Flamineo's Machiavellianism proves imperfect:

> I have a strange thing in me, to th'which
> I cannot give a name, without it be
> Compassion.
>
> (v iv 113-15)

Flamineo's philosophy is simply that

> Knaves do grow great by being great men's apes.
>
> (IV ii 247)

He explains his own villainy by saying:

> I made a kind of path
> To her [Vittoria's] and mine own preferment.
>
> (III i 36-7)

Flamineo's attitude to women proves him a 'Courtier' of a very
different cast from Castiglione's ideal:

> I visited the court, whence I return'd
> More courteous, more lecherous by far.
>
> (I ii 325-6)

His attitude to women is that of 'the cynic'. He regards a woman's
modesty as 'but the superficies of lust' (I ii 18), and makes love to
Zanche 'just as a man holds a wolf by the ears' (v i 154) – to prevent
her from turning on him. He looks on women – and on all humanity
– as mere animals: 'women are like curst dogs' (I ii 198); human
love-making he regards as the coupling of mare and stallion.[1] There is
something peculiarly fiendish about his ironical comment, as he
eavesdrops at the love-making of Vittoria and Brachiano:

BRACHIANO: [enamoured] Nay lower, you shall wear my jewel lower.
FLAMINEO: [aside] *That's better – she must wear his jewel lower.*[2]

(I ii 227–8)

There is an infinite weariness in Flamineo's voice when he says:

O, no oaths for God's sake!

(iiv I 147)

The strident courage which Flamineo shows in dying –

Strike thunder, and strike loud to my farewell.

(v vi 276)

– is a quality which he shares with all Webster's Machiavellians; and
this, the one admirable quality in so many of his characters, manifests
Webster's peculiarly limited and deformed notion of ethics. We find
in Webster only the virtue of Hell: the courage of despair. The
stridency of this pagan courage is very evident when Brachiano cries:

. . . Monticelso,
Nemo me impune lacessit,

(III ii 178–9)

or when Francisco proclaims:

Flectere si nequeo superos, Acheronta movebo.

(IV i 139)

Denied insight into any virtue other than Stoical courage, Webster
tries to erect unflinchingly perseverance in evil into the sum of moral

1 There is little need to emphasize the remarkable amount of animal-imagery
in the two plays. As we should expect, most of the animals mentioned are
ravenous or sinister.
2 [Ian Jack's italics]

goodness. In the process he is disingenuous. As Lamb remarked, 'This White Devil of Italy sets off a bad cause so speciously, and pleads *with such an innocence-resembling boldness*, that we ... are ready to expect, when she has done her pleadings, that ... all the court will rise and make proffer to defend her in spite of the utmost conviction of her guilt'.[1] Vittoria is dishonourable: Webster simply makes her behave as if she were honourable. This is an artistic insincerity – a lie in the poet's heart – of which Shakespeare would not have been guilty; but Webster, having no profound hold on any system of moral values, found it easy to write for Vittoria dissembling verse which in its righteous simplicity seems to proclaim her honesty in the face of her accusers.

It is consonant with Webster's unbalanced outlook that the distinguishing mark of his Machiavellian 'heroes' is their individualism. In Shakespeare individualism is an infallible mark of villainy:

Richard loves Richard; that is, I am I.

(Richard III, v iii 236)

Like Richard III, Iago, and Edmund in Shakespeare, Lodovico, the Cardinal, Bosola, and Flamineo are all individualists, and all villains.

The atmosphere in which Webster's characters live is the atmosphere of a corrupt court. The description of 'France' at the beginning of *The Duchess of Malfi* sets off the scene of Webster's play by contrast:

In seeking to reduce both state, and people
To a fix'd order, their judicious king
Begins at home ...

(1 i 5)

To point the contrast, Bosola – who is one of the 'dissolute and infamous persons' (1 i 8–9) who are banished from any healthy court – enters just as this speech is finished. If Webster were an orthodox Elizabethan, the rest of the play would be an illustration of what happens in a state of which the Prince himself is evil:

Death, and diseases through the whole land spread.

(1 i 15)

1 *Specimens of English Dramatic Poets who Lived about the Time of Shakespeare; with Notes* [Ian Jack's italics].

But while the atmosphere of the play is precisely the atmosphere described in these opening lines, there is in Webster, as we have already mentioned, no convincing statement of the positive aspect of Degree; we do not for a moment believe that when the Duke and Cardinal are dead the state of Amalfi will return to a condition of health and normality. While the atmosphere of Webster's plays is as unhealthy as that of 'Vienna' in *Measure for Measure*, there is in Webster no Messianic Duke to return and save the state from chaos. The 'mist' of the two plays is all-embracing: we can form no notion of another world which will be revealed when the rottenness of Amalfi has come to a head and been purged away. Comfortable words spoken at the end of *The White Devil* and *The Duchess of Malfi* carry no conviction; if we take evil away from Webster's world, nothing is left.

This explains the curious futility of all Webster's characters. When Bosola is asked how Antonio was killed, he answers:

In a mist: I know not how –
Such a mistake, as I have often seen
In a play.

                                          (v v 94–6)

Very similar in tone is the reply of the Duke in *The Duchess of Malfi*, when he is asked why he brought about the death of the Duchess; he replies that he had hoped to gain

An infinite mass of treasure by her death.

                                          (iv ii 285)

This explanation is so off-hand and perfunctory that it can only be termed an *excuse*: the Duke is in fact at a loss to find any plausible reason for his actions.

All Webster's characters, indeed, and particularly his most consummate 'politicians', have only the most tenuous hold on reality; they are characterized by the same 'motiveless malignity' that Coleridge noticed in Iago. But whereas Iago is a subordinate character in *Othello*, so that we are prepared to accept the convention by which he is simply 'The Villain', a man who desires evil because it is his nature to do so, Webster's plays are almost entirely peopled by such characters.

Without adopting the attitude of the 'naturalistic' critic, we must

maintain that there are too many inconsistencies in Webster's plays;
and whereas inconsistencies are readily passed over when – as in
Shakespeare – they are subservient to some important dramatic purpose, in Webster there is no deeper purpose than to make our flesh
creep, and we feel an inevitable resentment.

There is in fact something a trifle ridiculous about Webster. When
we have seen his two plays we have indeed 'supp'd full of horrors',
and overheard 'talk fit for a charnel'. An irruption of real humour –
humour of the Shakespearean sort – would knock Webster's wax-
works into a cocked hat. He is too evidently bent on exploiting the
emotions of his audience.

Webster, that is to say, is a decadent. He is decadent in the sense
that he is incapable of realizing the whole of life in the form in which
it revealed itself to the Elizabethans. By concentrating exclusively on
the narrow aspect of life revealed in one mood, he threw the relations
of the whole out of harmony. In his work the proper relations between
the individual and society, between God and Man, are overthrown.
The sensationalism of his plays is the stigma of an outlook on life as
narrow as it is intense. Webster sees the human situation as a chaotic
struggle, lit indeed by flashes of 'bitter lightning', but fated to sink
again into a mist of confusion and sub-human activity.

(38–43)

Gabriele Baldini

'John Webster and the Language of Tragedy' from *John Webster e il
linguaggio della tragedia* 1953 (Translated from the Italian by
Lorraine Whitehead, Judy Rawson and G. K. Hunter.)

The death of Brachiano brings Webster's usual method of building
up effects in layers and by means of imagery to its full fruition. The
pretext comes from the immediate situation, the assassination of the
Duke, which provides the deformation of reality and so the ground
out of which Webster's imagery burgeons. The phrase

O my brain's on fire

(v iii 4)

dominates the whole scene with its force; the reader finds himself in
the middle of it all, almost without knowing how. In this first terrible
cry of Brachiano's we should notice, first of all, how we take pleasure
in finding a physical correspondence to the mental situation – the mixture of intellectual and sensual in the torment. Brachiano's 'brain
on fire' provides the pretext and the basis for the whole train of
distorted and dazzling images of reality that appear in the scene that
follows.

The free-wheeling and fantastic nature of the imagery is everywhere subordinated to the pursuit, the uncovering, the layering of
emotion.

> ... the infection
> Flies to the brain and heart. O thou strong heart!
> (v iii 12–13)

The splendour of the imagery is not produced as an end in itself, as,
for example, in Tourneur, savoured for a moment and then quickly
absorbed in the images which follow; it is always justified by the
effort to portray emotions. Webster aims basically at a delineation in
which the psychological elements are presented in pictorial terms.
Instead of the fluent and busy play of ideas – I am thinking especially
here of certain passages in *Measure for Measure* and *Troilus and
Cressida* – he piles up tones and colours whose total effect is much
more than the sum of its parts. When Brachiano pursues the imagery
of suffering which moves from his 'brain' (the centre of his understanding) to his 'heart' (the seat of his feelings) and is there fulfilled in
the worst, almost unbearable, torture – 'O thou strong heart!' is one
of Webster's most vivid and dramatic statements, and gives the measure of both his strength and his tenderness – he is expressing one of
the writer's own tendencies, to pick out the salient points of the
emotions without bothering to give us the connecting links between
them. The image of Vittoria appears – like that of Shakespeare's
Cleopatra – with the splendour of worlds thrown away, in a typically
baroque universe:

> ... had I infinite worlds
> They were too little for thee. Must I leave thee?
> (v iii 17–18)

But this is quickly absorbed in a new and violent emotion: the consciousness that every earthly power must wither away, the relish even (more scornful than truly tragic) of the loss which is both unforeseeable and fatal:

> I that have given life to offending slaves
> And wretched murderers, have I not power
> To lengthen mine own a twelve-month?
> (v iii 23-5)

The attempt, later on, to exalt a kind of nostalgia for virtue only succeeds (we should notice) in confirming the hopeless nature of the life of the senses, as that appears in the ravings of the Duke's final moments.

> O thou soft natural death, that art joint-twin
> To sweetest slumber: no rough-bearded comet
> Stares on thy mild departure: the dull owl
> Beats not against thy casement: the hoarse wolfe
> Scents not thy carrion. Pity winds thy corse . . .
> (v iii 29-33)

When Webster adds to this last line a change of direction – 'Whilst horror waits on princes' – which justifies the images as part of a moral design, he obeys convention, as happens only occasionally, instead of following his poetic instinct. The succession of images is exhausted in the fifth line of the speech, and one feels that the addition impoverishes and disturbs the tone and feeling which attaches to the rest. These five lines offer, one might say in common speech, a sample-card of the basic Webster colours, his essential palette. These colours are not the most vivid nor the most delicate ones, perhaps not even the most forceful, but they are certainly some of the most typical. Were it not for the opening line and a half, and the final phrase which hold in a more gentle context, so that they seem to restore a balance of tones, that series of images that shriek out at us, the comet, the screech-owl, and the wolf, we would say that the effect was calculated and artificial. Even an ear which has superficial acquaintance with the Elizabethans cannot help registering in these five lines, with surprising accuracy, the timbre of Webster's speaking voice and catching the individual quality of his style. For Brachiano in his death-throes the sound of words carries an anguished echo:

On pain of death, let no man name death to me,
It is a word infinitely terrible, –

(v iii 39–40)

The Duke is carried off-stage for a moment, as if to allow for the more subdued dialogue between Flamineo and Francisco, which could not take place while the pitch of emotion was screwed up to such a frenzy. In this scene Flamineo maintains a lower tone, avoiding brilliance. The theme of Brachiano comes almost to a halt; there is a pause in preparation for his final entry. This is announced by Lodovico who re-enters soon after:

He . . . descends
To the most brain-sick language. His mind fastens
On twenty several objects, which confound
Deep sense with folly.

(v iii 71–5)

'These speeches are several kinds of distractions and in the action should appear so' states an unusual and rather visual stage-direction; I take this to be important, not so much as a prompting for the actor, who will know instinctively how to lose himself in the gestures of a madman, but rather for the reader, who must in his imagination superimpose over the movement of the images a suitable set of gestures, used almost to beat out the tempo. This 'distraction' of Brachiano offers another opportunity for the free play of composition, for the feelings follow on from one another, are superimposed one on top of another, without having to depend on any logical pattern; but while we are attending in this way we are following as well a line of abstract construction. The theme of the life of the senses, supported as it is by the food imagery, draws attention to Brachiano's physical weight:

BRACHIANO: Let me have some quails to supper.
FLAMINEO: Sir, you shall.

BRACHIANO: No: some fried dog-fish. Your quails feed on poison –

(v iii 91–2)

It has been observed that at the time of his acquaintance with and marriage to Vittoria, the historical Brachiano was almost fifty and so fat that he had, from the Pope, a dispensation from kneeling before him. At this stage in the dying Duke's hallucinations it is possible to suppose that an echo of such rumours reached Webster's ears. But here it is of no interest to us to know how much the poet took from his sources; we rather wish to know how much he was able to profit from the themes that lent themselves to his purpose. It is clear that by giving to the dying Brachiano the feature of physical bestiality, which becomes more and more prominent, Webster adds rather than takes away from the sensuality of Vittoria.

The apparition which follows is of the devil,

In a blue bonnet, and a pair of breeches
With a great codpiece. Ha, ha, ha,
Look you his codpiece is stuck full of pins
With pearls o'th'head of them. Do not you know him?
FLAMINEO: No, my Lord.
BRACHIANO: Why 'tis the devil.
I know him by a great rose he wears on's shoe
To hide his cloven foot. I'll dispute with him.
He's a rare linguist.
                                        (v iii 98–105)

This completes, this central image both obscene and precious, those features of bestiality that Webster was interested in ascribing to Brachiano, writhing on his death-bed. We should notice that such features avoid any reference which is not strictly attached to the life of the senses; and notice also how they tend to make the moral horizon of the Duke's last moments narrower and narrower.

In comparison with the figure of Brachiano, that of Flamineo becomes gradually hazier; he is seen as a rope-dancer with two pouches of money, one in either hand:

BRACHIANO: See, see, Flamineo that kill'd his brother,
Is dancing on the ropes there: and he carries
A money-bag in each hand, to keep him even,
For fear of breaking's neck.
                                        (v iii 109–12)

It is clear that this new figure represents a development out of the earlier one, and that Brachiano's bemused imagination tends to confuse, or rather to superimpose the figure of the devil over that of Flamineo, so that in this overlapping the fearfulness of the devil and Brachiano's repugnance for Flamineo both lose their definition. The devil is 'a rare linguist', that is a master of eloquence, more like Voltaire than Milton, more of the Enlightenment than of the Romantic period – hence the confusion with Flamineo. Between these fluctuating figures, and the scarcely noticed and quickly reabsorbed figure of the lawyer with his gown edged in velvet (ll. 112–15) – a recurrent figure in Webster's poetic world – Vittoria appears in one of her most moving transformations:

Ha, ha, ha. Her hair is sprinkled with arras powder,
that makes her look as if she had sinn'd in the pastry.
(v iii 117–18)

The figure of the white but aged and drooping devil that appears to Brachiano in his final hysterical moments is certainly one of the most vivid and affecting in the whole play. The critics rather indulge themselves over this. Greg is of the opinion that 'much living' has whitened Vittoria's hair; and Lucas suggests a parallel with Mary Stuart who was prematurely white before she went to the block; but he immediately withdraws this idea and reaffirms that that proud erect head of Vittoria's had to be still intact when it fell in the final scene, in full splendour, to the dagger of Lodovico. 'After all, Brachiano's ravings are not evidence.' The fact that Vittoria's head fell 'in untouched splendour' fits very well with the dishevelled apparition 'as if she had sinned in the pastry' that the Duke describes. In that last struggle in the arms of his fatal enemy the Duke becomes aware of the frailty of humankind and how little even he himself is able to preserve the passion which was nourished and indulged on a sensual level. Vittoria's beauty is disfigured, becomes wrinkled; and to fulfil and set a seal on imagery of physical decay, the motif of food comes back with a wry twist of the mouth – that imagery of food that is so much used by the mature Shakespeare.

The next image – of a drunken clergyman,

. . . th'argument is fearful when churchmen stagger in't.
(v iii 121–2)

brings flashing across his mind once again the phantom of a return
of conscience; but only so that he can defend himself against it: 'He
will be drunk: avoid him' – and over this he superimposes a new
image:

Look you; six grey rats that have lost their tails,
Crawl up the pillow, – send for a rat-catcher.

(v iii 123–4)

The space around Brachiano's litter is crowded with more and more
figures, suffused with colours, swarming, twitching, throbbing:

I'll do a miracle: I'll free the court
From all foul vermin.

(v iii 125–6)

until, as if trying to break down this fiction of Brachiano's brain on
fire, the image of the crucifix arises from the shadows together with
Lodovico and Gasparo dressed as Capuchin friars, half real and half
imaginary, like the rest of the figures:

FLAMINEO: See, see, how firmly he doth fix his eye
Upon the crucifix.
VITTORIA: O hold it constant.
It settles his wild spirits; and so his eyes
Melt into tears.

(v iii 131–4)

Flamineo, with a mind weighed down by forebodings (compare 127–
9) watches with terror the fixed stare of Brachiano; in him it is only
the physical fear of death that is speaking, for which the crucifix is a
kind of mediating symbol. The reaction of his sister forms a contrast
to this – one of Webster's masterly touches in this marvellous characterization of a woman. She is once more the Vittoria of the trial
scene, in all her masculine firmness and decisiveness, in all her feminine
softness. She feels spiritually close to and responsible for Brachiano, to
a degree he has not known before. Vittoria's devotion and loyalty
reaches into the most secret regions of her lover's mind, exhorting him
in the final and eternal moments with a resolute yet with a sweet and
persuasive voice charged yet with some of the old sensuality, so that
his eyes mist over with a film of tears – 'his eyes Melt into tears'. But

scarcely are these moments expressed and felt when, suddenly, all is submerged in a new wave of gloomy fantasies. The mournful Latin litany of Lodovico and Gasparo begins in a way which, in musical terms, would be called *largo*; after the frenzy and the excitement of the preceding imagery – the rats, the worms, the crucifix – this produces a splendid rhythmical effect. The same rhythm comes in again, after the Latin responses, when Lodovico and Gasparo are finally left alone with Brachiano – notice the pungent pretext for this:

> . . . pray stand all apart,
> And let us only whisper in his ears
> Some private meditations, which our order
> Permits you not to hear.
>
> (v iii 146–9)

This adds a slight note of irony to the scene – a note which is carefully held and brought out here and there during Brachiano's delirium. Lodovico and Gasparo then take off their disguises in order to make the Duke's torment more piercing, and to cap his physical suffering with psychological torture. Webster is a master of such situations and this scene is a pendant to that famous one in the fourth act of *The Duchess of Malfi*. In *The White Devil* there is a greater amount of explicit cruelty; the technique is more refined, and the scene seems to make its impact with greater directness, either because the instruments of torture themselves (Lodovico in particular) are acting more on their own behalf than as proxies – we must not forget that Bosola is not responsible for the murder but is merely an instrument, and as such is the first to feel pity – or because the victim does not (as happens in *The Duchess of Malfi*) passively accept undeserved punishment, so arousing feelings of pity and anger, but has to submit against his will to a punishment which perhaps he has really deserved. If one wished to analyse the tempo of this scene, one would notice, as I have said, that it continues the rhythm of the Latin litany, which should be considered as the Intonation, from which the following tempo develops. Merciless images of death, of the torments in hell, of the vilest moral degradation, pile up one on top of the other. From these only two moments stand out, shrieked rather than whispered, to beat out this slow tempo. One is the condemnation, spoken by Lodovico and drily echoed by Gasparo:

LODOVICO: Devil Brachiano. Thou art damn'd.
GASPARO: Perpetually.

(v iii 151)

The other is the last scream of the Duke before being strangled:

Vittoria? Vittoria!

(v iii 167)

– a scream charged with passion, immediate and absolute. Webster is one of those poets who can discover a whole gamut of psychological reactions and provoke a decisive and lasting effect with the minimum of means. One might say that that name pronounced twice in a loud and desperate voice is an elementary and easy device, but we must feel how the whole scene that leads up to it fills it with significance, making it vibrate with innumerable different shades of meaning. The image of Vittoria, mortified momentarily, returns like a dazzling blaze of light at the last moment; and it is in fact that image of vivid splendour which the 'true-love-knot' of the Duke of Florence extinguishes in the enflamed mind and dazzled eyes of Brachiano.

The episode of Brachiano's death offers one of the most characteristic examples of Webster's common method. He leads one of his characters to the threshold of delirium and then once free of any rules about the composition of images, he relies on their free and therefore insidious play.

A similar scene, as we have suggested, occurs in the fourth act of *The Duchess of Malfi*, with the difference that in the latter the victim preserves her clarity of mind, and the range of images has to be sought instead in those who wish to stir up the madness – Bosola and the retinue of fools. The procedure if not the actual result is the same in the two cases. But a more obvious parallel with Brachiano's death is given by the episode of Ferdinand's lycanthropy in the same play. In fact an attempt to repeat the formula seems evident from a number of details: notice just one example, the six snails in *The Duchess of Malfi* (v ii 47ff.), directly related to the six rats with chopped-off tails in Brachiano's hallucinations. It also seems to me to be necessary to admit that the passage in *The Duchess of Malfi* emerges as inferior to that in *The White Devil*. In the first place, for reasons connected with the structure of the play and its plot development, in *The Duchess of Malfi* Webster was forced to break up the episode and insert between the two parts the long and elaborate scene with Bosola and the Cardinal and the murder of Julia, and the other scene of the echo among the ruins. Once the unity has gone the episode loses its strength for it has lost its centre; as we have already seen, interruptions also occur in the scene of Brachiano's death; but these should be seen as pauses rather than interruptions for, as we have tried to show, they are meant to link up and justify the 'episodes' in a rhythm which has been foreseen and calculated instead of breaking them up and limiting their range, as is the case with Ferdinand's lycanthropy.

Another factor which reduces the effect of the episode in *The Duchess of Malfi* as against that in *The White Devil* is that Vittoria, the major cause of the madness, is present on the stage while the Duchess is absent. I believe that one of the most poetic and dramatic modes of the episode is the way he caresses the image of Vittoria, rejects it, again invokes it, sometimes despairingly sometimes scornfully, in the alternation of contrasting emotions, in the way he builds up her image, then breaks it down into its component parts, in the way he flatters, exalts, and humiliates her in turn. The lycanthropy of Ferdinand, on the other hand, even though it seems to have been caused by the horror of having sensed the truth about his own incestuous love, and by his having put an end to it by murder – seems none the less to have destroyed in him almost every memory of the duchess. Ferdinand just remembers her in the last speech before dying:

My sister, O! my sister . . .

(v v 71)

But this is to identify her as the cause that led to his own death; it cannot in any way compare with the desperate cry of Brachiano. In Ferdinand's lycanthropy Webster seems to have sought deliberately to underline the comic aspect, those aspects which only served as counterweights in Brachiano's madness, to balance the structure. Throughout we seem to see the colours of Flemish painting. If Brachiano's madness takes its colours from the grotesqueries of a Breughel, the lycanthropy of Ferdinand assumes the more candid and innocently comic tones of a Bosch; the doctor is perhaps Webster's only completely comic figure, and his function is in effect to arouse laughter in its most immediate and elementary forms.

(95–104)

Travis Bogard

'Tragic Satire', *The Tragic Satire of John Webster*   1955

As Webster darkens the world of his tragedy, life appears to become
an increasing agony. What had been aberration to the earlier satirists
becomes to Webster the norm. Each evil is a symbol of death, each
abuse a step toward it. In the end, what his satire revealed of the true
nature of life is fused with the outcome of his tragic story. The ultimate tragedy of Webster's world is not the death of any individual
but the presence of evil and decay which drags all mankind to death.
The function of the satire is to reveal man's common mortality and
his involvement in evil; the tragic story is the story of a few who find
courage to defy such revelation. In their defiance there is a glory for
mankind, and in their struggle and assertion lies the brilliance of
Websterian tragedy.

Yet it is important to realize that Websterian tragedy is great because of its fusion of satire and tragedy. Had this fusion been incomplete, the effect would have been destroyed. A lack of reality or of
proper heightening, a failure to integrate the satiric comment – and
the accusation could justly be made that these spectacles were merely
sensational shows to please the vulgar. As it is, taking the dramas in
their own time, in the light of the carefully developed techniques
which produced them, the accusation seems in all significant instances
to lack justification. Webster has created an integrated, important
world through his tragic action which makes his plays a profound comment on life. Second only to Shakespeare (and, with the essential
differences understood, the Shakespeare comparison can be safely
resumed), Webster has found what William Butler Yeats named
'Emotion of Multitude'. Yeats wrote, 'Indeed all the great Masters
have understood, that there cannot be great art without the little
limited life of the fable, . . . and the rich, far-wandering, many-
imaged life of the half-seen world beyond it.'

Shakespeare, concentrating on character, traces the wellsprings of
his tragic hero's inner being to its deep source in common humanity.
From this root comes generality – 'Emotion of Multitude' – which an
audience may not always consciously understand, but to which it rarely

fails to respond. Webster, forgoing significant inner revelation, traces the outer patterns of men struggling with one another, de-emphasizing the individual aspects of his 'fable', and relating its action explicitly to the action of men everywhere. It is when the light of satiric generality shines across the plane of tragic action and throws that action into relief that the immense shadows of the protagonists fall across the face of life itself. Through the 'Emotion of Multitude' thus achieved, *The White Devil* and *The Duchess of Malfi* speak as eloquently today as in the past.

The tragedies will not appeal to all audiences. Their horror at life, their preoccupation with death have been termed unhealthy obsessions in times characterized by ethical steadiness and spiritual faith. Yet many twentieth-century poets have found Webster congenial because they saw in their world a correspondence with the world depicted by the dramatist. Values crumpled in their hands as they had for Webster and his contemporaries three centuries earlier. From the very lack of values there sprang an affinity.

There comes a time, however, when denial of value has to cease. Man must find, or convince himself that he can find, something in the world which is not prey to rot and human bestiality. It has proved so with the poets of the 1920s, and possibly something of the kind happened with Webster. Perhaps the lost drama *Guise*, which he mentions in the preface to *The Devil's Law-Case* in connexion with the twin tragedies, might have told more of what happened to him in his search for ethical value. As it is, all that can be stated is that the fire, which struck out of his despair and forced him to set forth on the stage what he saw in the world, died suddenly. *The White Devil* and *The Duchess of Malfi* are the only plays that have the tragic sweep, the full 'Emotion of Multitude'. His later tragedy grows conventional, his comedy increasingly foolish. The plays after 1614 are few, and none of them attain the tragic heights. Sometime after 1635, Webster disappeared from the scene, swallowed 'in a mist' as effectively as any of his characters.

In all probability, nothing more will be learned of the man than his two tragedies revealed. But that is enough by which to know him. While his despair flamed, he presented life as he saw it, and although what he saw was undoubtedly distorted in that half-light, for the short space of Webster's life it was an aspect of the truth. His view of life was one-directional, but it was profound. He looked a long way into darkness. His characters buffet their course against a black panorama, and in the end are swallowed in shadow. Only a few, before the storm of terror breaks, can find the courage to assert the essential dignity of man. But this, as it is in any degree a picture of a world men must recognize, is, despite its horror, the stuff of tragedy.

(147–9)

Hereward T. Price

'The Function of Imagery in Webster', *P.M.L.A.*, vol. 70   September 1955

For many generations symbolism has dominated the poetry of America and Europe. In time, of course, the critics found out what was happening and they began to investigate the movement. They have carried their investigations further and further afield over the literature of the last four centuries and in the process they have enormously widened our knowledge of poetry. Through their labors we read with clearer eyes and a deeper enjoyment than before.

Shakespeare has, naturally, received a great deal of attention. He is indeed the center of a lively controversy about the exact function which he intended imagery to perform. One body of critics sees the Shakespearian play as a symbol at large made up of many smaller symbols. Such integration into a coherent form does not, of course, constitute for this school the whole truth about a play. They do not ignore the other structure of plot or of characterization. But they assert that a study of the elaborate interdependence of Shakespeare's images will afford us a valuable key to his meaning. Other critics refuse to recognize in Shakespeare any planned and complex correlation of imagery. Some even treat the idea with scorn.

We ought to approach this problem not as if it were something peculiar to just one writer but from the viewpoint of general Elizabethan practice. Not enough work has been done on other Elizabethans. We may perhaps obtain some light on Shakespeare by studying the technique of his contemporaries. Possibly, by establishing likeness or difference, by comparison or contrast, we shall come to see Shakespeare's characteristic tendencies more clearly. I have chosen

Webster to investigate because in the depth, the subtlety, and the complexity of his imagery he comes nearer than any other Elizabethan dramatist to the power of Shakespeare. Moreover his sombre rendering of life's terrors provides something that our generation can respond to immediately and with perfect comprehension.

While Webster approaches Shakespeare in many aspects of his imagery, there can be no comparison between them in range. Shakespeare wrote a large number of plays over a long period of time. Webster, on the other hand, is known chiefly for *The White Devil* and *The Duchess of Malfi*, which were written fairly close together. They resemble one another in the nature of the symbols used. In fact *The Duchess of Malfi* even takes over symbols from *The White Devil*. The resolute consistency with which Webster elaborates an extended sequence of diverse but interrelated images distinguishes *The White Devil* and *The Duchess of Malfi* not only from Webster's other work but also from the rest of the Elizabethan drama. It is because of their unique quality that I single out these two plays for discussion and ignore all else that Webster wrote. I say unique because the other plays, either alone or in partnership, do not display that contexture of imagery which we find in *The White Devil* and *The Duchess of Malfi*. Except in the two plays I have chosen for discussion there is no chain of related imagery that is in itself a form of construction and that reinforces the construction of action.

Before we begin, we must first point out that there was a stock of images common to all Elizabethan drama. We must, for instance, train ourselves to recognize proverbs.[1] Elizabethan critics regarded them as an ornament of style, readers delighted in them, and poets would try to give pleasure by interweaving proverbs or reminiscences of proverbs into their work. Many figures that appear to be brilliant inventions turn out on inspection to be old proverbs. When Bosola says: 'Thou sleepest worse then if a mouse should be forced to take up her lodging in a cat's ear' (*The Duchess of Malfi*, IV ii 136–7), he appears to have hit upon a striking figure. In reality he is only employing a proverb well known to the Elizabethans. They would approve of the passage because Webster gave to an old saw a novel application.

I pass over shortly the question of Webster's debts to contemporary

1 See Morris Palmer Tilley, *A Dictionary of Proverbs in England in the Sixteenth and Seventeenth Centuries* (Ann Arbor, 1950).

authors. He notoriously lifted his images from a large number of writers, especially from Sidney and from Montaigne. But it is also true that he rarely borrows without improving on his source. His mind was a sieve through which only the essential elements passed. He trims his borrowings so closely as to achieve the utmost economy and sharpness of phrase. At other times Webster uses what in his source is flat or merely logical in order to show his characters turning to passion or violence, and in Webster it sounds like the grinding of teeth in a curse. Or elsewhere by a slight change in rhythm or wording he transforms the prosaic into haunting poetry. When he conveyed other people's bright ideas, Webster was following the conventional Renaissance practice of imitation, and he could plead the conventional justification that he put his imitation to very good use. Whatever he took he worked into the essential substance of the play.

If we then ask what really distinguishes Webster from other Elizabethans, we find it in his consistent use of a double construction, an outer and an inner. He gives us figure in action and figure in language. These he fuses so intimately as to make the play one entire figure. Now it is possible to say that this would be true of all drama. But, if we except Shakespeare, no other dramatist works so resolutely as Webster at making figure in action and figure in word conform to one another all the way through. Most Elizabethan dramatists tend to use figure for its power of enhancing a speech, a scene, or a particular moment in a play. But in *The White Devil* and *The Duchess of Malfi* a figure is usually one of a series of figures, all of which are focussed on the same control point. The verbal images dovetail into one another exactly as they closely parallel the figure in action, rising and falling with it, inseparable from it. Webster is important in the history of English dramatic art just because of this exact and sustained correlation. The severe self-discipline necessary to achieve Webster's superb uniformity of effect is most unusual among writers in England. It might almost be called un-English; it is certainly un-Elizabethan.

For Webster the figure-in-words appears at first sight to be the more important. The action gives the impression of being loose, and while it leads up to violent explosions, as for instance, murders, Webster does not primarily exploit such happenings for their value as sensation. Like every dramatist he keeps us hanging in fear and hope about the thing that is to happen, but he interests us far more in what moves the minds of his characters. He works up to a sudden speech or perhaps only to a sudden line to reveal as by lightning the essential quality of a life or even the meaning of the whole play. That is his *grand coup*. In his two great plays a cruel villain plans to destroy a group of people. The event interests us, of course, but we are much more deeply occupied in watching Webster turn inside out the minds of good and bad characters in a successive, deep, and rich revelation. It is only after inspecting the play very carefully that we discover how much our interest in character has been kept up and repeatedly stimulated by Webster's skilful manipulation of action, his use of contrast, and especially by his superb timing.

The general function of imagery in Webster is of course the same as in all other drama. It is the most pregnant expression of truth. It reveals character, it does the work of argument, it emphasizes mood, and it prefigures the events to come. In Webster the foreshadowing is typically ironical. The good that is promised turns out to be evil. Webster especially uses imagery to convey the basic conflict of his drama, the conflict between outward appearance and inner substance or reality. He gives us a universe so convulsed and uncertain that no appearance can represent reality. Evil shines like true gold and good tries to protect itself by putting on disguise or a false show. What is hidden rusts, soils, festers, corrupts under its fair exterior. The devil is called the 'invisible devil'.

Most powerfully of all Webster uses poison to express the relation between fair show and foul truth. Poison kills all the more certainly because it is not seen or even suspected. In *The White Devil* Webster weaves into his lines about thirty references to poison. Parallel to this the action itself contains a number of notable poisonings. In addition Webster uses *devil* as a key-word. In *The White Devil* it occurs twenty-six times. The relentless repetition of the same kind of figure, the heaping up of the same words, time and again, cannot be accidental. Such frequency of occurrence shows that there must be method, conscious and deliberate.

I begin with *The White Devil*. Lucas explains the meaning of the title, 'a devil disguised under a fair outside' and he backs up his definition by many quotations.[1] The *N.E.D.* gives the following

1 *The Complete Works of John Webster*, ed. F. L. Lucas (Chatto & Windus, 1927), vol. 1, pp. 193-4.

meanings for *white*: morally pure, stainless, innocent; free from malignity, beneficent; propitious, auspicious, happy; highly prized, pet, darling; fair-seeming, specious, plausible. In the conflict between these meanings lies the irony of the title. Probably Webster also had in mind two Elizabethan proverbs, *The White devil is worse than the black* (D 310 in Tilley) and *The devil can transform himself into an angel of light* (D 321 in Tilley). The very title of the play, then, is a figure of the sort we have been discussing. Vittoria is the white devil: white to outside view, inside the black devil.

Lodovico opens the play with a series of figures that express the relation between deceptive appearance and the bitter reality. (He is to end the play by sacrilegiously putting on the disguise of a friar in order to commit a series of murders.)

LODOVICO: Fortune's a right whore.
If she give aught, she deals it in small parcels,
That she may take away all at one swoop.
This 'tis to have great enemies, God quite them:
Your wolf no longer seems to be a wolf
Than when she's hungry.
GASPARO: You term those enemies
Are men of princely rank.
                    (I i 4-10)

Here we have two themes at which Webster labors persistently, both pertaining to the difference between seeming and being. First we have Fortune that makes a show of favor in order to deceive. Secondly, the rich and powerful are not regarded as wolves, however wolfish they may be. Only the penniless and hungry adventurer is looked upon as a beast of prey. The magnificence of rank covers a multitude of sins. The unrelenting repetition of this kind of figure binds all the scenes of the play into a whole of the highest possible unity. Webster varies the figure to include hidden disease or indeed any kind of rottenness that develops unseen.

Webster then introduces that particular theme of hidden corruption, of magnificent rank covering sin, that is the overt subject of the play. Brachiano now lives in Rome, 'And by close pandarism seeks to prostitute | The honour of Vittoria Corombona' (I i 41-2). Close pandarism is, of course, hidden pandarism, pandarism that is kept close.

Act I Scene ii is concerned most of all with the *close* pandarism. Here is corruption of the vilest sort. Vittoria's brother, Flamineo, undertakes to corrupt his sister's honor. He asks Brachiano to conceal himself, using an ominous word that foretells the end: 'Shroud you within this closet, good my Lord' (I ii 35). He then goes on to seduce Vittoria from her husband Camillo and win her over for Brachiano. At the same time Camillo is tricked into believing that Flamineo is persuading Vittoria to come back to him. The scene that follows may appaer to be the ordinary stuff of Elizabethan drama. Flamineo tricks Camillo, and the trick is everywhere in Elizabethan comedy and tragedy. Camillo stands apart, watching Flamineo and Vittoria talking, and commenting on what he sees. That also is common form in Elizabethan drama. Camillo's most important comment is: 'A virtuous brother a' my credit' (145). The difference between Webster and other Elizabethans lies in the exact correspondence between his figures-in-word and figures-in-action. Camillo is entirely deceived by appearances, the seeming good cloaks horrible evil. Webster uses the old tricks of the stage but he fills them with his own meaning.

And now Webster follows up with figures that promise happiness, only to deceive. Flamineo foretells for Vittoria the delights which the affair with Brachiano will bring to her: 'Thou shalt lie in a bed stuff'd with turtles' feathers, swoon in perfumed linen like the fellow was smothered in roses – so perfect shall be thy happiness, that as men at sea think land and trees and ships go that way they go, so both heaven and earth shall seem to go your voyage. Shalt meet him, 'tis fix'd, with nails of diamonds to inevitable necessity' (I ii 154-60).

These lines contain one of the main ironies of the play. Webster grants Brachiano and Vittoria no happiness. While for a brief moment 'heaven and earth *seem* to go their voyage', only Flamineo's last prophecy comes true. Necessity binds them all together in a way Flamineo did not foresee. And what horror and revulsion Webster conveys in the one word *happy*, coming from the mouth of the brother and pander and used of the sister he is seeking to prostitute.

For the rest of the scene Webster pursues the difference between appearance and reality in a long series of figures. He piles up these figures especially to describe the fair outside of Camillo that covers only a 'lousy slave' (48-51, 135 f).

Then Webster makes Vittoria narrate a dream in which she suggests

to Brachiano how he may murder her husband and his own wife. She
invents the figure of a yew tree to represent the marriages of Vittoria
to Camillo and of Brachiano to Isabella. Vittoria speaks of the *yew* to
Brachiano and of course she means *you*. As we shall see Webster repeats the figure of the *yew* later on (IV ii 120-23). The marriages
represented by the yew were rooted in decay and could not prosper.

In connexion with the dream Webster identifies Vittoria for the
first time as the devil. Flamineo says: 'The devil was in your dream'
(I ii 250) and follows almost at once: 'Excellent devil.|She hath
taught him in a dream|To make away his duchess and her husband'
(256-8).

A little later Cornelia introduces the first mention of poison:

> O that this fair garden,
> Had with all poisoned herbs of Thessaly,
> At first been planted . . . rather than a burial plot,
> For both your honours.
>   (I ii 274-8)

Flamineo sums up the scene by speaking of the ways of policy as
winding and indirect, flowing like rivers with 'crook bendings' and
imitating 'the subtle foldings of a winter's snake' (352). 'Subtle' implies deceit, and a snake, 'anguis in herba', strikes from concealment
and kills by poison.

The happiness they are all so confident of turns out to be Dead Sea
fruit. In the case of Vittoria and Brachiano Webster defers the ironic
event, but in the next scene (II i) with Isabella he makes it follow upon
the too confident forecast at once. Isabella is certain she can win
back Brachiano:

> I do not doubt
> As men to try the precious unicorn's horn
> Make of the powder a preservative circle.
> And in it put a spider, so these arms
> Shall charm his poison, force it to obeying
> And keep him chaste from an infected straying.
>   (II i 13-18)

Notice the themes of *poison* and *infection*. Poison kills without being
seen, infection corrupts long before its effects are visible – here are the

two most frequent themes of the play. Of course, Isabella's attempt to recover Brachiano is a complete failure.

ISABELLA: You are as welcome to these longing arms
As I to you a virgin.
BRACHIANO: O your breath!
Out upon sweet meats, and continued physic!
The plague is in them.
ISABELLA: You have oft for these two lips
Neglected cassia or the natural sweets
Of the spring violet. . . .

                              (II i 162–7)

She fails, and notice that Brachiano in this speech can no longer see her as she is. Not only does Webster show evil disguised, he shows us also that Brachiano's foulness prevents him from seeing the good.

Brachiano curses his marriage and cruelly casts Isabella off. But she, in her love for her husband, pretends that it is she who has broken up the marriage. She 'puts on an act' of spiteful jealousy and rage and convinces her brother the Duke that she is but a 'foolish, mad, and jealous woman'. Here again Webster gives us the appearance that deceives. But this time it is purest goodness that cloaks itself in evil. Webster's world is so corrupt that goodness itself works to deceive. No appearance is true.

The next scene is full of figure-in-action. In two dumb-shows a conjurer reveals how the Duchess and Camillo are murdered. In the one show villains lay poison on the picture of Brachiano – and depart laughing. The Duchess kneels before the picture, does three reverences to it, kisses it thrice, and the poison on it kills her. Brachiano, watching the dumb show, exclaims, 'Excellent'. Such pitiless confrontation of opposites is the strongest of irony. In the second dumb-show Flamineo, Camillo, and others drink healths. Flamineo and Camillo 'compliment' one another as to who shall first use the vaulting-horse, and then Flamineo breaks Camillo's neck.

And now that Brachiano has lost his wife and Vittoria her husband, the way seems clear for the promised happiness. But Flamineo and Vittoria are arrested immediately. Here is Webster's method. Vittoria is promised happiness if she submits to Brachiano, Isabella thinks she can 'charm the Duke's poison', 'keep him from an infected straying'.

Both are deceived by the event. Isabella dies of Brachiano's poison, Vittoria is arrested even before she sees Brachiano. Webster builds his figures into the construction of the play, the whole of the play is in them, and that gives them their power.

But there is more in this scene. Here we see the characteristic polarity of Webster's method in the extreme. The murderers 'depart laughing', Isabella is all humility, devotion, and love, and even in her dying agony manages to prevent anyone else from being poisoned by the picture. Brachiano sees his wife's supreme love and the tortures of her death, and remarks, 'Excellent, then she's dead.' The principle of polarity is clear.

This polarity is seen in the figures of appearance and reality all through the play.

In the famous trial-scene (III ii) Vittoria faces her accuser with superb intellectual resource. Judge and defendant fight one another with figure, and for every figure the Cardinal hurls at Vittoria, she immediately retorts with another. The Cardinal proceeds to strip her of her fair-seeming in order to show the foul heart inside. He will point out her follies in more 'natural red and white' than that upon her cheek. She seems to be goodly fruit but is like the apples of Sodom and Gomorrah, so that when he touches her, she will fall to soot and ashes. Night by night she counterfeited a prince's court. Again and again he comes back to that word *counterfeit*. 'This whore, forsooth, was holy', 'Ha,' exclaims Vittoria, 'whore, what's that?' It is her only blunder. In twenty lines the Cardinal informs her with abundant detail :

> They are first,
> Sweet-meats which rot the eater : in man's nostril
> Poison'd perfumes. They are coz'ning alchemy
> Shipwrecks in calmest weather . . .
> . . . counterfeited coin . . .
> You, gentlewoman?
> Take from all beasts, and from all minerals
> Their deadly poison.
>
> (III ii 79–104)

Again Webster's figures show the polarity – or the irony – he loves. Sweatmeats which rot, shipwrecks in calmest weather, the stretch between these opposites is the source of Webster's strength.

The Cardinal also fixes on Vittoria the name of devil.

> I am resolved
> Were there a second paradise to lose
> This devil would betray it.
> VITTORIA: O poor charity!
> Thou art seldom found in scarlet.
>
> (III ii 68-70)

> MONTICELSO: You know what whore is – next the devil, Adult'ry,
> Enters the devil, Murder.
>
> (108-9)

> If the devil
> Did ever take good shape behold his picture.
>
> (216-17)

That is, she is the White Devil.

She retorts with spirit and throws back at him the reproach of falseness: 'These are but feigned shadows of my evils.| Terrify babes, my lord, with *painted* devils' (146-7). But this only strengthens Webster's theme of appearance and reality. She displays a splendid spirit, she is magnificent in intellect and courage, and she is – a whore and a murderess.

The Cardinal in passing sentence again insists on her rottenness: 'Such a corrupted trial have you made| Both of your life and beauty ...' (260-61). Vittoria raves at him and leaves the court with a figure that reverses the ideas of appearance and reality in Vittoria's favor: 'Through darkness diamonds spread their richest light' (294). Again we see the polarity of Webster's figure, the stark contrast of darkness and rich light. This line also shows Webster's habit of summing up a movement in its closing words. The light will become rich through the darkness, in adversity Vittoria's character will show its richest light.

In the next scene (III iii) Webster continues to harp on the theme of corruption. Flamineo is the chief speaker: 'A Cardinal ... there's nothing so holy but money will corrupt and putrify it' (25-7). 'Religion; O how it is commeddled with policy. The first bloodshed in the world happened about religion' (38-40).

In the next scene (IV i) the Cardinal and the Duke play at fence, trying to deceive one another. The Cardinal preaches dissimulation, the false front, the concealed intrigue: 'We see that undermining more prevails|Than doth the cannon' (13–14). He lends the Duke a black book in which he has collected the names of notorious offenders in the city. The list is so large that it demonstrates the immense rottenness of Society. And again Webster rams into us his idea of corruption concealed by outward show: 'See the corrupted use some make of books:| Divinity, wrested by some factious blood,|Draws swords, swells battles, and o'erthrows all good' (95–7).

In the next scene the Duke sends a love-letter to Vittoria, suggesting that she should elope with him. He hopes it will be played into Brachiano's hands. This is exactly what happens. Brachiano believes Vittoria has been unfaithful and his rage with her brings insight.

> Your beauty! O, ten thousand curses on't.
> How long have I beheld the devil in crystal!
> Thou hast led me, like an heathen sacrifice,
> With music, and with fatal yokes of flowers
> To my eternal ruin.
>
> (IV ii 87–91)

The *devil in crystal* is the White Devil. Music and flowers lead to ruin. Here again the principle of polarity is clear. Vittoria answers Brachiano:

> What have I gain'd by thee but infamy?
> Thou hast stain'd the spotless honour of my house . . .
> I had a limb corrupted to an ulcer,
> But I have cut it off; and now I'll go
> Weeping to heaven on crutches.
>
> (IV ii 107–23)

A stain on honor, corruption, the ulcer: here Webster pursues relentlessly the same themes.

But the letter has a second effect. Brachiano and Vittoria make up their quarrel and then resolve to adopt the suggestion in the letter and run away to Florence.[1] Again the trick succeeds, appearances deceive, they deceive most dangerously when they flatter. The suggestion to elope to Florence seemed wonderful. It promised to Vittoria and Brachiano liberty and the enjoyment of their love. But when the

1 Actually Padua. [Ed.]

Duke hears that they have fled, he exclaims that is exactly what he has been aiming at. 'Thy fame, fond duke,|I first have poison'd; directed thee the way| To marry a whore; what can be worse?' (IV iii 54–6).

The word *poison'd* links this piece of treachery with the other poisonings in the play. The Duke has destroyed by means of something whose apparent sweetness concealed its deadliness. He has really taken the Cardinal's hint and 'undermined' the lovers.

Meanwhile the Cardinal has been elected Pope. He sees Lodovico talking with the Duke and warns him to conjure from his breast that cruel devil. He especially warns him against his plan to kill Brachiano: '. . . like the black, and melancholic yew tree,|Dost think to root thyself in dead men's graves,| And yet to prosper?' (IV iii 120–2). Here, as we have already mentioned, Webster recalls Vittoria's fable of the yew tree in I ii and this links the beginning with the end of the play, one murder with the other. But after the Pope has left, the Duke sends a servant to Lodovico with a thousand crowns. Lodovico can only think that they come from the Pope. He soliloquizes on the art of great ones in concealing their designs. Here again Webster gives us the figure of false show in action. Such a trick may be common enough in Elizabethan drama, but the sharp irony of it has an intricacy that is peculiar to Webster. Lodovico believes that the holy churchman is dissembling with him. In reality it is the Duke who is fooling him. This world is so full of false shows that we deceive ourselves even when we recognize that trickery is afoot.

The deceitfulness of appearances dominates the close of the play. Villainy is cloaked under a show of holiness, and again events that seem to promise happiness turn to disaster. In IV iii Lodovico takes the sacrament to prosecute the murder of Brachiano and Vittoria in their place, i.e. he uses the false show of holiness for murder. Webster opens V i by a magnificent wedding procession of Brachiano, Vittoria, and their household. Flamineo remains on the stage. He speaks: 'In all the weary minutes of my life,|Day ne'er broke up till now. This marriage|Confirms me happy.' HORTENSIO: ''Tis a good assurance. |Saw you not yet the Moor that's come to court?' (V i 1–4). Even at the first moment of Flamineo's happiness, Webster shows him about to be destroyed. The Moor is the Duke in disguise and he has brought with him the murderers Lodovico and Antonelli disguised as holy men, as Capuchins. Disguise is not, as it may be elsewhere, merely a convention, something to be expected in a play of blood. It is the meaning of the play that these murderers use the mask of holiness to kill.

Again we see the polarity of Webster's method. The brilliant marriage-procession and Flamineo's assurance of happiness are immediately followed by a dialogue between the three disguised murderers. Flamineo, with unconscious irony, sums up this passage with a commonplace about the deceitfulness of appearances: 'Glories, like glow-worms, afar off shine bright | But look'd to near, have neither heat nor light' (41–2). The couplet has many facets. The glow-worm may point at the marriage, at the happiness so soon to be blasted. It may also refer, as Mr Lucas's note shows, to 'persons of paltry eminence'. But it all illustrates Webster's method. The situation is figure-in-action reinforced by figure-in-words.

Act v Scene ii opens with a typical mixture of figure-in-action and figure-in-word. Cornelia enters with her son Marcello. She is wearing a crucifix. Marcello says: 'I have heard you say, giving my brother suck, | He took the crucifix between his hands, | And broke a limb off.' CORNELIA: 'Yes: but 'tis mended' (v ii 11–13). At this point Flamineo enters and runs his brother Marcello through. This incident, again, shows Webster's characteristic polarity. The mother is giving suck to her child: he breaks the crucifix. Since the crucifix has been mended, she is entirely without fear: at that very moment: Enter Flamineo. *Flamineo runs Marcello through.* The thought is mirrored twice, in the language, and in the action.

Cornelia is at first deceived by appearances. She cannot believe that Marcello is dead, 'he is not dead, he's in a trance' (v ii 27). There is a tragic chasm here between appearance and reality. Brachiano enters and Cornelia, in a moment of superb greatness, lies to him in order to save Flamineo's life. She is torn between two emotions, love for the murdered son and love for the son that murdered him. The only thing that could come out of these twisted emotions was the lie. And now to illustrate the sharpness of Webster's irony, we are compelled to reproduce the text as it stands.

FLAMINEO:[*to the* DUKE] At your pleasure.
　　[LODOVICO *sprinkles* BRACHIANO's *beaver with a poison.*]
Your will is law now, I'll not meddle with it.
　　　　　　　　　　(76–7)

Webster mingles many figures in this short passage, all focused on the falseness of appearances. Brachiano's will is law *now*, in a few seconds he will be dead. At the same time Lodovico secretly sprinkles poison into the strong helmet that Brachiano will put on his head in order to protect his life. And of course there is the treachery of Lodovico, disguised as a monk, and therefore honored as a guest, evil concealed under a robe of religion.

At the moment of death Brachiano repeats the actions of his wife as she was dying. She had prevented those about her from touching the poisoned picture. Brachiano says to Vittoria: 'Do not kiss me, for I shall poison thee' (v iii 26). In this repetition there is terror. The moral law has not been mocked, it has vindicated itself with a resolute exactness. 'An eye for an eye . . .' But further, Brachiano speaks the horrible truth about his love. It was poison for Vittoria.

At the end of Brachiano's life he sees the false show dissolve and he is confronted with the terrible reality. He is made to see the full horror of his life and of death. In death, 'horror waits on princes' (34). His agonized ravings seem to be nonsense but they make grim sense. He speaks of quails (i.e. loose women) who feed on poison. He sees the Devil come to visit him. And when Vittoria says 'here's nothing', he answers: 'Nothing? rare! nothing! when I want money, | Our treasury is empty; there is nothing, | I'll not be us'd thus' (v iii 105–8). So far as he is concerned, this answer sums up the play. His adventure with Vittoria promised happiness and he has had nothing.

And then comes the last false show. The two assassins enter, disguised as friars. They hold up the crucifix to him. Then they throw off their disguise and reveal themselves to him. They add to his torments by piling reproaches on him, they call him devil, they say his art was poison. They glory in detailing to him the poisons that are melting his brains. But on the very threshold of death Brachiano's love finds its final great expression. He shouts 'Vittoria? Vittoria!' His love is still undefeated and in his extremity he calls to her for help. It reminds one of 'Pompilia, will you let them murder me'.[1]

Here Webster achieves a level of greatness in understanding the depth of a man's soul which he sustains throughout the play. Brachiano has murdered his wife and the husband of his mistress, but he is yet

---

1 Browning, *The Ring and the Book*, Book II (Guido), l. 2427. [Ed.]

capable of a deep and selfless love for the woman he dishonors. Appearances deceive in two ways; they disguise the good as well as the evil. It would appear that two people so debased and ruthless as Vittoria and Brachiano must be incapable of a great love. But in Webster no one is thoroughly evil. After Vittoria and Brachiano have committed all their crimes and their expectations have turned against them, this love, a source of so much evil and suffering, remains a thing of strength and beauty. Probably in his final cry 'Vittoria? Vittoria!' Brachiano transcends his crimes and brings salvation upon himself. Webster shows the same transfiguration in Vittoria, who, on learning of Brachiano's death, exclaims, 'O me! this place is hell.'

Vittoria comes running in but the pretended friars push her out of the room. 'What? will you call him again | To live in treble torments? *for charity*, | *For Christian charity*, avoid the chamber' (171-3). Once more the grim irony, the fairest of appearances is used to conceal the foulest of crimes. As quickly as possible, to prevent any more interruptions, Lodovico strangles Brachiano with 'a true love-knot' sent from the Duke of Florence.

In the concluding scenes Webster rings the changes on the figures he has been employing throughout the play. Lodovico and Gasparo enter, still disguised as churchmen, and confront Vittoria and Flamineo with the horrible truth that they are to die. Vittoria pleads:

> O your gentle pity:
> I have seen a blackbird that would sooner fly
> To a man's bosom, than to stay the gripe
> Of the fierce sparrow-hawk.
> GASPARO: Your hope deceives you.
> (v vi 183-6)

This is a terrible speech, fundamental to the play. Man, made in the image of his Creator, is false to this image. He is viler in his cruelty than the beasts. And hope in this play always deceives.

Webster repeats the idea of false show when he makes Vittoria appeal to Lodovico: 'You, my death's-man; | Methinks thou dost not look horrid enough, | Thou hast too good a face to be a hangman' (209-11). But Lodovico is as pitiless as Gasparo. In his turn he calls her 'thou glorious strumpet', that is, she is still the white devil, her glorious beauty covering only foulness. But the truth is, she is now really glorious. Both she and Flamineo are great in death. Webster plays on the word *glorious*. Flamineo says:

> Th'art a noble sister –
> I love thee now . . .
> Know many glorious women that are fam'd
> For masculine virtue, have been vicious,
> Only a happier silence did betide them.
> She hath no faults, who hath the art to hide them.
>
> (241–7)

Part of this problem of appearance and reality arises from the greatness of soul which is revealed or uncovered in the 'devils' of the play. Strip some veils of appearance from them and they are foul, strip those other veils from them and their hearts are seen to harbor an inviolable greatness.

Webster does not leave us without reverting to another principal figure – the deceitfulness of fortune.

> VITTORIA: My soul, like to a ship in a black storm,
> Is driven I know not whither.
> FLAMINEO: Then cast anchor.
> Prosperity doth bewitch men seeming clear,
> But seas do laugh, show white, when rocks are near.
>
> (248–51)

Finally the end of the play curiously echoes the beginning. Giovanni has the last word: 'Let guilty men remember their black deeds, | Do lean on crutches, made of slender reeds.' To the last bitter word of the play men's trust is deceived. In *The White Devil* Webster was something of a pioneer. Rich as Elizabethan drama is in imagery, nobody before Webster had elaborated a system of figure so intricately linked and so profound.

In *The Duchess of Malfi* Webster brings the system to perfection. In his first speech Webster gives to Antonio a long figure comparing by implication the French court with the Italian. The French court is kept clean of infamous persons, however,

> [in] a Princes Court
>   . . . if't chance

Some curs'd example *poison't* near the head,
Death, and diseases through the whole land spread.
(1 i 11–15)

Bosola enters and Antonio characterizes him as 'the only court-gall' [sore or ulcer] (23).

Webster now gives us the figures-in-action. The Cardinal and the Duke begin their work. The Cardinal, who years ago suborned Bosola to murder, advises the Duke: 'Be sure you entertain that Bosola | For your intelligence: I would not be seen in't' (225–6). 'I would not be seen in't' – Webster introduces here the motif of hidden corruption that is to pervade the play. Bosola thus describes the Cardinal and the Duke: '[They] are like plum-trees that grow *crooked* over standing pools [i.e. stagnant]; they are rich, and o'er-laden with fruit, but none but crows, pies, and caterpillars feed on them' (49–52). Then Antonio closes this movement by an analysis of Bosola, saying that he is very valiant, but his melancholy will poison his goodness, an immoderate sleep rusts the soul, his want of action will eat him up, like moths in cloth. Thus in the first eighty-four lines of the play Webster has done far more than introduce certain characters, he has established the idea of treachery, poison, and slow corruption working in individuals and in the state.

Antonio goes on to characterize the Cardinal and the Duke in the same way. The Cardinal is a brave fellow, but 'such flashes hang superficially on him, for form: but observe his inward character . . . the spring in his face is nothing but the engendering of toads . . .' (156–8). Of the Duke it is the same, 'What appears in him mirth, is merely outside' (170). The two brothers are twins 'In quality'.

Webster then turns to the other corrupt characters. Like Fortune, the Court promises and deludes. Bosola complains that his service at Court has been badly rewarded: 'What creature ever fed worse than hoping Tantalus? . . . places in the Court, are but like beds in the hospital, where this man's head lies at that man's foot' (1 i 56–68).

After Bosola's exit Delio reveals that Bosola had served seven years in the galleys for the murder which the Cardinal had suborned him to commit.

Ferdinand now sets about corrupting Bosola anew. He persuades him to be a spy in the household of the Duchess by procuring for him the Provisorship of the Horse to the Duchess. Bosola accepts: 'For the good deed you have done me, I must do | All the ill man can invent! Thus the devil|Candies all sins o'er' (274–6), and later, 'What's my place?|The provisorship o'th' horse? say then, my corruption|Grew out of horse-dung: I am your creature' (285–7).

Then the Cardinal and Ferdinand take the Duchess in hand and in a string of metaphors hint strongly at the dangers of her marrying again. They warn her against a honey-dew of the court that is poison and especially against hypocrisy, against making her face belie her heart. In the behavior of the two brothers we see the figure-in-action, fair seeming never covered falser hearts.

They make no impression on the Duchess. As soon as they leave, she proclaims her intention of essaying this dangerous venture of marriage. She tells her secret to Cariola, who answers: 'I'll conceal this secret from the world|As warily as those that trade in *poison*,|Keep *poison* from their children' (352–4). In the famous wooing-scene that follows, Webster shows the Duchess, in contrast to her brothers, as a candid and open nature. Webster uses the figures of falseness and deception to show that they do not apply to the Duchess or Antonio. The Duchess says to Antonio:

You were ill to sell your self –
This dark'ning of your worth is not like that
Which tradesmen use i'th' city – their false lights
Are to rid bad wares off.
                                        (431–4)

Again speaking of those born great, she says:

              . . . we
Are forc'd to . . . leave the path
Of simple virtue, which was never made
To seem the thing it is not.
                                        (444–8)

When at last the Duchess and Antonio pledge their troth, Webster shows the falseness of their hopes by the irony of the words he chooses. When the Duchess kisses Antonio, she says 'I sign your *Quietus est*' (464), a double-edged phrase significant of death. When she speaks of danger from her brothers, she lightheartedly challenges her fate: 'time will easily|Scatter the tempest' (471–2). As we shall see, this prophecy will be terribly reversed. When she proclaims their absolute marriage, she adds: 'Bless, heaven, this sacred Gordian, which let violence| Never untwine' (480–81). But the Gordian knot was not untwined; Alexander severed it with a blow of his sword. And to celebrate their contract, Antonio and the Duchess sing their loves in the sweetest music and the most delicious figures Webster can invent. (482–93). The whole love-scene is so strong because the image in word is completely fused with the image in action. The ironic hints leave no doubt that the trust in Fortune, which both the words and the action show, would in time be cheated. In order to make his irony quite clear Webster concludes the scene with a speech by Cariola:

Whether the spirit of greatness or of woman
Reign most in her, I know not, but it shows
A fearful madness; I owe her much of pity.

(504–6)

Thus from this one scene we see how Webster shifts his kaleidoscope round about, displaying in many different patterns the irony of specious appearance hiding bitter reality. An inexorable logic links the figures, giving the scene its unity and making it a most powerful intellectual construction. All the persons in the play, their every word, everything they do, are symbols of one idea.

In the next scene Webster invents a conversation between Bosola, Castruchio, and an Old Lady, apparently in order to lead up to the speech:

What thing is in this outward form of man
To be belov'd? . . .
Though we are eaten up of lice and worms,
And though continually we bear about us
A rotten and dead body, we delight
To hide it in rich tissue.

(II i 45–58)

Webster follows this up with an image-in-action. Bosola, suspecting the Duchess to be pregnant, offers her some apricots, they are 'wondrous fair ones'. Bosola says that the knave gardener 'did ripen them in horse-dung' (140). Notice the echo of I i 287 where Bosola says his corruption grew out of horse-dung.[1] The Duchess eats the apricots greedily and they bring on the pangs of labor. She bears a son and Bosola sends the news to Rome to her brothers Ferdinand and the Cardinal, who now begin to plan her death. The interconnexion of events is clear from the fruit, ripened out of horse-dung, that was so 'wondrous fair' but so disastrous in effect, right along to the wild rage of Ferdinand in Rome. Through these scenes Webster scatters images continuing the idea of secret corruption and false show. Antonio says of Bosola 'This mole does undermine me' (II iii 14). Bosola ends the scene with the couplet: '*Though lust do mask in ne'er so strange disguise,* | *She's oft found witty, but is never wise*' (II iii 76–7). He misunderstands the Duchess completely. Appearances deceive in many ways. They prevent us from seeing the good as well as the evil. But immediately the next scene shows us the Cardinal with Julia, his mistress, and the Cardinal says to her: 'Thou art a witty false one' (II iv 5), and the application of Bosola's words is clear.

Delio, at the end of the scene, speaking of Antonio, says 'unfortunate Fortune' (80). In this oxymoron he expresses the chief irony of the play.

With Act III Ferdinand moves upon the Duchess. Antonio is afraid:

He is so quiet, that he seems to sleep
The tempest out, as dormice do in winter –
Those houses that are haunted are most still,
Till the devil be up.
(III i 21–4)

Here there is a double echo: the 'tempest' linking this speech with the words of the Duchess, and 'dormice' echoing Ferdinand's admonition to his spy, Bosola, to be 'like a politic dormouse' (I i 282). Then Webster invents the figure-in-action. Ferdinand completely deceives the Duchess about his intentions and she exclaims *aside*: 'O bless'd comfort! | This deadly air is purg'd' (55–6). Again the irony of too confident hope that will be defeated.

Webster continues this figure-in-action in the next scene where he

---

1 Charles Williams has already called attention to this echo in his Introduction to *The Duchess of Malfi* (London, 1945), pp. xviii–xix. He also calls attention to the use of the word *dung-hill* (IV i 65).

shows the Duchess, Antonio, and Cariola harmlessly laughing and making fun of one another. The Duchess exclaims: 'When were we so merry? my hair tangles' (53), and then: 'Doth not the colour of my hair 'gin to change?|When I wax gray . . .' (III ii 58–9).

The next minute she turns and sees Ferdinand with a poniard, which he gives her, saying: 'Die then, quickly!|Virtue, where art thou hid? what hideous thing|Is it that doth eclipse thee?' (71–3). That is to say, while in other parts of the play the good do not see the vice hidden by hypocrisy, Webster twists the idea of appearance and reality to show that Ferdinand, on the other hand, cannot recognize virtue when it stands before him in its most beautiful form.

At the end of the scene Webster invents the image-in-action again when Bosola's defense of Antonio sounds so genuine and warm that he dupes the Duchess into confiding in him and learns that Antonio is her husband. He advises her to go 'to feign a pilgrimage' to Loretto so that her flight may *seem* a princely progress. Cariola is against this jesting with religion, 'This feigned pilgrimage', but the Duchess will not listen to her. The virtuous Duchess is not good at feigning; that is Bosola's job, and by making her feign Bosola sends her to her doom.

In III iii Webster leads up by a series of concentrated images to a new climax of power. The two brothers have just heard that the Duchess is going on a feigned pilgrimage, and Webster uses his favorite method of describing them through bystanders.

SILVIO: He [the Cardinal] lifts up's nose, like a foul porpoise before
      a storm.

(III iii 52–3)

Notice the link with the Duchess's carefree contempt for any storm the brothers could raise (I i 471–2).

It is difficult for us to recapture the effect of this figure of the porpoise on Webster's audience. It is built up on the proverb, 'The porpoise plays before the storm.' Since we have lost contact with proverbs, we can no longer feel their power.

PESCARA: These are your true pangs of death,
The pangs of life that struggle with great statesmen –
DELIO: In such a deformed silence, witches whisper
Their charms.

(56–9)

Surely this figure is so tremendous because it bears the weight of the whole play.

CARDINAL: Doth she make religion her riding-hood
To keep her from the sun and tempest?
(60–61)

Notice Webster's consistency in the characterization by figure. He gives the Cardinal figures strong by reason of their conciseness. Notice he repeats the idea of *tempest*.

FERDINAND: That!
That damns her: – methinks her fault and beauty,
Blended together, show like leprosy,
The whiter, the fouler: – I make it a question
Whether her beggarly brats were ever christened.
(III iii 61–5)

It is part of Webster's irony that the Duchess, by allowing herself to be duped into feigning a pilgrimage, has outraged the deepest religious feelings of those two pillars of the Church, the Cardinal and Ferdinand. They are both murderers, and the Cardinal keeps his mistress, but to go on a feigned pilgrimage they regard as utterly unpardonable. Webster brings it home to us that their religion is entirely external, a matter of show, without inner depth. Again, when Ferdinand speaks of her fault and beauty showing like leprosy, the whiter the fouler, we have the same twisted irony as before. Ferdinand sees her whiteness and imagines it is evil. He cannot see the reality and he misjudges the appearance.

FERDINAND: *Antonio!*
A slave, that . . .
. . . ne'er in's life, look'd like a gentleman,
But in the audit-time.
(III iii 71–4)

The irony of this is obvious. He misjudges Antonio by his appearance as certainly as he does the Duchess. The line is rich in its sardonic humor because it states with such a cutting edge the typical attitude of the conventional aristocrat towards the middle class. Thus in these few figures Webster has shown us that these two brothers are base, formidable through their treachery, and contemptible through their littleness of soul and mind.

The dumb-show in III iv is another figure-in-action. The Pope has appointed the Cardinal to be a general in his wars and so the Cardinal comes to the shrine of Our Lady of Loretto to lay aside his vestments as a man of God and to put on the armor of a soldier. To the same shrine come Antonio, the Duchess and their family. Choirs of priests sing to solemn music the praises of the Cardinal. The Duchess and her party, however, are banished from the shrine, and we are told the Pope has seized her dominions into his protection. The Church blesses the priest who goes out to kill but to the good it denies the consolations of religion and robs them of their property. To go back to I i 'the curs'd example', poisoning the state and the church 'near the head', is spreading disease through the whole land.

In III v Bosola brings the Duchess a letter from the Duke, promising as he avers 'All love and safety'. The Duchess answers:

> Thou dost blanch mischief,
> Wouldst make it white: – see, see, like to calm weather
> At sea, before a tempest, false hearts speak fair
> To these they intend most mischief.
> [*Reads*]
> *Send Antonio to me; I want his head in a business:*
> A politic equivocation!
> He doth not want your counsel, but your head;
> That is, he cannot sleep till you be dead.
> And here's another pitfall, that's strew'd o'er
> With roses ...
>   (III v 24–33)

Eternal repetition of the same theme of evil hidden by fair show. Bosola retires and the Duchess and Antonio take their eternal farewell of one another.

In IV i Bosola pretends to offer the Duchess comfort, she answers: 'I will have none :| Pray thee, why dost thou wrap thy poison'd pills| In gold and sugar' (IV i 18–20). In the ensuing passage Ferdinand tries to break her spirit by a series of horrors. He first insists on seeing the Duchess in a completely darkened chamber. He offers her apparently his hand to kiss, it turns out to be a dead man's hand which he has brought with him. Then '*is discovered behind a traverse the artificial figures of Antonio and his children; appearing as if they were dead*'. Finally there is a dance of madmen with 'music answerable'.

All these are figures-in-action, attempts to deceive and to strike down by false show. In contrast to this, Bosola can torture her still more by pointing to reality.

DUCHESS: I could curse the stars . . .
And those three smiling seasons of the year
Into a Russian winter: nay the world
To its first chaos.
BOSOLA: Look you, the stars shine still.

> (IV i 96–100)

He points to the stars, indifferent to her curses, pitiless, terrible – surely this line is among the greatest ever written.

In the next scene Webster goes even further. In a famous passage, marked by his characteristic polarity, confronting character with character, he makes the Duchess say:

Who am I?
BOSOLA: Thou art a box of worm-seed, at best, but a salvatory of green mummy: – what's this flesh? a little crudded milk, fantastical puff-paste . . .
DUCHESS: Am not I, thy Duchess?
BOSOLA: Thou art some great woman, sure, for riot begins to sit on thy forehead clad in gray hairs twenty years sooner than on a merry milkmaid's. Thou sleepest worse than if a mouse should be forc'd to take up her lodging in a cat's ear . . .
DUCHESS: I am Duchess of Malfi still.
BOSOLA: That makes thy sleeps so broken:
Glories like glow-worms afar off shine bright,
But look'd to near, have neither heat, nor light.

> (IV ii 123–45)

Here we see Webster's technique. No speech, however glorious, is allowed to stand without its swift riposte. And again the same motif in a different figure, appearance and reality still quarrel, the beautiful body is but a box of worm-seed. And he takes over a couplet from

The White Devil to show that as the great lady grows grey, the glories of the Duchess have neither heat nor light.

A little later executioners enter and Bosola sings a dirge for the Duchess in which he brings together two motifs in a couplet: '*Their life, a general mist of error,*| *Their death a hideous storm of terror*' (188–9).

The executioners strangle her and Ferdinand enters. Fate has given him what he demanded of her. Bosola points to the dead Duchess and says: 'She is what| You'd have her' (226–7). And now that Ferdinand has achieved what he has planned, he exclaims: 'Cover her face: mine eyes dazzle: she died young' (264). I do not wish to rush in where angels fear to tread and endeavor to improve on this famous line. But I am obliged to point out that it is not 'merely' superb 'poetry'. It is strong because it is built into the construction of the play. Ferdinand has never known his sister, and only now, when he has murdered her, and she is lying dead at his feet, does reality strike him and he sees her for the first time. William Archer will have none of this line. He says: 'It is not difficult to hit upon sayings which shall pass for highly dramatic simply because they are unforeseen and unlikely.'[1] It is curious that a famous critic who spent his life in writing about plays should know nothing about the construction of a play. Webster has taken infinite pains to lead us up to this line. He foresaw it and when it comes, we recognize it was inevitable that it should come. It is the climax of the play, the watershed, the dividing line.

Bosola now claims his reward from Ferdinand, but in vain. Again hope is completely deluded. Bosola sums up:

Your brother and yourself are worthy men;
You have a pair of hearts are hollow graves,
Rotten, and rotting others . . .
        I stand like one
That long hath ta'en a sweet and golden dream.
I am angry with my self, now that I wake.

                (IV ii 318–25)

Bosola is converted and turns from evil, but he can do no good. He desires more than anything to help Antonio and then – another figure-in-action – by mistake he stabs Antonio in the dark. In dying Antonio repeats the constant theme: 'In all our quest of greatness . . .| Like

1 *The Old Drama and the New* (New York, 1926), p. 61.

wanton boys, whose pastime is their care|We follow after bubbles, blown in th' air' (v iv 64–6).

Webster continues his figures-in-action. The Cardinal gives order to his retinue not to come to his aid if they hear calls for help. Such calls will probably come from the mad Ferdinand. When Bosola attacks him, he does cry for help, but his retinue only exclaim, 'Fie upon his counterfeiting!' (v v 20). And for his counterfeiting the Cardinal dies. Bosola stabs him repeatedly at his ease – no one interferes. Ferdinand, who has gone mad, now enters. In his madness he thinks the Cardinal is the enemy and he therefore helps Bosola. He stabs the Cardinal and in the scuffle gives Bosola his death-wound. Bosola still has strength before he dies to kill Ferdinand. All this the Cardinal might have prevented but for his 'feigning'. Their lives are a 'mist of error'.

In a final figure Delio sums up the theme of empty show that runs through the play.

> These wretched eminent things
> Leave no more fame behind 'em than should one
> Fall in a frost, and leave his print in snow –
> As soon as the sun shines, it ever melts,
> Both form, and matter: – I have ever thought
> Nature doth nothing so great, for great men,
> As when she's pleas'd to make them lords of truth:
> *Integrity of life, is fame's best friend,*
> *Which nobly beyond death shall crown the end.*
>
> (v v 113–21)

I have given these figures in such detail, as they occur, in order to make quite clear the nature of Webster's structure. Figure-in-action and figure-in-word reinforce one another. He repeats his theme tirelessly, spinning innumerable variations with his figures of the magnificent outer show and the inner corruption, of life, fortune, hopes that look so fair and delude us utterly, of the many bitter, twisted ironies of the difference between appearance and reality.

Webster's coordination of the figure-in-word with the figure-in-action makes his position in drama unique. Marlowe's figure runs parallel to his action; he rarely fuses the two. Ben Jonson devotes his attention to developing the action, to which figure is subsidiary.

Chapman is neither clear-headed nor patient enough to work out an elaborate pattern like Webster's. The only possible comparison is with Shakespeare. There can be no doubt that Webster profited by Shakespeare's example. But even Shakespeare could in his turn have learned something from Webster's skill in interlacing long chains of figure and action in order to express an irony so varied, so subtle, and so profound.

But to come back to where we started from, it is extremely important that all students of Shakespeare's art should familiarize themselves with Webster's technique. Perhaps if modern critics recognized the stern consistency with which Webster developed his elaborate imagery, they would be able to see that Shakespeare was doing very much the same sort of thing. They would no longer refuse to believe that Shakespeare coordinated his images. They might even come to admit that Shakespeare used plan and system in the development of his imagery, and that while he appears on the surface to be more simple than Webster, he plumbs to depths that Webster never reached.

(717–39)

Inga-Stina Ekeblad (Mrs I.-S. Ewbank)

'The "Impure Art" of John Webster', *Review of English Studies*, n.s. vol. 9 1958

'The art of the Elizabethans is an impure art. . . . The aim of the Elizabethans was to attain complete realism without surrendering any of the advantages which as artists they observed in unrealistic conventions.'[1]

Obviously *The Duchess of Malfi* is an outstanding example of the 'impure art' of the Elizabethans. Here, in one play, Webster plays over the whole gamut between firm convention and complete realism: from the conventional dumb-show –

Here the ceremony of the CARDINAL'*s instalment, in the habit of a soldier: performed in delivering up his cross, hat, robes, and ring, at the shrine; and investing him with sword, helmet, shield, and spurs:*

1 T. S. Eliot, *Selected Essays* (New York, 1950), pp. 96, 97.

Then ANTONIO, *the* DUCHESS, *and their children (having presented themselves at the shrine) are (by a form of banishment in dumb-show, expressed towards them by the* CARDINAL *and the state of* ANCONA) *banished.*

(III iv)

to the would-be realistic pathos of

I pray thee, look thou giv'st my little boy
Some syrup for his cold . . . ;

(IV ii 203–4)

or from the horror-show of '*the artificial figures of Antonio, and his children, appearing as if they were dead*' (IV i) to the realization of a character's psychological state, in such lines as Ferdinand's much-quoted 'Cover her face: mine eyes dazzle: she died young' (IV ii 264) or Antonio's 'I have no use | To put my life to' (v iv 63–4).

So Webster's dramatic technique needs to be understood in relation to the 'confusion of convention and realism' which Mr Eliot speaks of; and indeed many critics would in this 'confusion' see the key to Webster's alleged failure as a dramatist. They would say that Webster's method of mixing unrealistic conventions with psychological-realistic representation leads to lack of structure in his plays as whole.[2] It seems, in fact, to have become almost an axiom that when Webster uses conventional dramatic material – such as the various Revenge play devices – it is for show value, 'for effect', and not because the progress of his dramatic action, and the meaning of the play, are vitally tied up with that convention – as they are, for example, in *The Revenger's Tragedy* or *The Atheist's Tragedy*. While Tourneur's 'bony lady' is simultaneously an incentive to revenge and a tool for moralizing, the *memento mori* and centre of meaning of the play, Webster's wax figures seem to have no other function than Madame Tussaud's. And while Tourneur's famous speech, 'Does the silkworm expend her yellow labours | For thee? . . .', is closely dependent on, and interacts with, the skull on the stage, Webster's dramatic meaning would appear to inhere in his poetry – such as Bosola's '. . . didst thou ever see a lark in a cage?' – irrespective of the dramatic devices employed. Is it, then, only when his poetry fails to do the trick that Webster 'falls

2 Cf. M. C. Bradbrook, *Themes and Conventions of Elizabethan Tragedy* (2nd edn, Cambridge, 1952), pp. 187, 194, 211.

back on showmanship',[1] such as 'all the apparatus of dead hands, wax images, dancing madmen, and dirge-singing tomb-makers in *The Duchess of Malfi*'?[2]

Now, while recognizing that in other Elizabethans than Webster (for example Tourneur) the dramatic form is more firmly and consistently controlled by established conventions, we must, on the other hand, not blind ourselves to the richness which may inhere in the very 'confusion' of convention and realism. The two can be confused; but they can also be fused. And I hope to show that Webster – though he often leaves us in confusion – does at his most intense achieve such a fusion, creating something structurally new and vital. This something, however, is very much more elusive to analysis than the more rigidly conventional structures of Tourneur, or the more clearly 'realistic' structure of Middleton (as in *The Changeling*).

I wish to examine *The Duchess of Malfi*, iv ii – the Duchess's death-scene. It is a part of the play to which no critic of Webster has been indifferent; it stirred Lamb's and Swinburne's most prostrate praise and Archer's most nauseated denunciation, and later critics have only less ardently condemned or lauded it. Its complexity has been sensed, but hardly satisfactorily analysed.[3]

No one, I think, would deny that this scene contains Webster's most penetrating piece of character-analysis. Through language where juxtaposition of sublime and lowly suggests the tremendous tension in her mind:

Th' heaven o'er my head seems made of molten brass,
The earth of flaming sulphur, yet I am not mad:
I am acquainted with sad misery,
As the tann'd galley-slave is with his oar

(iv ii 25–8)

---

1 *The Age of Shakespeare*, Pelican Guide to English Literature (London, 1955), p. 352.
2 W. A. Edwards, 'John Webster', *Scrutiny*, vol. 2 (1933), p. 20. Cf. also Ian Jack, 'The Case of John Webster', ibid., vol. 16 (1949), pp. 38–43.
3 Miss Bradbrook sees this scene as largely symbolical: it represents the Duchess's Hell, or Purgatory (*Themes and Conventions*, p. 197). Miss Welsford, in *The Court Masque* (Cambridge, 1927), pp. 295–6, has some suggestive, though not very clear, comments on symbolical features in this scene.

we follow the Duchess's inner development towards the acceptance of her fate; till finally, though 'Duchess of Malfi, still', she humbly kneels to welcome death. And yet, in the midst of this representation of human experience, Webster introduces a pack of howling madmen, to sing and dance and make antic speeches; and as they leave the stage, the whole apparatus of 'dirge-singing tomb-makers', etc., is brought in. How are we to reconcile such apparently opposed elements? The commonly accepted answer is that this is only one more instance of Webster's constant letting us down, his constant sacrifice of unity of design, in order to achieve a maximum effect. But, in a scene which is so clearly the spiritual centre of the play, which verbally – through poetic imagery – gathers together all the chief themes of the play and thus becomes a kind of fulcrum for the poetry, ought we not to devote particular attention to the dramatic technique used, before we pronounce it as grossly bad as the answer suggested above would indicate?

In fact, if we pursue the question why Webster inserted a masque of madmen in a would-be realistic representation of how the Duchess faces death, we shall find that the madmen's masque is part of a larger structural unit – a more extensive masque. Within the scene, this larger masque is being developed on a framework of 'realistic' dramatic representation – the framework itself bearing an analogous relationship to the masque structure. The action of the scene is grasped only by seeing both the basic framework and the masque structure, and the progressive interaction of the two. It is this structural counterpointing of 'convention' and 'realism', this concentrated 'impurity' of art, that gives the scene its peculiar nature; indeed, it contains the meaning of the scene.

By 1613–14, the years of the composition of The Duchess of Malfi, the introduction of a masque in a play was a long-established dramatic device. In the Revenge drama, from Kyd onwards, masques were traditionally used to commit revenging murder[1] or otherwise resolve the plot. Furthermore, in the years around the writing of The Duchess of Malfi the leading dramatists show a strong interest in the marriage-masque – we need only think of the elaborate showpiece inserted in The Maid's Tragedy, or the masques of The Tempest and The Two

---

1 Cf. Vindice's words: 'A masque is treasons licence, that build upon; | 'Tis murder's best face when a vizard's on' (The Revenger's Tragedy, v i 196–7).

Noble Kinsmen. During these years, any play which includes a marriage seems also almost bound to contain a marriage-masque.[1]

Now, in *The Duchess of Malfi* it is the Duchess's love and death, her marriage and murder, which are the focal points of the dramatic action. And in IV ii Webster has, by the very building of the scene, juxtaposed – counterpointed – the two. He has done so by drawing on masque conventions. To see how, and why, we must proceed to a detailed analysis of the scene-structure.

The essence of the masque, throughout its history, was 'the arrival of certain persons vizored and disguised, to dance a dance or present an offering'.[2] Although the structure of the early, Tudor, masque had become overlaid with literature (especially, of course, by Ben Jonson) and with show (by those who, like Inigo Jones, thought of the masque primarily in terms of magnificent visual effects), the masques inserted in Jacobean plays – if at all elaborated on – stay close to the simpler structure of the Elizabethan masque. That structure, we may remind ourselves, is as follows:

1. Announcing and presenting of the masquers in introductory speeches (and songs).
2. Entry of masquers.
3. Masque dances.
4. Revels (in which the masquers 'take out' and dance with members of the audience).

   A further contact between masquers and audience – especially common when the masque is still near to its original form: groups of disguised dancers suddenly intruding into a festive assembly –

1 The two traditions of revenging-murder masque and marriage-masque sometimes meet. See, for example, Middleton's *Women Beware Women* (1625?), where the cupids' arrows are literally deadly, and the antimasque of Hymen includes the presentation of a poisoned cup.
2 Welsford, *Court Masque*, p. 7. In discussing the masque I also draw on R. Brotanek, *Die englischen Maskenspiele* (Wien, 1902); P. Reyher, *Les Masques anglais* (Paris, 1909); E. K. Chambers's chapter on 'The Masque' in *The Elizabethan Stage* (Oxford, 1923), i, pp. 149–212; the chapter on the masque in C. H. Herford and Percy Simpson's edition of Ben Jonson (Oxford, 1925), ii, pp. 249–334; and Allardyce Nicoll, *Stuart Masques and the Renaissance Stage* (London, 1937).

can be the presenting of gifts by the masquers to the one, or ones, to be celebrated.

5. Final song (and speeches).

These features all appear in *The Duchess of Malfi*, IV ii.

As the scene opens, the 'wild consort of Mad-men' is heard off-stage as a 'hideous noise'. The verbal imagery is preparing for the consciously scenic quality of what is to come. The Duchess turns immediately from her both ominous and ironic remark,[1] 'And Fortune seems only to have her eyesight, | To behold my tragedy', to the question, 'How now! What noise is that?' Here a Servant enters, to perform the function of the Announcer of the masque: 'I am come to tell you, | Your brother hath intended you some sport,' and the Duchess answers, by a phrase which in terms of the plot only would seem absurd — for what is her power to give or refuse entry? — but which is natural when coming from someone about to be 'celebrated' with a masque: 'Let them come in.' The arrival of the masquers in *Timon of Athens*, I ii, may serve to show that the opening of the scene follows the traditional pattern for the reception of unexpectedly arriving masquers:

TIMON : What means that trump?
  [*Enter* SERVANT.]
SERVANT : Please you, my lord, there are certain ladies most desirous of admittance.
TIMON : Ladies? What are their wills?
SERVANT : There comes with them a forerunner, my lord, which bears that office to signify their pleasures.
TIMON : I pray let them be admitted.

Now the Servant in IV ii becomes the Presenter of the masque and delivers a speech introducing each of the eight madmen-masquers:

1 Ironic because it echoes back to the wooing-scene, where the Duchess tells Antonio, 'I would have you lead your fortune by the hand | Unto your marriage bed' (I i 495–6). She is here thinking of the traditionally blind figure of Fortune and merely making a playful conceit. Yet unwittingly she is expressing her own blindness to the consequences of her action. And when the image is repeated in IV ii it is to make the tragic irony explicit. Now Fortune is no longer blind, nor is the Duchess; but what they see is only suffering and death. The Fortune image is used so as to point the almost literal opening of eyes that the action has brought about. Cf. F. L. Lucas's comments on this passage.

There's a mad lawyer, and a secular priest,
A doctor that hath forfeited his wits
By jealousy: an astrologian,
That in his works said such a day o'th' month
Should be the day of doom; and failing of't,
Ran mad: an English tailor, craz'd i'th' brain,
With the study of new fashion: a gentleman usher
Quite beside himself, with care to keep in mind
The number of his lady's salutations,
Or 'How do you', she employ'd him in each morning:
A farmer too, an excellent knave in grain
Mad 'cause he was hinder'd transportation:
And let one broker that's mad loose to these,
You'd think the devil were among them.

                                             (45–58)

This product of Webster's grim comico-satirical strain is, of course, in
terms of realistic plot totally out of place here. Not so, however, if
seen in the relevant tradition. From 1608 or 1609 practically every
court masque was preceded by an antimasque, often danced by
'antics': 'O Sir, all de better, vor an antick-maske, de more absurd it
be, and vrom de purpose, it be ever all de better.'[1] In each of the
earlier antimasques, the antic figures were all of a kind, and there was
no attempt to differentiate them. It is in the masques performed at the
Princess Elizabeth's wedding, in February 1613,[2] that individualized
comic characters first appear. It is worth noting that Campion's
'twelve frantics . . . all represented in sundry habits and humours' in
The Lord's Masque – such as 'the melancholic man, full of fear, the
school-man overcome with phantasy, the overwatched usurer . . .' –

1 Vangoose in Ben Jonson's The Masque of Augures. With the Severall Anti-
masques Presented on Twelfe-Night, 1622.
2 Three masques, by Campion, Beaumont, and Chapman respectively, were
performed on the occasion. The possibility that Webster directly imitates
Campion's masque of madmen has been pointed out; and John P. Cutts,
'Jacobean Masque and Stage Music', Music and Letters, vol. 35 (1954), p. 193,
suggests that 'it is Robert Johnson's music which is involved in the transference
. . . of the madmen's antimasque from The Lord's Masque to The Duchess of
Malfi'. What I am concerned with here, however, is not imitation or adaptation
as such, but the fact of a common tradition.

as well as Beaumont's various figures in the second antimasque of *The
Masque of the Inner Temple and Gray's Inn*, are described in much the
same manner as Webster's eight madmen. Webster is here working in
an antimasque tradition which was to have many uses in the drama
after him. We see it, for instance, in Ford's *The Lover's Melancholy*
(1628), which in III iii has a masque of the same shape as the madmen's
interlude in *The Duchess of Malfi*: six different types of Melancholy
are described and present themselves; their antic talk is given; and
then the Dance, 'after which the masquers run out in couples'.

After the presentation, the masquers themselves appear – '*Enter
Madmen*' – and one of them sings a song to what the stage directions
describe as 'a dismal kind of music'.[1] Even without the music, there
is plenty of dismalness in the jarring jingle of the words:

O let us howl, some heavy note,
  Some deadly dogged howl,
Sounding as from the threat'ning throat
  Of beasts, and fatal fowl!

(IV ii 61–4)

Webster's audience had the benefit of the musical setting, which,
according to Mr Cutts, 'makes a vivid and forceful attempt to convey
the horror of the imagery of owls, wolves and harbingers of death'.
The antimasquers at the court of James frequently appeared in the
shape of animals;[2] and it seems that, for example, the madmen-
masquers ordered for the wedding of Beatrice Joanna in *The Changeling* were to wear animal disguises. Stage directions in *The Changeling*
tell us: '*Cries of madmen are heard within, like those of birds and beasts*',
and the explicit comments on this are:

Sometimes they [madmen] imitate the beasts and birds,
Singing or howling, braying, barking; all
As their wild fancies prompt 'em.

(III iii 206–8)

1 The setting, which had been broken in two in B.M. Add. MS. 29481 and
wrongly catalogued, has recently been reassembled by John P. Cutts. He
ascribes it, conjecturally, to [Robert] Johnson. See *Music and Letters*, 33 (1952),
pp. 333–4.
2 Cf. A. H. Thorndike, 'Influence of the Court-Masque on the Drama, 1608–
15', *P.M.L.A.*, vol. 15 (1900), pp. 114–20.

Here, then, is another antimasque tradition drawn upon in *The Duchess of Malfi*. The bestiality of these madmen comes out chiefly in the imagery of the song:

As ravens, screech-owls, bulls, and bears,
We'll bill and bawl our parts.

(IV ii 65–6)

But we may be helped by other madmen-antimasquers to imagine, visually and aurally, how the song, and indeed the whole interlude, was executed.

Directly after the song various madmen speak for themselves, in a series of disjointed speeches which verbally link this episode with main themes of the whole play. Images of hell-fire, of madness and bestiality (preparing, of course, for Ferdinand's lycanthropy) – to mention only the most important – are concentrated here. After the speeches follows '*the dance, consisting of 8 Madmen, with music answerable thereunto*'. It is left to us to imagine the lumbering movements and discordant tunes which this passus must have contained; yet we should not forget that, though there is only a bare reference to it in the stage directions, the dance must have been the climax of the madmen's interlude. Now, it is not 'from the purpose', but truly meaningful, that in the centre of *The Duchess of Malfi* there should be this antic dance, accompanied by these incoherent words and discordant tunes. We know that to the Elizabethans the unity and coherence of macrocosm and microcosm alike was naturally expressed as a dance:

Dancing, the child of Music and of Love,
Dancing itself, both love and harmony,
Where all agree and all in order move,
Dancing, the art that all arts do approve,
The fair character of the world's consent,
The heav'n's true figure, and th' earth's ornament.[1]

And so the climactic dance would be particularly significant in the marriage-masque, the purpose of which was to celebrate the union brought about by the power of Love. Ben Jonson built his *Hymenaei*

1 Sir John Davies, *Orchestra*, ll. 666–71.

(1606) round this idea,[1] and the central dance of that masque is a 'neat and curious measure', accompanied by the following chorus:

Whilst all this *Roof* doth ring,
And each discording string,
With every varied voice,
In Union doth rejoice.
                              (306–9)

The dance in *The Duchess of Malfi*, on the contrary, acts as an ideo-graph of the *dis*-unity, the *in*-coherence, of the Duchess's world. It acts as a visual and aural image of what the action of the play has led to, the difference between the happiness and unity of the wooing-scene, imaged as the most perfect movement and melody:

ANTONIO: And may our sweet affections, like the spheres,
Be still in motion.
DUCHESS: Quick'ning, and make
The like soft music.
                              (I i 482–4)

and this scene where the Duchess herself has found that

          ... nothing but noise and folly
Can keep me in my right wits.
                              (IV ii 5–6)

By now it should be possible to say that the madmen's masque is not just 'Bedlam-broke-loose', as Archer, and with him many, would have it. Nor do we need to excuse this interlude, as has been done, by saying that Webster is not alone in it; that there are plenty of madmen in Elizabethan drama, and Webster's Bedlam stuff is as good as any. Such an excuse does not save the scene, as a piece of dramatic art, from damnation. But we are beginning to see the masque as peculiarly functional in the play. We have seen its connexions with antimasque conventions; now we must see how it is related to the events that are represented on the stage.

1 There is an admirable discussion of the theme of Union in *Hymenaei* in D. J. Gordon's '*Hymenaei*: Ben Jonson's Masque of Union', *Journal of the Warburg and Courtauld Institutes*, vol. 8 (1945), pp. 107–45. See esp. pp. 118–19.

In fact, there are reasons to believe that in this masque there is a nucleus of folk tradition, the bearing of which on the action of the play justifies the inclusion of the masque.

The widowhood of the Duchess is much stressed throughout the play – from the brothers' interview with her in the very first scene, around the motto, 'Marry! they are most luxurious|Will wed twice' (1 i 297–8). It is well known that objections to second marriages were still strong at the beginning of the seventeenth century. We need go no farther than Webster's own *Characters*, 'A Virtuous Widow' and 'An Ordinary Widow',[1] to get a notion of how strong they were. Early in 1613 Chapman's satiric comedy *The Widow's Tears* (1605–6), in which the 'luxury' of two widows provided the plot, had had a successful revival. The general attitude to widows' marriages was to see them as 'but a kind of lawful adultery, like usury permitted by the law, not approved; that to wed a second was no better than to cuckold the first'.[2] And in Webster's source, Painter's translation of Belleforest's story of the Duchess of Malfi, the Duchess is an *exemplum horrendum* to all women contemplating a second marriage:

> You see the miserable discourse of a Princess' love, that was not
> very wise, and of a Gentleman that had forgotten his estate, which
> ought to serve for a looking glass to them which be over hardy in
> making enterprises, and do not measure their ability with the
> greatness of their attempts . . . foreseeing their ruin to be example
> for all posterity. . . .[3]

Webster's Duchess, newly widowed, marries again, and marries a man in degree far below her – in fact one of her servants. Those are the facts on which the plot of the play hinges; they comprise her double 'crime'. But they also explain the point of the mental torture which, in the coming of the madmen, Ferdinand has devised for his sister.[4] For the madmen's interlude – such as we know it from

1 *The Complete Works of John Webster*, ed. F. L. Lucas (Chatto & Windus, 1927), vol. 4, pp. 38–9.
2 *The Widow's Tears*, II iv 28–31 (in Chapman's *Comedies*, ed. T. M. Parrott, London, 1911).
3 William Painter, *The Palace of Pleasure*, ed. J. Jacobs (London, 1890), vol. 3, p. 43.
4 One meaning of the device is, of course, to drive the Duchess mad, the irony of the scene being that it has exactly the opposite effect: it leads to terrifying

Webster's stage directions, and such as we divine it from the sung and spoken words – is strikingly similar to a kind of *ludus*, one of the predecessors of the masque proper, namely the *charivari*.

Du Cange defines *charivarium* thus: 'Ludus turpis tinnitibus & clamoribus variis, quibus illudunt iis, qui ad secundas convolant nuptias', and O.E.D. refers to Bale's *Dictionnaire*: 'A Charivari, or Mock Music, given to a Woman that was married again immediately after the death of her husband.' The *charivari* as such was a French *ludus*, or marriage-baiting custom, dating from the latter part of the Middle Ages,[1] 'originally common after all weddings, then directed at unpopular or unequal matches as a form of public censure'.[2] But the practice which the word stands for was not limited to France. English folk-customs and folk-drama knew the equivalent of the French *charivari*[3] – indeed a descendant of it was still known when Hardy put his skimmington-ride into *The Mayor of Casterbridge*. In the early seventeenth century a widow in an English village, marrying one of her late husband's servants, might well be visited by a band of ruffians, showing their disapproval through clamour and antic dances. Often we can trace the antimasque of a courtly masque back to village *ludi*. Clearly the connexion between the grotesque dances of anti-masques and various popular celebrations was, as Miss Welsford says,

clearness of vision and composure of mind in the Duchess. See Ferdinand's motivation in IV i 126: 'And 'cause she'll needs be mad I am resolv'd . . .'. But this still does not explain why the scene was given just the form it has.

1 The most famous *charivari* of all is the one at the French court on 29 January 1393. A wedding was taking place between 'un jeune chevalier de Vermandois' and 'une des damoiselles de la reine', who was a widow. Disguised as 'hommes sauvages', King Charles VI and five of his lords suddenly entered the ball of the festivities, making queer gestures, uttering wolfish cries, and per-forming an antic dance. (Cf. Welsford, *Court Masque*, p. 44.) In the end the masquers caught fire; and though the King himself survived, he never quite recovered from the shock. See Froissart's account in *Collections des Chroniques Nationales Françaises* . . ., ed. J. A. Buchon (Paris, 1825), vol. 13, pp. 140–49, particularly Buchon's note, p. 142: 'Le moine anonyme de St. Denis dit que "C'était une coutume pratiquée en divers lieux de la France, de faire impuné-ment mille folies *au mariage des femmes veuves* et d'emprunter avec des habits extravagants la liberté de dire des vilenies au mari et à l'épousée".' [My italics – I.S.E.]

2 Funk and Wagnall, *Standard Dictionary of Folklore, Mythology and Legend* (New York, 1949), vol. I, p. 212.

3 See E. K. Chambers, *The Medieval Stage* (Oxford, 1903), vol. I, p. 393.

'still felt, if not understood, in the seventeenth century' (*Court Masque*, p. 29). And so I do not think it too far-fetched to assume that the spectators at the Globe and the Blackfriars would have seen in the 'clamoribus variis' of Webster's madmen a kind of *charivari* put on to 'mock' the Duchess for her remarriage. They would then have seen a meaning in Ferdinand's (and Webster's) device which totally escapes us when we see it as just one Bedlam episode among many. For, if seen as related to the *charivari* tradition, the madmen's masque becomes a contrivance of cruel irony on the part of Ferdinand: in a sense, the Duchess is here being given her belated wedding entertainment. The Duchess is of 'royal blood', and the wedding of such an elevated person would have had to be celebrated with some show allegorically bearing on the occasion. The year 1613, because of the spectacular celebrations of the Princess Elizabeth's wedding, was, above all years in the period, a year of marriage festivities. So the audience would be particularly prepared to respond to the masque-features of this Webster scene. And in that response would be the realization of the dissimilarities of this masque from such masques as did honour to the Princess and her Count Palatine, or the one Prospero put on for Miranda. The Duchess's masque, as far as we have followed it, is all antimasque, all a grotesque mockery; but that is not in itself the point. It is the cruel twist of this mockery, as the madmen's interlude turns out to be merely the antimasque prelude to a kind of main masque, which strikes home.

Traditionally, after the masquers had danced 'their own measure', they would be ready to 'take out' members of the audience to dance. It is this feature – the involving of the spectators in the proceedings – which more than anything else distinguishes the masque as an art form from the drama. And now the Duchess is indeed 'taken out'. For directly upon the madmen's 'own measure', Bosola, masqued '*like an old man*', enters, and his 'invitation', or summons, to the Duchess is as conclusive as could be: 'I am come to make thy tomb.' The Duchess has for a while been as much a passive spectator as anyone in the audience. Now, with a sudden change, she takes part in what is happening. Bosola's disguise is like that of the traditional masque image of Time;[1] and his appearance, while again focusing our atten-

---

1 Cf. for example Time in Jonson's masque *Time Vindicated*; or Queen Elizabeth's coronation, when in a pageant 'issued one personage, whose name

tion on the Duchess, turns the mock wedding-masque into what reminds us of a Dance of Death. The text of this 'dance' is Bosola's words:

Thou art a box of worm-seed, at best, but a salvatory of green mummy: – what's this flesh? a little crudded milk, fantastical puff-paste; our bodies are weaker than those paper prisons boys use to keep flies in; more contemptible, since ours is to preserve earthworms.

(124–8)

From the point of view merely of plot this is a rather extravagant way of saying: 'Like all men, you are a worthless creature', or something of the kind. But we see now that this speech is as much fed with meaning by the masque structure around it as is Tourneur's skull-speech by the presence of the *memento mori*. Webster's practical joke is not as spectacular as Tourneur's, and there is none of the grotesque fun of the 'bony lady' in it; but it has some of the effect of Mutability entering into an Epithalamium, or of the skeleton Death joining the masque-dancers at the Jedburgh Abbey marriage feast.[1] In the lines just quoted there is all the medieval sense of the perishable nature of all things, and this sense deepens as Bosola's focus widens:

Didst thou ever see a lark in a cage? such is the soul in the body: this world is like her little turf of grass, and the heaven o'er our heads, like her looking-glass, only gives us a miserable knowledge of the small compass of our prison.

(128–33)

There is a pointed consistency in the movement of thought, through associatively linked images,[2] from the nothingness of the Duchess's

was Time, apparalled as an old man, with a scythe in his hand . . .' J. Nichols, *The Progresses of Queen Elizabeth* (London, 1823), vol. 1, p. 50.

1 Alexander III of Scotland in 1285 married Joleta, daughter of the Count de Dreux. At their marriage-feast in Jedburgh Abbey, 'while a band of maskers danced before the king and queen, Death in the form of a skeleton appeared in their midst and struck terror into spectators and performers alike' P. Hume Brown, *History of Scotland* (Cambridge, 1902), vol. 1, pp. 128–9. Cf. R. Withington, *English Pageantry* (Cambridge, Mass., 1918–20), vol. 1, p. 103.

2 The box containing worm-seed (the pun on the two senses of 'anthelmintic medicine' and 'seed-producing maggots' should be noticed, for in the sense of

body to the despicableness of all flesh, to the plight of the soul in the body and of man in the universe – the correspondence between microcosm and macrocosm enabling Webster to move from one to the other in the last image. All that remains is to be absolute for death.

But the end of the masque is not yet reached. In the course of Bosola's and the Duchess's dialogue, horrible life is given to the masque convention of presenting gifts:

Here is a present from your princely brothers,
And may it arrive welcome, for it brings
Last benefit, last sorrow.
(166–8)

The gifts are '*a coffin, cords, and a bell*', presented by the Executioner. One is reminded of a passage in *The White Devil* where Brachiano, who is about to be strangled – also for a love-crime – is told, 'This is a true-love knot | Sent from the Duke of Florence' (v iii 174–5). The parallelism is such that it is tempting to see in the earlier image the seed of an idea worked out more fully in *The Duchess of Malfi*.[1]

By this time we are ready for a change of guise in Bosola. He becomes 'the common bellman' (who used to ring his bell for the condemned in Newgate on the night before their execution), and accompanied by the bell he sings his dirge: '*Hark, now every thing is still.*' The situation has turned like that threatened by the King in *Philaster*, v iii:

I'll provide
A masque shall make your Hymen turn his saffron
Into a sullen coat, and sing sad requiems
To your departing souls.

The dirge would answer to the concluding song of the masque; and it

'medicine' the image is parallel to the subsequent 'salvatory of green mummy') becomes the paper prison with flies in it, the flimsiness of which was prepared for by the intervening 'puff-paste'. The paper prison becomes the birdcage (which image has an extra layer of meaning because of its connexion with the actual dramatic situation of the imprisoned Duchess). Each image derives from, but adds to and develops, a preceding image.

1 Cf. also the notion of masque in the last scene of *The White Devil*: Lodovico and Gasparo, 'disguised', entering to murder Flamineo and Vittoria, introduce themselves ironically: 'We have brought you a masque' (v vi 169).

is here part and conclusion of the Duchess's masque. In fact, through the death-imagery of Bosola's song, we hear epithalamic echoes. The invocation,

The screech-owl, and the whistler shrill,
Call upon our dame, aloud,

(IV ii 179-80)

refers, of course, to the harbinger of death so often mentioned in Elizabethan-Jacobean drama and poetry. But is also stands out as the very reverse of the traditional epithalamic theme of averting evil in the shape of birds[1] – as in Spenser's *Epithalamion*, 345-6:

Let not the shriech Oule, nor the Storke be heard:
Nor the night Rauen that still deadly yels,

or the last stanza of the marriage-song in *The Two Noble Kinsmen*, I i:

The crow, the slanderous cuckoo, nor
The boding raven, nor chough hoar,
Nor chattering pie,
May on our bridehouse perch or sing,
Or with them any discord bring,
But from it fly.

Further, the Duchess is bidden to prepare herself:

Strew your hair with powders sweet,
Don clean linen, bathe your feet.

(IV ii 190-91)

Preparation for death, this is; and the strewing of her hair could be taken as a penitential act, or simply as referring to the new fashion[2] – a cruel echo of her happy chatting in the bedchamber scene, just before disaster descends:

Doth not the colour of my hair 'gin to change?
When I wax gray, I shall have all the Court
Powder their hair with arras, to be like me.

(III ii 58-60)

1 See J. A. S. McPeek, *Catullus in Strange and Distant Britain* (Harvard, 1939), ch. vii.
2 Powdering the hair was just coming into fashion in England at this time (F. L. Lucas in *Works*, vol. I, p. 255).

But one may also hear an echo of Ben Jonson's *Hymenaei* where the 'personated Bride' has her hair 'flowing and loose, *sprinkled with grey*' (my italics)[1] – an idea which was to be taken up by Donne in the fourth stanza of his *Epithalamion* on the Earl of Somerset's wedding on 26 December 1613, to be made the basis of a witty conceit:

Pouder thy Radiant haire,
Which if without such ashes thou would'st weare,
Thou which to all which come to looke upon,
Art meant for Phoebus, would'st be Phaeton.

So the Duchess's preparations for the 'laying out' of her dead body have cruel reminiscences of those connected with the dressing of the bride. And, finally, the end and climax of the dirge,

'Tis now full tide, 'tween night and day:
End your groan, and come away,
(IV ii 194–5)

strongly suggests the traditional exhortation at the end of the epithalamium, referring to the impatiently awaited night of the bridal bed: Catullus's lines 'sed abit dies : | perge, ne remorare' (*Carmen*, lxi 195–6) and their echo through practically every Elizabethan-Jacobean epithalamium, as – to give only one example – the final lines in Campion's *The Lord's Masque*:

No longer wrong the night
Of her Hymenean right,
A thousand Cupids call away,
Fearing the approaching day;
The cocks already crow:
Dance then and go!

And so the Duchess goes, not to an ardent bridegroom, but to 'violent death'.[2] It is the culminating irony of the scene.

1 That Jonson had most likely misinterpreted his source-books and made a mistake when he described the Roman bride as having her hair strewn with grey does not alter the argument (see my note on *Hymenaei*, N. & Q., vol. cci (1956), 510–11).
2 It need hardly be said that the parallel death-bed/bridal-bed is often drawn on in the drama of these years. The most spectacular instance is perhaps in *The*

There is clearly a close kinship between IV ii and the wooing-scene
in Act I. While the death-scene is interwoven with marriage-allusions,
Death is very much there in the scene where the marriage *per verba de
presenti* takes place. We hear, for instance, of the Duchess's will (playing, of course, on the two senses of 'testament' and 'carnal desire'),
of winding-sheets, and of a kiss which is a *Quietus est*; of the 'figure
cut in alabaster | Kneels at my husband's tomb', and of a heart which
is 'so dead a piece of flesh'. There is, however, one crucial difference
between the two scenes. In the wooing-scene, the counterpointing of
marriage and death is entirely verbal: it is through 'uncomical puns'
and apparently irrelevant images that sinister associations are fused with
the dramatic situation. In IV ii, on the other hand, Webster has used
the very building of the scene to express something of that typically
Jacobean paradox which is contained in the two senses of the word
'die'. The masque elements in the Duchess's death-scene, then, are
truly functional. Unlike, say, the masque in *The Maid's Tragedy*,
which is a self-contained piece of theatre (it is justified in the play as a
whole by acting as an ironic foil to the actual wedding-night which
follows), the masque in *The Duchess of Malfi* gathers into itself all the
essential conflicts of the play. And it does so on all levels: from the

Maid's Tragedy, II i, where the deserted Aspatia helps to put Evadne to bed, the
two women being played off against each other as 'bed' against 'bier'. It was
such exquisite horror that was inherited from the Jacobeans by Beddoes – see,
for example, *Death's Jest Book*, IV iii 230–57 (ed. H. W. Donner, London,
1950), where Athulf sings a song intended to be simultaneously his own dirge
and his beloved's epithalamium:

> A cypress-bough, and a rose-wreath sweet,
> A wedding-robe, and a winding-sheet,
> A bridal-bed and a bier.
>
> . . . . .
>
> Death and Hymen both are here.

But one might note that the parallel, or contrast, could also be used in the most
matter-of-fact manner:

> Lift up thy modest head,
> Great and fair bride; and as a well-taught soul
> Calls not for Death, nor doth control
> Death when he comes, come thou unto this bed.

(Sir Henry Goodere, 'Epithalamion of the Princess' Marriage', 1613; in *English
Epithalamies*, ed. R. H. Case, London, 1896.)

pure plot conflict between the Duchess and her brothers, involving questions of revenge and persecution, to the deep thematic clashes of love and death, man and Fate, which much of the poetry of the play is nourished by.

So Act IV Scene ii of *The Duchess of Malfi* gives an insight into Webster's 'impure art'. The scene as a whole neither fits into a realistic scheme of cause and effect or psychological motivation, nor does it consistently embody convention. It balances between those two alternatives. It is a precarious balance, and at other points we see Webster losing it. But in this scene he holds the tension between the two and draws strength from both sides – the kind of strength which tempts one to suggest that Webster's art is most 'impure' at the centres of meaning in his plays; that his peculiar skill, not only as a dramatic poet but as a poetic dramatist, lay in the ability to utilize the very impurity of his art.

But when, finally, we try to see how Webster holds the balance between convention and realism, we seem to find that it is by poetic means: within the scene, the masque is related to the 'realistic' dramatic representation of what happens, in the manner of a poetic analogy. That is, the Duchess's marriage, leading to her murder, is like a marriage-masque turned into a masque of Death. The two chief structural components of the scene are: (1) the plot situation – the Duchess imprisoned and put to death, because she has remarried, and (2) the *charivari*-like antimasque of madmen, developing into a masque of Death. In pursuing the interconnexion between these two, we have come to see that they are best understood as two halves of one metaphor, certainly 'yoked by violence together', but in the end naturally coming together, to give the full meaning of the scene. Conventional masque elements – such as Webster's original audience would have known from other plays – have helped to give Webster a structure on which to build up the most pregnant irony. The irony is there in the basic analogy between the represented human situation and the masque. It is clinched at individual points, when the analogy is most forcible – that is, at each new stage in the masque. And the irony culminates when the two parts of the analogy become interchangeable: the Duchess becomes 'involved' in the masque, and her fate becomes one with the progress of the masque. Also, as in any effective metaphor, the implications reach beyond the immediate situation: in

Bosola's worm-seed speech not only the Duchess but – in the manner of the *Danse Macabre* – all flesh and all things are involved. What Webster wanted to say here he could say in no other way. What he does say we can understand only by grasping the technique of the scene.

(253–67)

R. W. Dent

from the Introduction to *John Webster's Borrowing*   1960

We already know for certain that the extent of Webster's borrowings was extraordinary even for the age in which he wrote. Unfortunately, at present we know very little about many of the most famous scenes and passages. The bulk of Webster still cannot be traced to specific sources, and for much of that bulk we lack even source-implying parallels. Yet anyone examining the extant evidence must admit that a great deal of source material obviously remains undiscovered. It is difficult to guess how much. I hesitate to believe that we will ever find unmistakable sources for Webster's most frequently quoted lines in *The Duchess of Malfi*, lines depending for their effect almost wholly upon context, and stripped to a bareness free of imagery or of any sententious element: 'I am Duchess of Malfi still', or 'Cover her face: mine eyes dazzle: she died young'. But with a few such exceptions, plus some of the occasional realistic topical satire, I suspect almost everything in Webster has a basic source. Every characteristic of style in the untraced portions suggests they were composed by the selfsame method traceable elsewhere in his work. This stylistic similarity of the untraced portions to the traced ones, joined with the degree of indebtedness already ascertained for parts of his work, makes extremely probable a density of borrowings unrivaled in English literature.

The probability of such density is supported by much of this introduction and by most of the commentary. A pair of illustrations may serve for the present. First, let us take *A Monumental Column*. This elegy for Prince Henry was written with a haste for which Webster apologizes; here, supposedly, he did write with a winged goosequill.

Nevertheless, although he shows signs of laboring at excessive speed, he composed the work bit by bit from sources, a line or two at a time, with commonplace book open. Also open, perhaps, was Matthieu's recently translated memorial for the assassinated Henry IV of France, the principal source for Webster's own memorial to a dead Henry. Thanks to Matthieu, we can trace a greater percentage of this work than we can for most of Webster, but the poem is by no means drawn from a single source. Of the first two hundred lines more than half are now traceable to thirty distinct borrowings from twelve different works. Examination will convince anyone that the entire memorial stems directly from such sources. And just as the known sources for the elegy have proved also to be sources for *The White Devil* and *The Duchess of Malfi*, so too the unknown sources probably provided material for the tragedies.

For a second illustration, let us move to the tragedies themselves, and to a part of Vittoria's famous trial scene (III ii 141–51). Here, a short speech of Monticelso's is followed by some of what Lamb misleadingly called Vittoria's 'innocence-resembling boldness'. Below, the source side indicates merely by author and quotation a part of the evidence that Webster is characteristically borrowing, bit by bit.

MONTICELSO: Well, well, such counterfeit jewels
Make true ones oft suspected.
VITTORIA: You are deceived;
For know that all your strict-combined heads
Which strike against this mine of diamonds,
Shall prove but glassen hammers, they shall break, –
These are but feigned shadows of my evils.
Terrify babes, my lord, with painted devils,
I am past such needless palsy – for your names
Of whore and murd'ress they proceed from you,
As if a man should spit against the wind,
The filth returns in's face.

Here we have dramatic conflict built principally from metaphorical sententiae. One fragment is already specifically traceable (that from Matthieu's portion of a French chronicle). A second, though it sounds proverbial, apparently comes from some one of the many accounts of Richard III based on More, perhaps from More's own. The remaining

More: 'many well counterfeited jewels make the true mistrusted.'

Matthieu of conspirators against Henry IV: 'those heads which shall strike against this rock of diamant will prove glass.'

Shakespeare: ''tis the eye of childhood|That fears a painted devil.'

Yver: 'Thou shalt be like him that spitteth against the wind, whose slaver fleeth in his own face.'

two parallels, although by no means commonplace in English, are definitely proverbial. Yet, as the commentary will show, it is becoming increasingly evident that Webster did not employ even the commonest proverbs without the stimulus of some specific work. Hence some immediate source for each of the above proverbs seems probable, and it is equally probable that that source will account for further passages as well (just as More and Matthieu do). Similarly, a few lines later in this same trial scene (lines 171–83), we know that the three elements composing Brachiano's defiance of Monticelso are paralleled, respectively, in accounts of Henry III of France, Stephen Gardiner, and Robert of Normandy. But for none of these elements do we know a plausible immediate source for Webster. There can be no doubt that he had one, however, and little doubt that again it would account for more than the single parallel.

That a good many such sources will be discovered in the future appears inevitable. Others, undoubtedly, are irrecoverably lost, either because the works are no longer extant or because Webster in part drew upon unpublished materials – hearing and recording parts of conversations, sermons, trials. Whether he did so at all, and if so how frequently, we can never adequately know, though we can be virtually certain that he occasionally used a comparable source – unpublished plays. But books, clearly, provided his primary reservoir. The man worked strangely, his creativity receiving some written stimulus at almost every turn. Sometimes he appears strikingly original, occasionally merely commonplace, but almost always – unless our present evidence is very misleading – he worked from sources. Such a fact need not convert Webster into some kind of freak, a creature whose eyes served only to look at the printed page, whose ears listened only to potentially usable materials, and whose other sensory organs operated only vicariously. But in an extraordinary degree he consciously – conscientiously, rather – depended on others for the language, the images, even the ideas out of which he built his plays. . . .

I have no desire to reduce Webster to some kind of mechanical man, dully proceeding by some single and simple method. But analysis of a few representative passages can illustrate some of the pervasive characteristics of his technique. In the first such passage, Julia is busily courting Bosola (and thereby serving once more as a foil to the

Duchess). All the quoted lines are based on parts of Sidney's *Arcadia*, which I identify by a parenthetical letter for easy reference, followed by volume and page in the Feuillerat edition. Lucas includes only (a) and (d) in his commentary.

JULIA: Compare thy form, and my eyes together,
You'll find my love no such great miracle:
Now you'll say,
I am wanton: this nice modesty in ladies
Is but a troublesome familiar,
That haunts them.
BOSOLA: Know you me, I am a blunt soldier.
JULIA: The better –
Sure, there wants fire where there are no lively sparks
Of roughness.
BOSOLA: And I want compliment.
JULIA: Why, ignorance
In courtship cannot make you do amiss,
If you have a heart to do well.
BOSOLA: You are very fair.
JULIA: Nay, if you lay beauty to my charge,
I must plead unguilty.
BOSOLA: Your bright eyes
Carry a quiver of darts in them, sharper
Than sunbeams.

. . . . .

JULIA: I am sudden with you;
We that are great women of pleasure use to cut off
These uncertain wishes, and unquiet longings,
And in an instant join the sweet delight
And the pretty excuse together.
                                   (v ii 167–96)

Admittedly, this is not one of the scenes on which Webster's fame
depends. Nevertheless, it is characteristic in many ways of his procedure:

(1) The striking degree to which the whole passage can be traced to
specific sources (the lines omitted by an ellipsis include at least one
further borrowing). Webster may improve upon his source in vigor,
rhythm, or conceit; but his imagination is initially stimulated by some
specific passage.

(2) The working in units only a line or two in length. The quoted
dialogue gives us a good chance to see Webster stitch them together

(a) II, 186: 'Let her beauty be compared to my years, and such effects will be found no miracles.'

(b) II, 31: 'the cumbersome familiar of womankind, I mean modesty'.

(c) I, 452 f. (of women's pleasure in rape): 'we think there wants fire, where we find no sparkles at least of fury'.

(d) I, 106: 'it seemed ignorance could not make him do amiss, because he had a heart to do well'.

(e) I, 403: Pamela protests against the compliment of 'Beauty, which it pleaseth you to lay to my (as I think) unguilty charge.'

(f) I, 107: of one suffering from 'the dart of Love', 'stricken by her, before she was able to know what quiver of arrows her eyes carried'.

(g) I, 452 (of women's pleasure in rape): 'For what can be more agreeable, than upon force to lay the fault of desire, and in one instant to join a dear delight with a just excuse?'

with more visible thread than he often employs. Julia's first speech is preceded by Bosola's saying 'this is wondrous strange'; from then on he provides the requisite transitions: 'I am a blunt soldier', 'And I want compliment', and 'You are very fair'. The result is fairly effective and plausible dialogue, although of course too compressed and too conceited to be 'realistic'. Webster's peculiar density and abruptness, his continuity by loose association rather than gradual and explicit transitions, are in part the consequence of the fragmentary elements with which he worked, however consciously he may have cultivated the resulting dramatic effect. Element after element might be cut without loss of meaning, continuity, or completeness. And although each part is (in the above passage) appropriate, one can see that Webster's sources are in some measure determining the dialogue.

(3) The presence of an element meaningful in the source but not in Webster. As just noted, the borrowings here are adapted fairly successfully to their new context. But heaven knows what Julia, in the final line, can mean by 'excuse'. Her speech *sounds* meaningful – sufficiently so that no audience would be distracted, and that critics could debate over possible interpretations – but is it?

(4) The considerable variation, from close verbal borrowing to imitation made probable only by the context in Webster and Sidney. In (a), of course, to fit the new context of a woman addressing a man, 'beauty' is changed to 'form' and 'age' to 'eyes'. Some such changes were essential. More significant is the shift in (a) from passive to active verbs, with the resulting greater directness, typical of Webster. This is akin to his preference for concrete rather than abstract nouns, and for concrete detail generally.[1]

Often, Webster's minor changes seem inconsequential, or nearly so. Two such changes appear in the adaptation of (g): the substitution of the monosyllable 'sweet' for 'dear' (slightly increasing the sensual element, while replacing Sidney's faint alliteration with consonance),

1 This latter characteristic is always cited, and generally exaggerated, by those who praise Webster for 'almost always' improving on his sources. He recognized the potential effectiveness of concreteness as well as any English instructor today, or as any satirical pamphleteer of his own day. Usually, the consequent alteration is an undeniable improvement; occasionally, however, it is either unnecessarily offensive or excessively developed. For examples of improvement, see on *The Duchess of Malfi*, I i 38–9, 242–3; II i 101–7; far more dubious are *The Duchess of Malfi*, II i 78–9, III iii 41–7.

and of the bisyllabic 'pretty' for 'just' (slightly altering the sense, while obscuring the metre by a typically Websterian abundance of unstressed syllables).[1] In this latter change, it may well be that Webster felt he had removed the inappropriateness of 'excuse' by changing its modifier.

(5) The dominant attraction to imagery, especially when combined with argumentative and sentential elements. Sometimes he retains little but the kernel of a witty image, as in (b), (e) and (f), or of a witty argument, as in (a); sometimes he keeps much of its original phrasing as well, as in (c) and (g); sometimes he repeats almost verbatim a pleasing formulation of what he surely knew was a commonplace or proverbial idea, as in (d). Generally, I suspect, he thought the resulting poetry, especially in its imagery, would sound impressively 'original' to his theater audience, his sources notwithstanding.

(6) The sententiousness. In the present passage the prevalence of metaphor, typically undeveloped, is obvious. Less obvious, perhaps, because the passage quite successfully conveys the impression of being dramatic dialogue, is the heavy sentential element, again typically undeveloped. Passage (d) has its proverbial origin concealed in both Sidney and Webster. Often, however, even when most successfully dramatic, Webster's inclination is to retain or even increase the sententiousness of his source. Here he converts (b) to a sententia, while increasing the sententiousness of (c) by dropping Sidney's 'we', and of (g) by introducing a 'we' of his own.[2]

1 It is tempting to seek some relationship between Webster's imitation and his very loose blank verse, which often scans no better than his prose, if it scans as well. Even for an age when dramatic blank verse was growing looser and looser, and when such poets as Donne intentionally violated accent for effect, Webster's verse is much of the time unusually jagged. Like Donne, he can write as regular a line as anyone when he chooses to do so. The problem is to account for the unpredictability of his so choosing – as in Julia's final four lines above, with two lines very irregular, one somewhat so, and one a perfect iambic pentameter (such as frequently appears, of course, in the midst of his prose). I have not been able to discover any convincing causal relationship between Webster's borrowing and his prosody.

2 It is interesting to see the company Webster keeps in a seventeenth-century collection of apophthegms from the drama. In 'John Cotgrave's "English Treasury of Wit and Language",' *S.P.*, vol. 40 (April 1943), 195 ff., G. E. Bentley provides a recapitulation of the 1,518 passages (from a total 1,686) he

(7) The concentration of borrowings from a single work, but from widely separated passages in that work. Such concentration occurs only occasionally, and rarely in this degree, but it is common in Webster's use of all his principal sources – Sidney, Montaigne, Guazzo, Alexander, Matthieu – and even in a few minor sources. It is especially common in the play where Webster first uses a source. Thus *The White Devil* concentrates its borrowings from Guazzo and Alexander, whereas the later tragedy does not. When considered in conjunction with (8) below, this is most plausibly explained if we imagine Webster sometimes working at first directly from his source, but more often employing a commonplace book, in one part of which quotations were arranged by author rather than topic.

(8) The appearance of borrowings re-used in Webster's later compositions. Passages (a) and (d), like several others from various sources, are copied more literally in their second appearance, again suggesting

---

has traced. The following dramatists provided Cotgrave with more than a hundred passages or more than twenty from a single play.

Author	Total Passages	Number of plays	Highest for 1 play	Title of Play
Beaumont & Fletcher	112	40	10	Queen of Corinth
Chapman	111	10	27	Byron
			27	Bussy D'Ambois
Daniel	49	3	24	Philotas
Dekker	63	10	26	Honest Whore
Greville	110	2	63	Alaham
			47	Mustapha
Jonson	111	11	33	Catiline
			28	Sejanus
Shakespeare	154	27	18	Hamlet
Tourneur[?]	30	2	25	Revenger's Tragedy
Webster	104	4	23	Devil's Law-Case
			36	White Devil
			40	Duchess of Malfi

Webster's tragedies contributed more than any but Greville's; his 'comedy' is rivaled only by Dekker's much longer work. Cotgrave was obviously interested in wit rather than in what Chapman called 'elegant and sententious excitation to virtue'. In Flamineo, Bosola, Julia, and the like, he found abundant inelegant but sententious excitation to vice. Many of the passages from Webster are of course traceable to sources.

the use of a commonplace book, at least at the time of their second use. Probably every repetition in Webster, including those not yet traced, stems from this notebook method.

A second passage will illustrate further characteristics of Webster's imitative procedure. Unlike the passage just examined, parts of it cannot yet be traced. Sources, or indications of sources, are identified by author only. The scene is that in which Antonio and the Duchess are separated:

DUCHESS: I had a very strange dream tonight.
ANTONIO: What was't?
DUCHESS: Methought I wore my coronet of state,
And on a sudden all the diamonds
Were chang'd to pearls,
ANTONIO: My interpretation
Is, you'll weep shortly, for to me, the pearls
Do signify your tears: –
DUCHESS: The birds that live i' th' field
On the wild benefit of nature, live
Happier than we; for they may choose their mates,
And carol their sweet pleasures to the spring: –
    [*Enter* BOSOLA *with a letter*]
BOSOLA: You are happily o'erta'en.
DUCHESS: From my brother?
BOSOLA: Yes, from the Lord Ferdinand, your brother,
All love and safety –
DUCHESS: Thou dost blanch mischief,
Wouldst make it white: – see, see, like to calm weather
At sea, before a tempest, false hearts speak fair
To those they intend most mischief,
    [*Reads*] *Send Antonio to me; I want his head in a business:* –
A politic equivocation!
He doth not want your counsel, but your head;
That is, he cannot sleep till you be dead.
And here's another pitfall, that's strew'd o'er
With roses; mark it, 'tis a cunning one:
    [*Reads*] *I stand engaged for your husband, for several debts at Naples: let
not that trouble him, I had rather have his heart than his money.*
And I believe so too.
BOSOLA: What do you believe?
DUCHESS: That he so much distrusts my husband's love,
He will by no means believe his heart is with him
Until he see it:
                        (III v 12–40)

Many of the imitative characteristics already noted recur in this passage. The most noteworthy new aspect in Webster's use of historical

(a) Matthieu: 'Some few days before this fatal accident she [Henry IV's queen] had two dreams, the which were true predictions, whenas the Jewelers and Lapidaries prepared her crown [for her coronation] she dreamt that the great diamonds and all the goodly stones which she had given them to enrich it were turned into pearls, the which the interpreters of dreams take for tears.'

(b) Sidney: 'to have for food the wild benefits of nature.'

(c) Hall: *Fame is partial, and is wont to blanch mischiefs.*

(d) Cf. Tilley, C 24: 'After a calm comes a storm.'

(e) Bodin: 'Others distinguish upon the word, as king *Lewis* the 11, who making a show that he had need of the good counsel and advice of *Lewis* of Luxembourg Constable of France, he said, That he wanted his head.'

(f) Camden, of Richard III: 'when diverse shires of England offered him a benevolence, he refused it, saying, I know not in what sense; *I had rather have your hearts, than your money.*'

(g) Donne: 'we [Jesuits] consider . . . the entrails of *Princes*, in treasons; whose hearts we do not believe to be with us, till we see them.'

or professedly historical, materials, as in (a), (e) and (f). In whole or part, episodes are frequently indebted to such materials, probably far more frequently than the commentary shows, and often for elements modern readers regard as melodramatic. Once again, there is no reason to believe that Webster expected his average spectator to recognize the derivation of most such passages, but he did have the support of 'history' for much that may seem incredibly unreal to some of us today. The warrant of history may be no artistic justification, especially if the artist seizes only on its most bizarre elements, but it can at least qualify our judgements. No one, I suppose, would object to the Duchess's dream; nevertheless, it is somewhat reinforced and illuminated by its parallel from French history of Webster's own day. Ferdinand's letter, on the other hand, may well seem in the tradition of the wax-mustached villain. Yet the first of its equivocations, according to Comines, was used successfully by Louis XI, and the second Camden attributes to the traditionally crafty Richard III. Occasionally, Webster bases an episode on fiction (as in *The Duchess of Malfi*, II ii 36–48), where Nashe suggests a bit of low comedy), but the soberer elements are commonly suggested by history.

Secondly, the passage reflects Webster's infrequent borrowing of a mere phrase while radically changing its context. In such instances, of course, direct indebtedness may sometimes be to another source. Here he appears to have taken 'the wild benefits of nature' (which recurs in *Anything for a Quiet Life*, IV i 81–2) from (b). Similar are such expressions as 'tumultuary opinion' (*The White Devil*, I ii 169, from Matthieu), 'Under the eaves of night' (*The Duchess of Malfi*, I i 318, from Dekker or Adams), 'state of floods' (*The Duchess of Malfi*, III v 128, from Shakespeare?), and, with less contextual alteration, 'more willingly and more gloriously chaste' (*The White Devil*, I ii 90–91, from Montaigne). But most borrowings of this kind, including some of those just cited, are not merely verbal; they involve some degree of metaphor. Thus they resemble the 'blanch mischief' drawn from (c) and merely re-emphasize Webster's attraction to unusual imagery.[1]

(9–19)

---

1 Of this sort are most of the parallels to Hall's *Epistles* and *Characters* in *The Duchess of Malfi*. A source-hunter feels reassured by the notebook borrowing reflected in Webster's much later *Monuments of Honour*, lines 297–303:

J. R. Brown

[*The White Devil* as Tragedy] from the Introduction to his edition of
The White Devil   1960

'Willingly, and not ignorantly', Webster turned his back on classical
example, and set before himself the achievements of poets of his own
age: by the light of Chapman, Jonson, Beaumont and Fletcher,
Shakespeare, Dekker, and Heywood he wished that what he wrote
might be read. And, in making this request in the preface to *The
White Devil*, he praised the classical drama in such repetitive and conventional terms that all his readers must instinctively be glad that he
rid himself of any duty he might have felt to write in that manner.
'Willingly, and not ignorantly' let it be – but it is also necessary to
observe for what he exchanged 'all the critical laws' of the ancients,
their clear form and 'grave' and 'heightened' sentiments. It was not to
one kind of drama that he committed himself; his avowed exemplars
derived their craft from European and classical writings as well as
English, from Christian and pagan religious rites as well as from secular entertainments; and they appealed not only to the audience of the
Globe Theatre of London, but also to exclusive groups of the learned
or the sophisticated, and to the pious, raucous, practical, or adventur-
ous citizen audiences of the Red Bull or the Curtain. They were both
experimental and old-fashioned, and they left no simple or single clue
to those who might wish to follow them. Moreover, the dramatists
whom Webster cited as his patterns make such a varied list that it
looks as if he has simply put down the first names that came into his

---

... his Faith and Charity
Was the true compasse, measur'd
   every part,
And tooke the latitude of his
   Christian heart;
Faith kept the center, Charity
   walkt this round,
Untill a true circumference
   was found;
And may the Impression of
   this figure strike
Each worthy Senator to do the
   like.

Epistles, IV vi: 'Charitie and Faith
make vp one perfect paire of Com-
passes, that can take the true latitude
of a Christian heart: Faith is the one
foote, pitcht in the centre vnmoue-
ably, while Charitie walkes about, in
a perfect circle of beneficence: these
two neuer did, neither can goe
asunder.'

head, as a kind of general recommendation, or 'puff', for his book: if one name did not recommend itself to any particular reader, another probably would. But a careful perusal of his play silences this thought, or, rather, relegates such a motive to the casual and accidental. Mr T. S. Eliot has remarked that one of the characteristics of Webster's generation of playwrights was

their artistic greediness, their desire for every sort of effect together, their unwillingness to accept any limitation and abide by it.[1]

This is especially true of Webster; the heterogeneous list of dramatists in the preface to *The White Devil* is but a beginning of the list that might be made of those in whose footsteps he followed. To understand the nature of his art, it may be best to follow his own advice and read his work 'by their light', to try to appreciate his power of using this native and multifarious inheritance in his own greedy way.

In setting his play in Italy, with dukes, cardinals, and mistresses for its characters, with passionate love, ambition, jealousy, and revenge for its motives, and with Machiavellian intrigues, poisonings, stabbings, and court ceremonial for its action, Webster was following well-known examples: Shakespeare's Iago and Iachimo are Italian villains in this tradition; Marston's *Insatiate Countess* and Middleton's *Women Beware Women* are set within it. Some dramatists used this hot-house setting – a northerner's view of Italy in the fifteen-seventies and eighties – for its own sake, and to exploit its opportunities for eloquence, passion, and suspense. For others, it was a setting in which to cry aloud for 'Justice', the wild justice of revenge, or the more severe and personal justice of a northern, puritan conscience. For Webster, the Italian setting had both appeals: he rose fully to its eloquence, passion, and suspense, and throughout his play – not always loudly, but persistently – there is the cry for justice and revenge. To the last scene, both dramatic appeals are maintained; we are amazed and awed by the spectacle of Vittoria and Flamineo passionately and ambitiously dying, and we are also caught up in the meting out of justice, not only to them, but also, through Giovanni, to their persecutors. Webster seems to have exploited greedily all possibilities, but, on reflection, we must also own that his amalgam is dexterously consistent.

1 *Elizabethan Essays* (1934), p. 18.

There are other modes of tragedy which Webster copied, as, for instance, the 'full and heightened style' of Chapman. His was a tragedy which took its form from a considered (if not very deep) view of court society and politics, and of stoical personal behaviour; basically its characters were examples of virtue and vice, and its climaxes were touched with sententious comment on human life in general. Webster praised Chapman and sometimes imitated him in his dialogue, and an even less 'popular' writer, William Alexander, he constantly used as a mine of sententious utterance for his own characters.[1] He followed both, certainly, in a tendency to generalize: the first 'sentence' is in the second line of *The White Devil*, and its last scene concludes with one. Webster's tragedy is not so obviously organized around a single theme as Chapman's, but its very title suggests that Vittoria is not only an individual but also a type; there is a general name which fits her, and which, it may sometimes seem, she is made to fit.

Webster's tragedy is also akin to various forms of narrative drama. Chronicle-plays are echoed in its episodes of the papal election and the wedding festivities, in its exploitation of supernumeraries such as lawyer, conjurer, courtier, or physician, and in its presentation of a sequence of events rather than a single crisis. And like the best history-plays – like Shakespeare's *Richard II*, *Henry IV*, or *King John* – it presents a series of related and contrasted figures, not a single hero, and is concerned with society as well as with individuals – although here it is an exclusively professional and court society. And, like Shakespeare in *Macbeth* or *Antony and Cleopatra*, Webster combined a chronicle-play technique with interests and devices derived from medieval narrative tragedy, and so presented the rise and fall of Fortune's wheel. Nor is that all, for when Flamineo turns to the audience and says:

> O men
> That lie upon your death-beds, and are haunted
> With howling wives, ne'er trust them, . . .
>
> (v vi 154–6)

Webster may have gone beyond Shakespeare's example and momentarily borrowed from plays like *Arden of Feversham* or Heywood's *A*

1 For Webster's more general debt to Chapman, cf. T. Bogard, *The Tragic Satire of John Webster* (Berkeley, 1955).

Woman Killed with Kindness – domestic tragedies of exemplary narrative which were immediately relevant to the everyday life of their audiences.

By borrowing some structural devices from chronicle-plays, Webster was bound to lose something of the concentration which is often considered a hallmark of tragedy; but apparently this did not concern him, for these devices are repeated in his following tragedy, *The Duchess of Malfi*. Moreover, he went outside tragic example for other features of *The White Devil*. Possibly there is something of the sophisticated sensationalism of Beaumont and Fletcher's tragi-comedies in some rapid changes in the attitudes of Monticelso, Vittoria, and Brachiano, and in Flamineo's feigned death. Certainly there is much of Marston's satiric mode in the comments of Flamineo, Lodovico, and Francisco, who are all, on occasion, satirical observers like the heroes of *The Malcontent*, *The Fawne*, or Sharpham's *The Fleire*.[1] Tourneur had also introduced a satirical observer into his tragedies, linking him, something in the manner of Hamlet, with the more old-fashioned revenger, and Jonson, while avoiding a single satirical mouthpiece, had chosen subjects for his tragedies which enabled satirical comments to accompany disaster. Webster may well have remembered all these examples, for the satire in *The White Devil* partakes of all these forms. Occasionally, when the relationship of Vittoria and Camillo, or even of Vittoria and Bracciano, is the object of the satire and Flamineo stands unengaged, manipulating the situation, it might even seem that Webster was indebted to the citizen comedies of cuckoldry which, earlier in his career, he had helped Dekker to write, and which – as his apparent borrowings from Sharpham's *Cupid's Whirligig* suggest – he was probably still reading with pleasure and interest.

Webster wrote a mongrel drama – one hesitates to call it 'tragedy' after such a recital – and as far as we know he was only able to succeed in it twice. That, perhaps, is more than could be expected, for such cormorant tendencies would normally ensure a muddled failure. But he was a careful, painstaking writer; he worked slowly and his restless mind was constantly leading him to repeat and modify what he had written. His compilations were not likely to be thoughtless; even if they were not perfect wholes, their various parts would be deeply and

1 For Webster's debt to Marston, cf. T. Bogard, op. cit.

minutely considered. And two further points follow: his plays are highly individual, for although he borrowed from others, few borrowed so widely as he; and highly complex, for few borrowed so repeatedly as he.

Faced with such complexity, we should observe the effect of *The White Devil* as a whole and inquire what the critics have deduced about Webster's overall purpose in writing it. Lord David Cecil was convinced that it is a 'study of the working of sin in the world': 'His characters are ranged in moral divisions; there are the good and there are the bad.' In this view, even Webster's 'wickedest characters' are forced to recognize before they die 'the supremacy of that Divine Law, against which they have offended'.[1] But not all critics can discern this simple plan: their admiration is so drawn towards Vittoria and Flamineo that Lord David's 'good' characters can provide no effective contrast or criticism. Mr Ian Jack, for example, has claimed that the play's 'background of moral doctrine' has nothing to do with its action, 'having been superimposed by the poet in a cooler, less creative mood than that in which Flamineo had his birth'. Mr Jack believed that this 'dissociation' was a fundamental flaw in Webster, and that his play has no purpose beyond that of 'making our flesh creep'; in short, Webster was 'a decadent'.[2]

In recent years an attempt has been made to find a moral purpose in the play which could account for the bias that Mr Jack and others have observed. Professor Travis Bogard has judged that Vittoria and Flamineo, and other characters, are 'alive on the stage' because of their struggle to 'keep themselves as they are, essentially'; in his view, Webster was not concerned with 'traditional divisions of good and evil', but with 'integrity of life'; this is 'the sole standard of positive ethical judgement in the tragedies'.[3] Professor Clifford Leech had earlier seen something of the same purpose, but he did not think that Webster accepted the stoical conclusion so consciously, or so simply:

1 *Poets and Story-Tellers* (1949), pp. 27–43 (see above, pp. 150–57). See also H. W. Wells, *Elizabethan and Jacobean Playwrights* (New York, 1939), p. 46, etc.
2 *Scrutiny*, vol. 16 (1949), pp. 38–43 (see above pp. 157–64). More recently Madeline Doran has accused Webster of an 'inveterate habit of emphasis on good theatre at the expense of artistic consistency, or on vivid sympathetic insights at the expense of ethical coherence' (*Endeavors of Art*, Madison, 1954, p. 355).
3 Op. cit., p. 40.

what comes after life may be uncertain, but there is a terrible certainty in the recognition of evil. That is the portion of Vittoria and Flamineo, and their power to stare it in the face gives them something of nobility. And this is worth ambition, though in hell.[1]

Dr Gunnar Boklund has suggested a further modification, for he has not felt sufficiently drawn by Vittoria and Flamineo to give them a central place in the drama; for him, Webster's purpose was to present 'a world without a centre':

a world where mankind is abandoned, without foothold on an earth where the moral law does not apply, without real hope in a heaven that allows this predicament to prevail.[2]

It is small wonder that for critics less intent on defining Webster's purposes, there has always been something 'inexplicable' in his art, or some unresolved contradiction in their praise of it. Mr F. L. Lucas has claimed that 'it sometimes seems as if [Webster] felt courage to be the one vital thing in life', but, being astute and sensitive, he qualified this uneasy statement by adding elsewhere that 'if Vittoria were mean, and Brachiano cowardly, and Flamineo a fool, then we might turn away' from the sight of them.[3] Rupert Brooke, an earlier critic, seems to have anticipated Dr Boklund's description of a 'world without a centre', but he wrote of it with less satisfaction; he saw Webster's characters as 'writhing grubs in an immense night. And that night is without stars or moon'; then he qualified this with 'But it has sometimes a certain quietude in its darkness', and qualified even this with 'but not very much'. Rupert Brooke, like Mr Lucas, saw something he could not fully explain.

Critical opinion cannot speak with certain or united voice about Webster's purposes; it has proved possible to talk of him as an old-fashioned moralist, as a sensationalist, as a social dramatist, as an imagist or dramatic symphonist, as a man fascinated by death, or a man halting between his inherited and his individual values. Where an artist's purposes are thus uncertain, and where he follows no simple or single tradition, we may proceed towards an understanding of his

1 *John Webster* (1951), p. 57.
2 Boklund, pp. 179–80.
3 Lucas, vol. 1, pp. 39 and 95.

art by another track, by trying to define more closely the nature of his individual style; for a dramatist this involves a study of his use of language and his dramatic technique – a study of the kind of dramatic experience he communicates to an audience.

For a start we may say that the plot or structure of *The White Devil* is loose and rambling, a gothic aggregation rather than a steady exposition and development towards a single consummation. It has something of the width and range of a history-play. It could be called a revenge tragedy, yet there is no single revenger: Monticelso is at first ready to 'stake a brother's life' for the sake of revenge, but later he says ''tis damnable'; Francisco is a revenger who works mostly through other men and escapes scot-free at the end; Lodovico is a revenger who satisfies his own pride while working for Francisco, and finally loses his life; and Giovanni stands for justice in revenge, inexperienced but fully resolved. The play may also be called a tragedy of passion, or of great deeds overthrown, but there is no single disaster: Brachiano, Marcello, and Cornelia take their several exits, and only at the last do Vittoria and Flamineo die together. As a satirical drama, as we have already seen, it has three commentators instead of the more usual single one. (Notice that, when we begin to analyse the nature of Webster's dramatic style, his heterogeneous debts to other dramatists begin to make sense; at least they all seem to serve a consistent technical purpose.) Such multiplicity is not found in any of the contemporary accounts of Vittoria which may have been Webster's sources; it was he who introduced the death of Marcello and the madness of Cornelia in the last act, who developed Flamineo's role, brought Francisco to Padua to act as commentator, gave Lodovico a personal motive for revenge, and added to the importance of Giovanni at the close.

It is popularly supposed that *The White Devil* is contrived to present the maximum number of deaths and horrors; but this is true, if at all, of the last act only. In the earlier acts all seems to be contrived to allow the maximum variety of comment. The deaths of Isabella and Camillo are carefully presented in dumb show, so that they forward the narrative without engaging our interest too closely with their victims. Our interest is chiefly claimed, at this stage of the play, by arguments and direct comment: the first scene is an argument, the second and third present a series of them; when action is called for, Flamineo or some other is present to describe it and fill out our understanding. It might be said that Webster indulged an almost literary zeal for description, to a degree dangerous in a drama. The third act is chiefly occupied with a trial scene, worked up from the slightest of hints in his source, and used, as so often in other plays, for the exciting exploration of a single situation – and in this play, the situation remains almost the same at the end of it as it was at the beginning. It is only in the last act of all that action and horrors press upon us; and even there, a commentary is maintained throughout. Whatever action takes place, there is always some one observing and commenting upon it: Francisco watches Brachiano's helmet being sprinkled with poison, and Flamineo joins him to watch Brachiano die; Lodovico watches Zanche make love to Francisco; Francisco and Flamineo observe Cornelia's madness, and the very assassins are chorus to the stabbing of Zanche, Vittoria, and Flamineo; Flamineo describes Vittoria's death and then, uniquely, he alone describes his own.

Our attention has passed from the structure of the play to the handling of individual scenes; this was perhaps inevitable, for they show similar techniques. As a commentator is always provided for the action, so in the course of a scene the speeches are continually turning from the expression of individual feeling to the expression of generalities. The poisoning of Brachiano may be taken as an example: even as he is speaking of his own pain and helplessness, our attention is drawn aside to the disguised Francisco ironically commenting 'Sir be of comfort', and to the despairing Vittoria who cries 'I am lost for ever'; but more than this, Brachiano himself draws our attention away from himself, towards all physicians, to all soft, natural deaths and to howling women, and, as soon as he moves off-stage, Flamineo takes up his theme, speaking of the solitariness of all dying princes. In this play, intimate feeling for a single character is intermittent only: none of its characters draws attention wholly to himself for more than a few consecutive lines;[1] as we tend to identify ourselves with one character, we are forced back, not only to observe the other characters on the stage and their relationships, but also to contemplate the relevance of the action to mankind in general.

It is a restless technique; besides insisting on the general, Webster

[1] It is noteworthy that the only two soliloquies of any length (at the ends of IV i and V iv) are sustained by making the soliloquizer address a vision or ghost of some other person.

seems to have aimed at a continual series of shocks, not only large *coups de théâtre* (though the play has its share of them), but brief, stinging changes of direction. One might instance Cornelia trying to explain away the death of Marcello and so defend the life of her remaining son, Flamineo:

> ... and so I know not how,
> For I was out of my wits, he fell with's head
> Just in my bosom.

There is a pause and she looks round for signs of belief, but a page speaks, 'This is not true madam.' 'I pray thee peace', flashes Cornelia, but at once she perceives that all is in vain, and she concludes in tame explanation:

One arrow's graz'd already; it were vain
T'lose this: for that will ne'er be found again.
(v ii 64–9)

More obviously theatrical are the changes of fortune in the last scene, where Webster, risking the serious reception of the play's last moments, introduced a bizarre, almost laughable, mock-suicide: Vittoria and Zanche think they are doomed, but then they see a chance of eliminating the newly dangerous Flamineo, and then are tricked into believing that they have succeeded, and then, finally, are shocked by Flamineo rising to his feet, having merely feigned death. (Webster was not like a photographer who composes a formal portrait or group, and carefully records it with a long exposure; he has recorded the movement of men rather than their composure, the strain as their wills conflict with their impulses, their reasons with their emotions.) And after so much excitement and movement, Flamineo draws our attention away again, to all men that lie upon their death-beds and to the cunning of all women. *The White Devil* presents its characters in flashlight moments, against a background as wide and general as continual choric comments can establish it.

Webster's use of language is in keeping with such techniques. Two characteristics stand out. First, the dialogue is often knotted and complex: in the more descriptive passages it sharpens towards the epigrammatic; its vocabulary and images are unexpected, various, punning, and sensuously evocative; the pulse of utterance alternately rushes, hesitates, tugs, and reiterates. Secondly, its fine passages – the poetic expressions which remain in the memory and have a winged validity both in and beyond their dramatic context – are for the most part extremely brief, a single image or phrase perhaps, or else are a little more extended, but nervously, almost hesitantly, expressed. There is, in short, little sustained poetic utterance; long speeches are either deliberate description (which is often in prose), or set-pieces like the telling of a dream or tale, or a considered statement in a law-court. The quarrel in Act IV, scene ii may be taken as an example:

VITTORIA: '*Florence*'! This is some treacherous plot, my lord, –
To me, he ne'er was lovely I protest,
So much as in my sleep.
BRACHIANO:　　　　　　　Right: they are plots. –
Your beauty! O, ten thousand curses on't.
How long have I beheld the devil in crystal?
Thou hast led me, like an heathen sacrifice,
With music, and with fatal yokes of flowers
To my eternal ruin. – Woman to man
Is either a god or a wolf.

(84–92)

There is an instantaneous change of thought at each dash marked in this passage; and within each train of thought there are progressions or minor changes of emphasis. The most extensive and powerful image is prepared for by another related to it (though more briefly expressed), and is itself presented, as it were, in two stages: 'With music, *and with* fatal yokes . . .' And immediately this statement has been attained, the pulse drops and Brachiano continues with a generalized aphorism. There follows, shortly, a more lengthy speech for Vittoria, but this is built up by a number of short questions, giving a breathless rather than a massive indictment. When Vittoria, like Bracciano, reaches a dominant image she expresses it in two, or possibly three, stages, and then changes the tone completely:

I had a limb corrupted to an ulcer,
But I have cut it off: and now I'll go
Weeping to heaven on crutches.—For your gifts,
I will return them all; and I . . .

(121–4)

An example of the complex descriptive passages is Flamineo's description of Camillo:

a gilder that hath his brains perish'd with quick-silver is not more
cold in the liver. The great barriers moulted not more feathers
than he hath shed hairs, by the confession of his doctor. An Irish
gamester that will play himself naked, and then wage all downward, at hazard, is not more venturous. So unable to please a
woman that like a Dutch doublet all his back is shrunk into his
breeches.

(I ii 27–34)

There is a connexion between all these details, yet the speaker is never
at pains to make it fully explicit; his utterance is staccato and often
grammatically incomplete or ironically casual; his images are unexpected and from widely differing sources, and his vocabulary is allusive ('all downward') and punning ('wage ... hazard ... venturous').
The effect of such a style is, as its nature, two-fold. First, it must be
followed closely to be fully appreciated; being subtle and complex, it
demands detailed attention – and this, of course, is in accordance with
the multiplicity of the play's structure, for its audience must be ready
to watch and hear many disparate yet related things. Secondly, our
appreciation must be nervous, ready to respond to momentary
stimulus.

A play's structure, scene-handling, and use of language all affect its
characterization. In *The White Devil* this also is impressionistic or
momentarily perceived, being repeatedly under the stress of conflict
or surprise; and there are contrasts and relationships between many
of the characters according to their roles of mistress, lover, Machiavellian, revenger. Vittoria is one of the dominant characters (if not,
as the title proclaims her, *the* dominant one), yet even she is presented
fragmentarily; there are only four scenes of any length in which she
appears and her mood, or tone, is very different in each of them. For
an actress, this presents a great difficulty, for there is no build-up of
presentation; each of Vittoria's scenes starts on a new note, with little
or no preparation in earlier scenes.[1] Flamineo is the most consistent

---

[1] The actor of Francisco has the same problem in becoming, suddenly, a passive figure in Act v, the actor of Monticelso in the abrupt transition to Paul IV,
and the actor of Lodovico on practically every appearance.

and continuously presented character, but his consistency lies in a mercurial nature; Webster made him draw attention to this:

It may appear to some ridiculous
Thus to talk knave and madman; and sometimes
Come in with a dried sentence, stuff'd with sage.
But this allows my varying of shapes, –
Knaves do grow great by being great men's apes.[1]

(IV ii 243–7)

So he varies shapes more quickly than other characters vary moods; the whole is fragmentary, subtle, intricate.

Such was Webster's dramatic style, the instrument he forged out of many elements. It is not the instrument to present, with massive assurance, types of good and evil; if a critic sees that in *The White Devil*, the assurance must come from him and not from the play. Nor is it an instrument for presenting a general society of men, or for varying the presentation of a number of general themes; if a critic sees only such things in the play, he must be insensitive to the immediacy of the dialogue which draws the audience momently towards individual characters. Yet there must have been some motive for creating so individual an instrument: it is good for variety, for shock and surprise; it is good for irony and detailed, critical humour; it is good for moments of poetic utterance and for the subtle, nervous presentation of human thought and feeling. Its disadvantages would seem to be – from the point of view of an easy success – its restlessness, its persistently small scale (in spite of presenting great events), and, finally, the demand it makes on its audience to pay attention minutely and unflaggingly. Since Webster created this dramatic style (and used it only slightly modified in his next play) we may suppose that he did not rate these disadvantages very highly; he may even have considered them to be advantages. Let us examine what is, perhaps, the most dangerous of its shortcomings, the demands it makes on the audience's close attention. If we can see how this could have appeared as an advantage to Webster, we may come close to defining the nature of his artistic purposes, the bias of his dramatic vision.

The very title, *The White Devil*, offers an immediate clue, suggesting that this play presents some person or persons who are not what

1 See also III i 30–31.

they seem, devils transformed into angels of light. In the play, this idea is repeated again and again: there are verbal echoes of it in 'We call the cruel fair' (I ii 213), 'If the devil Did ever take good shape' (III ii 216–17), and 'the devil in crystal' (IV ii 88). And the same idea is expressed in other images, in passages relating to other characters besides Vittoria:

> O the art,
> The modest form of greatness! that do sit
> Like brides at wedding dinners, with their looks turn'd
> From the least wanton jests, their puling stomach
> Sick of the modesty, when their thoughts are loose,
> Even acting of those hot and lustful sports
> Are to ensue about midnight . . .
>
> (IV iii 143–9)

or again:

> O the rare tricks of a Machivillian!
> He doth not come like a gross plodding slave
> And buffet you to death: no, my quaint knave,
> He tickles you to death; makes you die laughing . . .
>
> (V iii 193–6)

or more subtly and more comprehensively:

> I have liv'd
> Riotously ill, like some that live in court;
> And sometimes, when my face was full of smiles
> Have felt the maze of conscience in my breast.
> Oft gay and honour'd robes those tortures try, –
> We think cag'd birds sing, when indeed they cry.
>
> (V iv 118–23)

Those that 'live in court' – that is, all the characters of this play – may be deceitful; as they smile they may be murdering, as they sing they may be weeping. To recognize their deceit a minute and determined scrutiny will be necessary. Webster's choice of images reinforces the same point. He used, for example, an extraordinary number of animal images – on one count, over a hundred[1] – so that, behind the human

1 So Muriel Bradbrook, *Themes and Conventions of Elizabethan Tragedy* (1935), p. 194.

activity, sophisticated and courtly, the audience's attention is constantly drawn to an activity or habit which is animal. He also used many images associated with witchcraft, with illusions ('as men at sea think land and trees and ships go that way they go'), and with poisons ('the cantharides which are scarce seen to stick upon the flesh when they work to the heart'). And of course conjuring, poison, disguises, and dissimulation are not only images, but recurrent episodes in the very action of the play.[1] With so much emphasis on deception in the action, images, and ideas of this play, an audience must watch closely and subtly if it is to see, hear, and understand aright; here lies a justification for the demands Webster's dramatic style makes upon an audience.

As soon as we begin to respond intently, subtleties open up before us: when Brachiano vows to protect Vittoria, we become aware that he is vowing to execute two murders; when Flamineo decries women, we become aware that he is encouraging Brachiano to be his sister's lover.[2] Some deceptions are made abundantly clear by subsequent action – as Francisco's pretence that he will not revenge[3] – but others are hidden or partly hidden so that we hardly know how to respond: when Flamineo explains that he has not asked Brachiano for reward, we cannot be sure that that is not precisely what he has done.[4] Our response becomes subtle and intricate, and also insecure. The comments which are so often made upon the action in the course of the play are no longer straightforward or reliable: all the time we question the true intention of the speaker, asking whether he is ironic or deceitful, or, for some ulterior purpose, bluntly honest; the comments do not simplify the play for us, they involve us in it, and make us question the implications of its action and dialogue. And the more intently we observe individual characters, the less simple they become: which of Flamineo's many 'shapes' is his true one? when Brachiano cries on his death-bed 'Vittoria? Vittoria!', is it in anger,

---

1 This relation between the play's images and action has been demonstrated in detail by H. T. Price (*P.M.L.A.*, vol. 70 (1955), pp. 717–39 – see above pp. 176–202); he has claimed that such technique is uniquely elaborate in Webster.
2 These are two of many examples in an admirable discussion of this aspect of Webster's style by J. Smith (*Scrutiny*, 1939, vol. 8, pp. 265–80; see above, pp. 116–32).
3 Cf. IV i 3ff.
4 Cf. IV ii 222–42.

or in love and faith? Isabella has often been called one of the very few simply 'good' characters in the play; but such a view can scarcely survive a close scrutiny. Arriving in Rome,[1] she goes first to her kinsmen and not to her husband (one might not censure her for this if later she herself did not hotly deny that she had done, or ever would do, such a thing), and her thoughts and hopes are all for herself, none for her husband: the wrongs done to her are pardoned; her arms shall charm and force him to obey her, and prevent him from straying from her. All this is said in a quiet, lofty tone, without any criticism unless it be in Francisco's brisk 'I wish it may. Be gone.' When Isabella comes, as her kinsmen have arranged, face-to-face with Brachiano, neither he nor she can speak peacefully: 'You are in health we see,' he tries tentatively, but she answers with an innuendo, 'And above health To see my lord well.' At one and the same time, Isabella presumes the worst of him and presents herself as selflessly humble. Within half-a-dozen lines, their incompatibility is manifest; while Brachiano is self-defensively angry, Isabella is always praising herself and reminding him of his duties and shortcomings. Because she appears as a defenceless woman speaking in a submissive tone, and because he is openly angry, scornful, and brutal, the natural tendency is to side with Isabella. But on a closer, or more sensitive, view, it is impossible to side with either. There is perhaps a further subtlety: Isabella suggests laying the blame for their divorce on her 'supposed jealousy' and promises to deceive the others into believing this by playing her part with 'a piteous and rent heart', yet when she does put the blame on herself, she does it with such abandoned hatred towards Vittoria and in a manner so calculated to infuriate Brachiano (who must now, of course, say nothing) that we may be tempted to think she is indeed that which she seems, 'a foolish, mad, And jealous woman', perhaps deceiving herself.

The other supposedly 'good' characters are likewise vulnerable. Marcello says that his sister's chastity is dearer to him than her life, but, when Brachiano, by double murder, has made Vittoria his duchess and promised to advance her kindred, he at once leaves Francisco to follow Brachiano; there is indeed a touch of smugness and self-pity in Marcello's avowals of honesty and poverty, and in his question about his brother's misdeed when a child. Cornelia, so power-

1 Cf. II i 1ff.

ful and peremptory in reproof of vice, also takes advantage of Brachiano's fortunes; and in defeat she is deceitful, and in madness concerned, not with honour or virtue,[1] but with the preservation of her son's body; her regard for virtue has not been, we may suspect, for its own sake. This may all seem *too* subtle and uncertain; and one must grant that it would be hard to be conscious of all this during a performance. Yet the play's title, its imagery and incidental comments, its dissimulating action, the complexity of its plot and dialogue, all invite such a consciousness:

Know many glorious women that are fam'd
For masculine virtue, have been vicious . . .

(v vi 244–5)

May not Isabella or Cornelia be of this number?

One aspect of Webster's writing that was noticed earlier is the manner in which disparate ideas are expressed in a single speech, both in prose and verse, without any words bridging the gap between them. The only way to deliver such speeches satisfactorily in the theatre is for the actor to be conscious of the unspoken connexions; if this is not achieved – and a good actor delights to do it with dialogue so nervously and richly alive as Webster's – the speeches will remain a sequence of unrelated utterances and there can be no dramatic development. The essential thing is for the actor to be aware of the unspoken thoughts and feelings underneath, sustaining the utterance, and so to find some expression of them. Members of his audience may have very little conscious understanding of such subtleties – they have no time to ask questions and make explicit judgements – but, nevertheless, as they respond to the actor's *total* performance, they will, consciously or unconsciously, respond to those elements of it. So Webster's very manner of writing makes us aware, perhaps unconsciously, of that which is unspoken – and so why not of the hidden selfishness of Isabella or Cornelia?

Webster's characterization of Vittoria uses a similar 'undertow' of thought and feeling. The dominant impression she gives is of a passionate, courageous woman, and one who suggests that her lover

---

[1] As Ophelia is in her first mad-scene (the comparison is apposite, for Webster was indebted to *Hamlet* here).

should kill his wife and her husband. But her reaction to Cornelia's rebuke and curse in the first act hints at something else, at a regard for conventional morality underneath; having protested that nothing 'but blood' could have 'allayed' Brachiano's suit to her, she cries 'O me accurst' and rushes from the stage alone, and perhaps frightened. Her attitude here is sharply contrasted to both Flamineo's and Brachiano's. In the trial scene, on the defensive, she gives no sign of a hidden conscience, save only that she counterfeits innocence with alarming exactitude, as if she knew what it might be like. In the scene in the house of convertites, she shows that she can, painfully for Brachiano, give herself over to expressions of repentance; again she may be acting a part, but certainly she acts it to the life. Later when she yields and so regains Brachiano, we can only guess at her thoughts and feelings, for she does not speak at all, perhaps guilefully, knowing this will whet his appetite, or perhaps shamefully, wishing to keep something to herself. At her wedding festivities she is silent also, but when she realizes that Brachiano is poisoned she is horror-struck and, between her cries of grief and attempts to comfort him, we hear only 'I am lost for ever' and 'O me, this place is hell'; then she leaves the stage alone, as she had done after her mother's curse. Such hints that Vittoria feels the 'maze of conscience' (and they include silences as well as words) might escape many people's notice – except, certainly, an actress trying faithfully to perform the part – or if noticed they might be considered of little account. But the intent, involved audience must surely take account of other passages in the last scene, which become, at last, not hints, but bare statement. At the beginning of this scene, Vittoria is 'at her prayers', but when Flamineo enters and threatens her life she is successively scornful, accusing, and pleading; it is Zanche who thinks of a way of escape, and then Vittoria is quickly deceitful, cruel, and exulting – so far, all is unlike her former behaviour. When Flamineo rises from his feigned death, she is at first silent and then cries for help. At this point her true assassins enter, masked. Now facing death for the second time, she tries asking for mercy, but she speaks now with more pride; then she tries flattery, and then a proud show of courage and womanliness. As she commands silence and respect, she rises to her part, and, at first trembling, overcomes her fear at the thought of death:

> I am too true a woman:
> Conceit can never kill me: I'll tell thee what, –
> I will not in my death shed one base tear,
> Or if look pale, for want of blood, not fear.
>
> (v vi 223–6)

The stroke itself is felt:

> 'Twas a manly blow –
> The next thou giv'st, murder some sucking infant,
> And then thou wilt be famous.
>
> (232–4)

And then, in the moment of her greatest courage, comes another thought, quite different, but one which has been heard before:

> O my greatest sin lay in my blood.
> Now my blood pays for't.
>
> (240–41)

This implies no breakdown, for it is at this moment that Flamineo is drawn to her:

> Th'art a noble sister –
> I love thee now; if woman do breed man
> She ought to teach him manhood: ...
>
> (241–3)

Vittoria is silent for a time, and when she does speak it is clear that she has been thinking of life beyond death:

> My soul, like to a ship in a black storm,
> Is driven I know not whither.
>
> (248–9)

And then, finally, her 'greatest sin' reminds her of other lives; after another long silence her last words are:

> O happy they that never saw the court,
> Nor ever knew great man but by report.
>
> (261–2)

Taken by itself, this might be an expression of momentary weakness; but at such a moment, it may show courage, being the true expression

of Vittoria's deepest thoughts. We may think, as Webster suggested
at the beginning of this play, that:

> ... affliction
> Expresseth virtue, fully, whether true,
> Or else adulterate.
>
> (I i 49–51)

Certainly Vittoria's acknowledgement of her 'greatest sin', and of
the torment of her soul, expresses thoughts and feelings that have
earlier been heard only momentarily; those brief statements and
longer silences have all been sustained by a great undertow, and its
force she has felt despite her outward committal to a life of passion,
ambition, and cunning.

Isabella, Cornelia, and Marcello, hiding self-concern behind an appearance of goodness, Vittoria with a sense of sin behind her courage
and passion, Brachiano at once weak and steadfast in his love, perhaps
unable to reconcile all he knows within himself ('Where's this good
woman? . . . Away, you have abus'd me'[1]) – why was Webster so
concerned with such characters, and why did he present them in this
manner? Possibly Flamineo is there, at the end, to satisfy such a
question. He too has had his moment of truth:

> I have a strange thing in me, to th'which
> I cannot give a name, without it be
> Compassion . . .
>
> (v iv 113–15)

and soon afterwards he has admitted that 'sometimes', when his face
was 'full of smiles', he has 'felt the maze of conscience' in his breast.
But he has put such thoughts behind him, and in the last scene he
assumes more 'variety of shapes', to feed his own ambition and his
appetite for ceaseless activity. When death comes to him, he tries to
have done with all thought; he reiterates that he thinks of nothing:

> I remember nothing.
> There's nothing of so infinite vexation
> As man's own thoughts.
>
> (v vi 206–7)

1 v iii 17 and 82.

He tries to be concerned only with his immediate existence, for, in his state,

> While we look up to heaven we confound
> Knowledge with knowledge. O I am in a mist.
>   (259–60)

Yet, as he assumes his last 'shape' of defiant villainy, his denial of conscience is a reality for him, and a pain; he knows:

> This busy trade of life appears most vain,
> Since rest breeds rest, where all seek pain by pain.
>   (273–4)

In *The White Devil*, Webster has presented a 'busy trade of life', where judgement seems inescapable, not judgement by death merely, but by pain. He shows human beings who are not what they seem: those 'famed for masculine virtue' are not necessarily at peace in their inner consciousness; those who seem careless of consequence may have felt compassion; and the white devil herself may know what sin is, and, in her ultimate access of courage, know what fear and honesty are too. Man lives in a net: if he sins, directly, or by using the outward show of a virtue he has no desire for, or by failing to face the full truth about himself, some retribution must follow; he cannot deceive without bearing the consequence. Man's judgement is within, perhaps unknown to others, perhaps unrecognized as such by himself.

This is the kind of world which Webster has presented in his tragedy, and for which his unique dramatic style seems to have been created; his use of language, the pulse of his verse and prose, his images, the continual choric comment, ironic, humorous, and straightforward, the sensational happenings and sudden changes in action and sentiment, all seem entirely appropriate to this purpose. The multiplicity and looseness of his dramatic structure give a width of presentation; besides the characters that have already been examined here, Monticelso, who veers so suddenly in his attitude towards revenge, and Francisco, who several times so curiously accepts the role of compassionate observer, seem to be caught in the same net, and motivated, on occasion, by some undertow of hidden, and perhaps unconscious, thought and feeling.

There is, possibly, a further purpose in the multiplicity of the play's structure, for the various characters are not merely in apposition and contrast to each other; their stories are inextricably bound together, one event causing others. So Webster showed, it would seem, that man's actions do not influence only himself, but other men also, and that one ill deed brings others with it. For this reason, perhaps, he made Vittoria think in her last moments of those who have not lived where she has lived: in the intensity of her suffering, she may presume that mankind misuses mankind only at the court, that the rest of the world cannot be so dangerous. And when she is dead we are shown the course of hatred and retribution continuing, first in Lodovico's defiant, yet belittling, stoicism, and then in Giovanni's promise that justice shall pursue all the murderers. As his youthful voice points the moral:

Let guilty men remember their black deeds
Do lean on crutches, made of slender reeds.

(v vi 300–301)

we must surely listen to his words carefully and scrutinize his face; does he really have 'his uncle's villainous look already' as Flamineo has suggested? or is there any hope in his self-reliant, innocent voice that the 'bed of snakes is broke', that will has become purified and that underneath there is now no pride, or greed, passion or selfishness? There is no answer; the play leaves us with a sense of insecurity. The predicament which Webster presented is continual.

In writing such a play Webster took great risks, for he made great demands upon his own craft and imagination, upon the dramatic form, upon his actors and his audience. But as we watch, awed and insecure, we will feel pity in our hearts for those who suffer, for those who by pain seek pain; with its horrors, its deadly laughter and its intricacies, the dramatic experience is humane, and in Vittoria's end ennobling.

(xxxviii–lix)

G. K. Hunter

from 'English Folly and Italian Vice: John Webster', the original
version of the article published in *Jacobean Theatre*, ed. J. R. Brown
and Bernard Harris   1960

This treatment of Italy, as a mode of human experience rather than
as a country, may seem to apply less to Webster than to Marston and
Tourneur; since Webster's two Italian tragedies are probably the
greatest plays in the tradition, the exception would have some importance. F. L. Lucas has remarked: 'Again and again critics have cried
out at characters like Flamineo or Francisco or Ferdinand with the
refrain of Judge Brack – "But people do not do such things." And to
that the only answer is, "They did"; and the only remedy is to read
the history of the time' (vol. 1, p. 92). This may be true, but it has little
relevance to the art-form that Webster was working in, which can only
seem incredibly ramshackle if judged by the standards of any school
of historical realism. It is true that Morality structure is not obvious
in Webster: his characters do not generally have significant names
(though Zanche, Cariola and Doctor Julio seem to be exceptions).[1]
It is only possible to regard the plays in a realistic way, however, if
we disregard the explicit gnomic statements which stud every scene.
This is, of course, regularly done; Ian Jack tells us that the moral
statement 'has nothing to do with the action of the plays',[2] and
Professor Ellis-Fermor has explored this attitude quite fully. If we
approach Webster's plays via Marston's it is possible, however, to see
within his dramatic actions a structure and an attitude which may
reconcile their sententiousness with their liveliness. In Webster, as in
Marston, we have the political conditions of Guicciardini's *History of
Italy*, the mazes of princes and cardinals with their plots and counter-
plots, their dynastic ambitions and their ruthlessness, to provide a
natural milieu for the discontented scholar or 'spitting critic' who
stands at the centre and mediates all the action. Flamineo and Bosola,
like Malevole (and Vindice), are also the centre of the plays' gnomic
activity; they keep before us an idea of virtue which may be help less

1 See *Notes and Queries*, vol. CCII (1957), p. 55.
2 Ian Jack, 'The Case of John Webster', *Scrutiny*, vol. 16 (1949) (see above,
pp. 157–64).

in the world and therefore rejected, but which continues to exercise its appeal:

to scorn that world which life of means deprives.

They, like Malevole, are the individualists who know all the rules for individualists, know the meaninglessness of success, yet carry on, as if hypnotized by their own expertise. They indeed of all characters in the plays are least able to achieve any of their desired ends. As tool-villains they have to obey the rules of those who have hired them, and lack even the satisfaction of a Lodovico in 'limning' the night-piece of *The White Devil* – a satisfaction which seems to survive even when the artist himself is about to be 'dis-limbed'. They end their lives where the plays started them – intelligent, self-aware, disenchanted, poor, envious, and damned.

Webster's Malcontents, like Marston's, hold together in their minds a world which involves obvious logical contradictions and which (in another presentation) might fall apart – a world of greed, cunning, madness, ambition, melancholy, and contempt for the world, priggishness and cynicism – but since the play *is* what they see (and since the dramatist has found a compelling language for their vision of it) the play does not fall apart. Indeed we can see the dramatist altering his Italian narrative so that the pressure of real life will not obscure his obsessive rephrasing of it into Morality terms, so that it will fulfil what the Malcontents tell us:

This busy trade of life appears most vain
Since rest breeds rest, where all seek pain by pain.
(*The White Devil*, v vi 273–4)

The choice allowed here is so narrow as to be inadmissible in any but Morality terms, but it supplies the framework for Webster's Italy, where the only rest is the rest of innocuousness, unimportance, and death (the rest that Spenser's Despair offers Red Cross Knight), and where the only activity that is effective is what leads through 'policy' to wickedness and punishment.

Let us now look at this 'rephrasing', as it works out in the structure of the plays. *The White Devil* begins and ends with the figure of Lodovico. Why? Not because he is a central character, but because he depicts most clearly, as its undifferentiated victim (in both his activity and his passivity), the world of wickedness which envelopes the rest of the play. At the beginning, through Lodovico's violent responses, we are pitched headlong into a world which measures men not by their capacity for good or evil, but by their capacity to escape the consequences of evil, where some are criminals on a small scale – unwillingly enough – and are punished, while others (like Brachiano) are criminals who happen to be in control of rewards and punishments. At the end we see Lodovico (still too small-scale) dragged off to the torture-chamber:

> here's my rest –
> I limb'd this night-piece and it was my best.
>
> (v vi 296–7)

It is a splendidly defiant pose and has (like Vittoria's 'innocence-resembling boldness') been justly admired; certainly Lodovico has ensured that Brachiano, for all his greatness, has shared his own fate. But does the whole play ask us to admire this, or to treat it with ironic reserve? One scene seems to give a conclusive answer. In the middle of the play we see Lodovico first of all persuaded to murder by the Duke of Florence, then dissuaded by Monticelso, then re-persuaded by a trick and a gift. In the praise for the cunning politician which follows, we are shown political man rejoicing in his own dehumanization, in his reduction to the status of a mechanism (a process the imagery is never tired of describing). The morality of Monticelso and the conscience of Lodovico are alike at the mercy of gold and cunning, and we may see that the action has been organized to give this effect.

> O this gloomy world!
> In what a shadow, or deep pit of darkness
> Doth womanish and fearful mankind live!
>
> (*The Duchess of Malfi*, v v 100–102)

With this quotation in mind one can see why Webster organizes his action to place women at the centre; he sees the human lot as one in which any role that can be played against fate is bound to be passive:

> Fate's a spaniel,
> We cannot beat it from us.
>
> (*The White Devil*, v vi 177–8)

By choosing women as his protagonists, the point is half made in advance. But Webster's women are not merely passive victims. Beside their softer capacities and inferior status he notes their characteristic desire (and *need*, in a disorganized society) to air their individual wills, though they may be incapable of fulfilling them. By allowing his women to initiate action Webster is able to expose more poignantly how fate frustrates the individual will. Thus in wooing scenes he tends to give the leading role to the woman rather than the man. It is Julia who woos Bosola, not vice-versa; it is the Duchess who woos Antonio, Zanche who woos Florence. Even where it is the man who is alleged to be making the advances, as in the first scene of *The White Devil*, the real dynamism comes from the woman (in this case from Vittoria's dream of the 'Yew' tree). Webster's desire to pattern his material leads to a loving documentation of the obliquities which a world emptied of moral norms imposes upon the individual seeking to fulfil desires:

As rivers to find out the ocean
Flow with crook bendings beneath forced banks . . .
So who knows policy and her true aspect
Shall find her ways winding and indirect.

(*The White Devil*, I ii 342–54)

By arranging his wooing scenes in the unnatural order, he achieves this effect. Once again we can see him imposing his vision on his material.

Another favourite method of achieving this effect of labyrinthine frustration is to build up scenes to a climax where we expect confrontation or showdown, and then to conclude without resolving any of the personal tensions. The most brilliant example of this occurs in *The Duchess of Malfi* (III ii) where Antonio hides in jest from the Duchess and is then replaced by Ferdinand, with daggers in his words and his hands. Ferdinand never sees Antonio, though he talks to him through the arras, and Antonio only emerges when Ferdinand has disappeared. This scene has been much censured for its physical improbability; but I suggest that it conveys brilliantly the pattern that Webster is aiming at: the sense of human passions yearning for fulfilment, but never able to reach resolution, because never able to come into full-face contact with one another, and speak out directly. Throughout Webster's tragedies we are living in a world where the individual is powerless to publish his insights or to realize in any out-spoken way the integrity of his desires. There is a notable lack here (and throughout Jacobean drama) of that direct persuasion of one character by another which is such a feature of the earlier drama (e.g. Faustus and the old man). Mind is no longer in contact with mind through the common bond of shared presuppositions; characters rather appear to fit their speeches together like fragments of a mosaic, to complete the picture of a world too shattered and self-divided to be communicable in any other medium.

Let us see how this works in a single scene, from *The Duchess of Malfi* (ii ii):

[*Enter* BOSOLA.]

BOSOLA: So, so there's no question but her tetchiness and most vulturous eating of the apricocks are apparent signs of breeding –

[*Enter an* OLD LADY.]

Now?

OLD LADY: I am in haste, sir.

BOSOLA: There was a young waiting-woman had a monstrous desire to see the glass-house.

OLD LADY: Nay, pray let me go –

BOSOLA: And it was only to know what strange instrument it was should swell up a glass to the fashion of a woman's belly.

OLD LADY: I will hear no more of the glass-house – you are still abusing women!

BOSOLA: Who, I? No; only (by the way now and then) mention your frailties. The orange tree bears ripe and green fruit and blossoms all together: and some of you give entertainment for pure love; but more for more precious reward. The lusty spring smells well; but drooping autumn tastes well. If we have the same golden showers that rained in the time of Jupiter the Thunderer, you have the same Danäes still, to hold up their laps to receive them :– didst thou never study the mathematics?

OLD LADY: What's that, sir?

BOSOLA: Why, to know the trick how to make a many lines meet in one centre :– go, go; give your foster-daughters good counsel: tell them that the devil takes delight to hang at a woman's girdle, like a false rusty watch, that she cannot discern how the time passes.

[*Exit* OLD LADY.]

It is fairly easy to follow the drift of this conversation, but we do not follow through things spoken directly by one character to another. It is rather the sum of the obliquities that makes the point. The harping on lust and procreation keeps the Duchess and her child-bearing in our minds; the menace and probing intelligence of Bosola looms through the trivialities that he speaks, though (in his final remark) his conscience looms through as well. A complex web of divided characters, each involved in the others, and none able to cut out and go free, is constructed by conversations like this throughout the play. That Webster must have worked in this way, fitting together brilliant and oblique images, is clear from the nature of his borrowings from other authors.

Again and again Webster shows us men defeated in their attempts at communication, or given the power to communicate only in a form which is ironically useless to them. The echo which answers Antonio tells him the truth, but does not open any passage to escape from the doomed world in which he somnambulates. In like manner the madness of Brachiano and the lycanthropy of Ferdinand give them power to speak out directly, but in a form so removed from ordinary language that no one can use the communication or talk back to them. The Cardinal of Aragon, so sparing in his confidences, arranges so that his real cries for help are taken for a politician's ruse.

Webster organizes action, no less than words, so that the natural progression from intention to conclusion is lost in the mist of mis-interpretation which separates man from man. Nearly all the climatic actions of the plays are handled as rituals or dumb-shows, in such a way that the result is seen as remote from the intentions which pre-ceded it; the bungling expectations of individuals, indeed, come to seem strangely irrelevant to the world of Fate, where lives are desti-nies. The killing of Isabella is managed by a poison so clever as almost to reach the status of magic, and is anyway only observed through a magic mirror. The death of Brachiano is achieved at a wedding-tournament and then in a fake requiem. Antonio and the Duchess are banished from Ancona during the dumb-show of the Cardinal's 'enstallment' as a soldier. The most famous of these ritualizations is, of course, the torturing of the Duchess through masques of madmen, waxworks of death, and other quaint devices. This has often served as a point of departure for attacks on Webster's 'sensationalism'; but Miss Inga-Stina Ekeblad[1] has found terms to describe it which fit it into the prevailing pattern – as a *charivari* or mock wedding masque, suitable for a woman who married again immediately after the death of her husband. The violence and the cruelty of Webster's 'Italy', turn out to be the violence and cruelty of an expiatory ritual; and it would seem to be generally true that here, as in Marston, 'Italy' is little more than convenient shorthand to express a symbolic world where the individual is lost in the mazes of political activity, and where intelligence (the very word is ambiguous) cannot secure communication.

The Calvinist fervour of *The Revenger's Tragedy* and the anti-Puritanism of *The Malcontent* do not appear in Webster, but his combination of princes and cardinals, hunting in pairs, makes the same general point – and no doubt the Duke of Guise and the Cardinal of Lorraine made the point once again in the lost play of *The Guise*. The forces of organized religion in these plays offer no protection for the life of virtue, can supply no effective counter-weight against political evil. Webster's vision imposes on his narrative a deviousness of action and an abrogation of the free-will of his characters; action is too atomized by competing individualisms ever to be foreseen to a conclusion, and the individuals are too isolated from each other ever to make a community of purpose. But this is not to say he creates a world in which ultimate meaning is denied; indeed, the self-defeating quality of evil and the existence of a retributive Justice in Heaven is a point the commentary is never tired of making:

> Other sins only speak; murder shrieks out:
> The element of water moistens the earth,
> But blood flies upwards, and bedews the heavens.
>
> (*The Duchess of Malfi*, IV ii 261–3)

But though Webster affirms the existence and importance of the stars, yet he shows equally that any attempt to steer by them leads inevitably (in the misty conditions prevailing) to the shipwreck of worldly hope:

1 Inga-Stina Ekeblad, 'The "Impure" Art of John Webster', *Review of English Studies* n.s. vol. 9 (1958) (see above, pp. 202–21).

FERDINAND: ...some
Hold opinion, all things are written there. [in the stars]
BOSOLA: Yes, if we could find spectacles to read them.

                    (*The Duchess of Malfi*, III i 60–62)

The intense gnomic activity of the plays is not irrelevant to their
action; for the action is organized on principles that depend on such
gnomic understanding. Webster is obsessively concerned with certain
patterns of action which show man to be lost, isolated, or in a state of
servile subjection; but these patterns are only important if the author
can convey some sense of the values they exclude, the sense of loss in
the world of power, the tension between Virtue and Fortune, or (as
the Humanists would have put it) between *vita contemplativa* and *vita
activa*.[1] Webster carries to its logical extreme the concern with
Marston's 'what men were, and are'[2], assuming that it is only in
action that men are truly themselves, and that contemplation or pure
knowledge is beautiful but ineffective. This was the basic assumption
that the Humanists handed on to these dramatists and to the modern
world. The line of tragic drama from Marston to Webster explores
the assumption in terrifying detail, facing the Italianate or modern
world of success-at-all-costs with scorn and horror. The scorn and
horror remains relevant to us in the modern world of today.

Harold Jenkins

[Revenge in *The White Devil* and *Hamlet*] from 'Revenge in Shakespeare and Webster', *Shakespeare Survey*   1961

Webster does not construct like Shakespeare, and though this need
not mean that he constructs less well, I confess to thinking that he
does, since I have failed to discover in his apparent inconsequentialities
the design that others may see in them. It is as though his sources, with
the murder of Camillo as well as Isabella, and the revenge tradition,
with its ghosts and poisonings and mad scenes, have supplied him

1 See especially the *Dialogue between Pole and Lupset* by Thomas Starkey.
2 *Antonio's Revenge*, The Prologue.

with too much material, which his imagination cannot effectively control. And one reason why it cannot, I think, is that Webster is using the idiom of the revenge play when his imagination is really engaged by something else.

The direction in which his imagination is drawn is already clearly suggested by that dynamic opening which flings Lodovico on to the stage. This man of dreadful menace hurls his threat at Vittoria and Brachiano before *their* crimes take place. Though he is a revenger, he is an unholy one. We cannot suppose that in a play which begins like this revenge will have anything to do with even a wild justice. Francisco, with his sister's ghost, is a more orthodox revenger; but he recruits his assistants from the Cardinal's book of 'notorious offenders', 'agents for any villainy', and when he gloats over revenge achieved he says, 'Tush for justice'. The revengers share guilt with their victims. So it is not merely that Webster has changed the dramatic emphasis by centring his interest in the sufferers of the revenge; he has broken from that type of revenge situation in which Shakespeare could find imaged a contest between good and evil.

Vittoria and Brachiano suffer for their evil; but what drives them into evil is what drives them into love. They live superb in the vitality of their passion. This is their greatness, but it is also their fate. Is it not this which engages Webster's imagination – the progress of passionate life through its fulfilment to its inevitable destruction? In this imaginative rhythm the particular crimes, even those upon which the plot appears to turn, can become almost incidental. What may be as important to notice, though this too the plot structure does not emphasize, is that it is in the celebrations of his marriage that Brachiano receives his agonizing and terrible death. And his ghost bears like an emblem a pot of lily flowers which are rooted in a skull.

It is with the shadow of Lodovico already cast upon him that Brachiano first enters, saying 'Quite lost, Flamineo'. As he and Vittoria come together in delight, there is still the suggestion of their helplessness. Even Vittoria's dream which inspires the murders, since we must surely take it as a dream and not as a fabrication on her part, is something that arises in the mind unsought. Their guilt is born in their enchantment to begin their course towards ruin. The full complexity of this situation is suggested in that scene (1 ii) where Brachiano woos in talk of jewels, while Flamineo supplies accompaniment in gross jests of copulation and Vittoria's mother arises from the background with her curse. None of these things can we forget as we follow Vittoria, still splendid, to her trial, her imprisonment, and her death, till we behold her on the brink of eternity 'like to a ship in a dark storm' driven she knows not whither.

What the play expresses, then, most powerfully, through these central figures, is the doom that hangs upon their lives. In focusing upon the sufferers of the revenge, Webster has enlisted for them our pity and our admiration. But as they are still the perpetrators of crime, we still see Claudius and Gertrude in them. And although Webster has not based his plot upon the opposition of good and evil, he has not been able to free himself entirely from the predilections of such a design. On the contrary, as the opposition between good and evil disappears from the central conflict between murderers and revengers, we find him introducing it elsewhere. That this is done designedly is evident because it is done through episodes which are not offered by the original story. When Webster amalgamated in Flamineo the brother who murdered Vittoria's husband and the brother who died with her, he removed the need for any second brother at all. Yet he still retained Marcello as a good brother to set against the bad. As Flamineo is in the service of the wrongdoer, so is Marcello in the service of the revenger. He attacks Flamineo for his villainy and Flamineo kills him for his pains. Similarly, Brachiano's son is given a boyish virtue to contrast with his sinful father; he mourns his mother's death; he bids Flamineo be penitent; and when at the end he inherits, we see him dispensing justice. But this antithesis of good and evil which Webster has woven into his play, at any rate as I see it, does not complement, it rather criss-crosses that other pattern in which Vittoria and Brachiano appear as the hapless, if splendid, creatures of their human destiny. Some confusion, I think, is evident in the ambivalence with which all the chief characters are presented. The ambivalence of *The White Devil* is quite different from that of *Hamlet*. For when Hamlet appears both as revenger and as object of revenge, he has a dual role and a dual situation; and Vittoria has only a single ambiguous one. It was Lamb who spoke of Vittoria's 'innocence-resembling boldness' at her trial, and though the play never conceals that she is guilty, she is allowed to behave as if she were not. At the beginning of this famous scene she ridicules the prosecuting lawyer for his 'hard and undigestible words' in a passage that one might compare with Hamlet's mockery of Osric just before the fencing-match. But Osric is the villain's messenger and can be the object of our ridicule without upsetting the moral balance of the play. When the Cardinal accuses Vittoria, she wrests the initiative from him, and one of the ambassadors – significantly the English one – remarks that 'the Cardinal's too bitter'. All this has the effect of swinging us to her side, and when she is finally sentenced as a whore, her superb disdain of the judgement has the air of a moral triumph. It is very different from Gertrude's collapse when she is taxed with *her* sins. Earlier Vittoria's paramour has suffered the Cardinal's rebuke, in words that may remind us of the Ghost's about Claudius, for giving himself to a 'lascivious' and 'insatiate bed'; but he daunts his accusers with the authority of his bearing and all Webster's wit in retort. When Claudius sees his crime enacted, he is put into confusion, but Brachiano is never more majestic than when he leaves the trial – and his cloak – in scorn behind him. He retains his majesty even in terror of death – 'On pain of death, let no man name death to me: It is a word infinitely terrible' – whereas Claudius' death is wholly ignominious. Yet Brachiano is taunted and reviled as he goes into perpetual damnation. Vittoria recognizes the scene as 'hell', and at her own death she says, 'My greatest sin lay in my blood. Now my blood pays for't'. When her persecutors have disregarded justice and she is being driven she knows not whither, she sees perhaps too clearly that this is retribution. *The White Devil* does not, I suggest, like *Hamlet*. combine two patterns; it remains uncertain what its pattern is to be,

James L. Calderwood

'*The Duchess of Malfi*: Styles of Ceremony', *Essays in Criticism*, vol. 12   1962

In his review-article, 'Motives in *Malfi*' (*Essays in Criticism*, October 1959), McD. Emslie presents an interesting departure from what has been, until recently, a prevailing fashion in Webster criticism – the careful examination not so much of the plays themselves but of their literary failings. For critics with this sort of aim, Webster has been a fairly easy mark. Admissions are not difficult to make: Webster's plots are replete with the most un-Aristotelian contingencies and blind alleys; his verse, happily suited to the aphorism, is only rarely able to sustain itself well beyond a couple of lines; his action is uncomfortably near to being melodramatic; his characterization is often either vague or else too neatly Theophrastian; and finally – a fault for which some of his critics have been unable to forgive him – his plays were not written by Shakespeare. Underlying much of the specific criticism of Webster is a general distaste for his philosophy, or, more accurately, for his lack of a philosophy, for his failure to supply in his plays a governing moral perspective. For example, W. A. Edwards finds ['John Webster', *Determinations*, ed. F. R. Leavis (London, 1934), p. 176] that 'in Webster's tragedies there is no such internal scale [as that provided in *Hamlet*] to measure depravity.' Ian Jack holds a similar view ['The Case of John Webster', *Scrutiny*, vol. 16 (March 1949), p. 38 (see above, p. 158)]: 'If one reads through [both plays] noting down the *sententiae* and moralizing asides, one finds oneself in possession of a definite attempt at a "philosophy", a moral to the tale.' However, Jack finds that the tale itself is altogether too discrete from the attempted moral. He concludes (p. 164) that the plays exemplify Webster's 'artistic insincerity' and that Webster himself is a 'decadent in the sense that he is incapable of realizing the whole of life in the form in which it revealed itself to the Elizabethans'.

The argument of Edwards and Jack, however it may apply to *The White Devil*, seems wholly untenable with respect to *The Duchess of Malfi*. Certainly no one, I think, denies that the later play has an abundance of depravity and is embarrassingly rich in unintegrated moral comment, or that there are excrescences of plot and inconsistencies of character. But these faults can be granted without our having to concede either that the play is a dramatic failure or that Webster is morally despicable. On the contrary, the view offered here is that the play is, among other things, a powerful and subtle articulation of a thoroughly Elizabethan theme – the relationship between individual impulse and societal norms, specifically the religious and political doctrine of Degree. And I shall suggest that Webster, far from failing to present an 'internal scale to measure depravity', is entirely willing to test evil against good. His principal dramatic means to this end is his employment of ceremony and ritual for the evaluation of private action. My intention here is to examine several crucial scenes in order to suggest how Webster's use of ceremony helps clarify some of the rather vexing problems of action, motivation, and character.

In a play which focuses so largely upon revenge and violence, motivation is unusually important. In the corruption scene of Act I Ferdinand, referring to the Duchess, says to Bosola: 'she's a young widow,|I would not have her marry again.'

BOSOLA: No, sir?
FERDINAND: Do not you ask the reason: but be satisfied,
I say I would not.
                                            (I i 256–8)

Bosola, whether satisfied or not, does not ask the reason; but critics have not been so easily put off. What Ferdinand later calls his 'main cause' – his hope to have gained 'An infinite mass of treasure by her death' (IV ii 285) had she died without remarrying – has been unanimously disallowed by critics for having no dramatic confirmation elsewhere. On the other hand, most critics have acknowledged as at least plausible the case made by F. L. Lucas and supported by Clifford Leech that Ferdinand acts from incestuous jealousy. But Leech himself is not very happy with his proposal, for after all, he finds, 'Ferdinand leaves us perplexed, not quite certain of the dramatist's purpose' [John Webster (London, 1951), p. 105]. However, the perplexity which he complains of is discredited – or at least so I am convinced – by his own findings. A certain haziness of motivation need not result from a corresponding haziness of authorial purpose but may be deliberately built into a character: it is Ferdinand who is unsure of himself, not Webster. From Ferdinand's 'Do not you ask the reason' – certainly an answer that makes us want to ask the reason – we can assume either that he does not understand the grounds of his behaviour or that he prefers not to state them. But a flat refusal to discuss the matter is surely a poor means of concealing information, especially from a man who has been singled out precisely because he is an adept at ferreting facts. Ferdinand's brusqueness here suggests a lack of self-awareness, not so much an irritation at being questioned as a failure ever to have asked himself the same question.

It is in the following exchanges between the Duchess and her brothers that we should expect to find an indication of the motives underlying the demonic punishments of Act IV. There is clearly, even before the offence, a pressure behind Ferdinand's speech that is absent from his brother's. The Cardinal is willing to consider the prospect of remarriage provided it involves 'the addition, Honor'; Ferdinand categorically forbids it: 'Marry! they are most luxurious,| Will wed twice'. It is Ferdinand who harps upon the sensual temptations of remarriage – 'luxurious' (i.e. lecherous), 'those joys,| Those lustful pleasures', his Lamprey metaphor; and he associates sensuality with corruption and disease – 'Their livers are more spotted| Then *Labans* sheep' – an association which he dwells upon again, most significantly, later in the play. Taking a cue from the Cardinal, however, Ferdinand does insert one important non-sensual objection to the Duchess' possible remarriage: he likens private marriage to 'the irregular crab,| Which though 't goes backward, thinks that it goes right,| Because it goes its own way.' This is essentially an argument from Degree: the reliance upon private choice, especially when that choice descends upon an inferior, constitutes an infringement of the rigidly established social hierarchy and is, ultimately, an attack upon cosmological order.

There is by no means sufficient evidence here to persuade us one way or another about the brothers' opposition to a possible remarriage. However, the Duchess provides us a critical perspective to the scene when she suggests that the brotherly duet has been a piece of staged ceremony: 'I think this speech between you both was studied,| It came so roundly off.' The sequence of mutually supported and elaborated arguments has seemed impressive; but the stylization to which the Duchess calls attention enables us to observe a schism between the form and the content of their objections. For in actuality the brothers have offered only the appearance of an argument, not any logical grounds for opposition, but merely opposition. What they have said is simply that they do not want the Duchess to remarry, but their motives have been left unclarified. Ferdinand's emotional antagonism – we cannot at this point give it a more precise title – has been both partly obfuscated and superficially ennobled by the ritual formality of a 'studied' presentation. Since the brothers are wholly unaware that Antonio or anyone else is a potential, much less a favoured, suitor, their argument from Degree is entirely irrelevant, at best hypothetical.

But as we shall see, it is not irrelevant structurally: the hypothetical attack upon order becomes actual after the brothers' exit, when the Duchess reverses the courtly tradition in her wooing of Antonio. By comparing these two brief scenes, as well as others later on, we shall find that Webster, at times so cavalier in his disregard of dramatic consistency, can at other times unify apparently discrete elements of action by remarkably subtle nexuses of imagery and structure.

The Duchess conducts her courtship of Antonio as a staged ceremony which is in effect a casting off of the essential values represented in ceremony. As a depersonalized, formalized expression of belief and emotion, ceremony is necessarily in the service of supra-individual interests, and its participants make at least a gesture of endorsing those interests by voluntarily restricting the free play of private emotion to the symbolic pattern prescribed by the ceremonial role. Although ceremony and ritual are by no means prohibitive of individual expression – but merely impose a form upon the content of private experience – they are confirmations of order, of an order that exists to some extent regardless of the individual, even if the individual is a Duchess. Indeed, as Antonio's first speech in the play implies, it is precisely because the individual here is a Duchess – the political and moral exemplar who, if corrupt, causes 'Death, and diseases through the whole land' – that her conduct has serious and even tragic implications. For what the Duchess is engaging in here is not properly ceremony but ceremony-in-reverse, a form of deceremonialization by which she divests herself of the responsibilities of her social role.

The Duchess's defection from Degree is not simply the product of impetuosity; after her brothers' exit her determination to assert herself is couched in convincing terms: 'if all my royal kindred | Lay in my way unto this marriage: | I'd make them my low foot-steps.' Nor, as her last remark to Cariola indicates, is she unaware of the broader implications of her action:

> ... wish me good speed
> For I am going into a wilderness,
> Where I shall find nor path, nor friendly clew
> To be my guide.
>   (I i 358–61)

This journey beyond the restrictions, but also the safeguards, of

Degree into a 'wilderness' where her only guides are the dictates of private impulse cannot help reminding us of Ferdinand's warning about 'the irregular crab,| Which though 't goes backward, thinks that it goes right,| Because it goes its own way'. But the Duchess's 'own way' is not a random one. The 'wilderness' into which she goes may be thoroughly disordered, but her means of getting there are quite systematic.

She first establishes Degree with almost ritual formality. As Antonio enters, at her bidding, her greeting is an expression of superiority: 'I sent for you – sit down.' This is of course ironic, and charmingly so in the light of her intentions; but it is also the initial step towards a moral infraction the gravity of which charm fails to dissipate. It is also significant, particularly in a scene which makes a symbolic point of bodily positions, that at the beginning the audience is presented with a view of Antonio seated and the Duchess standing above him, prepared to dictate her 'will'. She quickly forces an opportunity to use the word *husband*, and then with considerable psychological subtlety suggests her concern about 'What's laid up for tomorrow', which, coming hard after the word 'expense', seems to regard Antonio in his inferior role as treasurer – and so he interprets it; but then she corrects him by explaining that she meant 'What's laid up yonder for me', that is, in heaven, which gently insinuates Antonio into an equality with her as fellow mortal. Further promptings by the Duchess, the most important of which are of a ceremonial nature – the transfer of the ring (415), the symbolic elevation of rank (429–30) – lead Antonio to realize 'whereto [her] favours tend'; but though he is tempted by ambition, he remains uncomfortably aware of his 'unworthiness', of his prescribed station in the hierarchy of Degree. To the Duchess, for whom Degree is by this time irrelevant, his hesitance is puzzling: 'Sir, be confident,| What is't distracts you?' Despite his later reminder about her brothers, it is not fear of violence that is troubling Antonio: it is made sufficiently clear that he is an excellent soldier, a man of proved courage and ability. It is also made sufficiently clear that he is an honourable man, one who would be honest, as he says, 'were there nor heaven, nor hell'. Indeed, his distraction here could only be felt by an honourable man, for it stems from a conflict between private desire and societal values. Part of the irony of the courtship scene is that the Duchess abandons Degree in wooing the one man who thoroughly endorses Degree: his opening lines in Act I displays his admiration for the French king who sought 'to reduce both State, and People|To a fix'd Order'. It is in the light of Antonio's reluctance to overturn Degree that Webster, by a kind of literary counterpoint, enables us to judge the nature of the Duchess' conduct. For the ceremonial revelation of her feelings to Antonio is necessitated by the inhibitions of Degree. The 'great', she says,

> Are forc'd to express our violent passions
> In riddles, and in dreams, and leave the path
> Of simple virtue, which was never made
> To seem the thing it is not.
>
> (I i 445–8)

It is surely a perversion of terminology when the 'path of simple virtue' – which echoes her earlier image of the pathless 'wilderness' – has become representative of uninhibited passion. Having discarded her own loyalties to 'fix'd order', she has nevertheless been utilizing until now the symbolic forms of order – ceremony and ritual – as psychological weapons designed to overcome Antonio's more entrenched loyalties and to release the passions which those loyalties have so far successfully constrained. Her final resort is to dispense altogether with ceremony and Degree; if he will not rise to her station, she will descend to his: 'I do here put off all vain ceremony,|And only do appear to you a young widow|That claims you for her husband.' It is a telling expedient, and with it Antonio's last resistance breaks. It is characteristic of him that he is unable either to deceive effectively – witness the way he falls apart in II iii, when forced into deceptions – or to cope with deception. But it must be admitted that the Duchess's techniques – first establishing, then suddenly relaxing the formalities of Degree – have been unusually subtle, and, coupled with his own desires, difficult to resist.

Near the conclusion of this movement away from Degree and towards the release of 'violent passions', we have another brief ritual gesture as the Duchess puts her arms around Antonio and then orders him to kneel. It is a fitting end, for the gesture is merely a gesture; far from endorsing ceremony and the values it represents, the Duchess engages in a profane parody, employing the ritual solemnities of Degree to confirm and sanction the autonomy of private impulse, the symbols of order to proclaim the ascendancy of disorder. Of her brothers she says:

> Do not think of them,
> All discord, without this circumference
> Is only to be pitied, and not feared:
> Yet, should they know it, time will easily
> Scatter the tempest.
>
> (I i 468–72)

The imagery here, and in the following passages which use musical metaphors (551–4), is strongly reminiscent of Ulysses' famous speech on Degree in *Troilus and Cressida*: 'Take but degree away, untune that string,| And, hark, what discord follows' (I iii 109–10 ff.).[1] Degree taken away, discord does indeed follow; but for the moment the lovers seek within the circumference of their own arms to create a private universe, to elevate 'violent passion' to the status of a self-sufficient moral law. The attempt may have its romantic appeal, but the Duchess's speech displays a disrespect for external realities which is, as the remainder of the play demonstrates, dangerously naïve. It is left to Cariola to conclude the scene on a note of ominousness: 'Whether the spirit of greatness, or of woman| Reign most in her, I know not, but it shows| A fearful madness. I owe her much of pity'.

If we are correct in assuming that Webster is using ceremony as a dramatic device to explore subtleties of character and action, we should expect it to be used again in other critical scenes. The tragic ironies of the Duchess's speech about 'discord' indicate that Webster was anticipating the dramatic future. The audience is prepared for the next appearance of Ferdinand and the Cardinal, is awaiting with a certain amount of suspense the brothers' reactions to the marriage. In

1 In some respects Webster's entire play is a comment on Shakespeare's passage, even to the point of Ferdinand's becoming, like 'appetite', a 'universal wolf' eating himself up in madness. Incidentally, there is another parallel with Shakespeare that has gone unmentioned: in IV ii Bosola, denied reward for his services to Ferdinand, says, 'I stand like one | That long hath ta'en a sweet, and golden dream. | I am angry with my self, now that I wake' (323–5), which appears to be an echo of Posthumous's speech in *Cymbeline* (v iv 127–9), 'And so I am awake. Poor wretches, that depend | On greatness' favour, dream as I have done, | Wake, and find nothing'.

II v, where those reactions are presented, Webster is clearly conscious of the logical and structural claims imposed upon him by Act I. The 'tempest' which the Duchess felt time would scatter has now arisen in the form of Ferdinand's intemperate anger; the association is made exact as the Cardinal says, 'Why do you make yourself | So wild a tempest?' and Ferdinand wishes the metaphor were literal fact: 'Would I could be one . . .'. Ferdinand also embodies the 'discord' of which the Duchess was so disdainful: he produces 'this intemperate noise', and is admonished by the Cardinal, 'Come, put yourself | In tune.' His anger, we may think, is perhaps a vastly amplified echo of Antonio's 'distraction' – that is, that just as Antonio hesitated to over-turn Degree, so Ferdinand rages because it has been overturned. But this would hardly explain the Cardinal's relative calmness, his utter inability to comprehend his brother's reactions: 'You fly beyond your reason'; 'Are you stark mad?' Only if we accept the unmistakable suggestions of incestuous jealousy in this scene does Ferdinand's behaviour become more understandable for us than for the Cardinal.

The psychological development here is roughly the reverse of that in Act I. Instead of casting off ceremony to reveal underlying passions, Ferdinand moves from passion to the cloaking of passion in cere-monial robes, from disorder to order. His opening line, 'I have this night digg'd up a mandrake', is meaningfully ambiguous, carrying not only the primary notion of madness but a secondary, sexual implication as well. What is merely implication at this point becomes manifest when Ferdinand's sense of injury shifts to the source of injury:

> Methinks I see her laughing –
> Excellent hyena! – talk to me somewhat, quickly,
> Or my imagination will carry me
> To see her, in the shameful act of sin.
>
> (II v 38–41)

To this point, and somewhat beyond it, Ferdinand seems wholly lack-ing in self-awareness; his jealousy receives direct expression in anger, but he is conscious only of anger, and mistakenly assumes that the Cardinal is reacting similarly. But when he tortures himself with images of the Duchess 'in the shameful act' he has clearly gone beyond anything that the Cardinal is feeling. The intensity of his experience

is attested by his failure even to hear the Cardinal's 'You fly beyond
your reason.' Lost to the immediate situation, he directly addresses
his sister from his imaginative station as voyeur (46–8). Dumbfounded
by this display, the Cardinal remonstrates with a metaphor that is
more accurate than he realizes:

> ... this intemperate noise,
> Fitly resembles deaf men's shrill discourse,
> Who talk aloud, thinking all other men
> To have their imperfection.
> (51–4)

Although Ferdinand is unconscious of the nature of his 'imperfection', he has supposed a similar violence of reaction on the part of his
brother. It is only now that he senses a difference between them.
Immediately he withdraws, knowing that he has somehow exposed
himself. His next lines – 'Have not you,│My palsy?' – mark an abrupt
shift of tone: outwardly directed anger recoils, turns inward, gives
way to self-suspicion. The question is wary, the diction ambiguous
enough to suggest shaking anger and perhaps also his half-awareness
of a deeper motivation springing from bodily disturbance. The
Cardinal's reply is significant:

> Yes – I can be angry
> Without this rupture: there is not in nature
> A thing, that makes man so deform'd, so beastly,
> As doth intemperate anger ...
> (55–8)

The thought moves from the personal to the general, from the
admission of private but controlled anger to an explanation of the
necessity of control. Disordered passions, whether specifically sexual
or not, represent a deviation from the nature of, from what is proper
to, man; it is not Ferdinand's impulse to violence that the Cardinal
objects to, it is the unrestrained disorder of that impulse. The parallel
with the Duchess is obvious: both have become threats to society by
departing from communal patterns of ordered behaviour, by representing the chaos of uninhibited private action. But the parallel ends
there. Ferdinand has not deliberately violated Degree in order to
release passion; indeed, his very lack of deliberation, the spontaneity

of his giving way to emotion, has released to the surface a deformity of man's nature. Although both of them enter a 'wilderness', the Duchess seeks to establish private order amid public disorder, to forge a circumference of harmony in the centre of discord. Secure of self, conscious of her own identity, she conceives of 'wilderness' as being purely external. But Ferdinand blunders into a chaos within himself. Nearly losing complete control of himself, he discovers a self he would prefer to lose. Ultimately he does lose himself all ways, in madness; and ultimately the Duchess retains her self, even triumphantly reasserts her identity despite all Ferdinand can do to destroy her.

Webster's problem now is a delicate one. Unless the prolonged torture and demonic killing of the Duchess have some amount of communal sanction, he will have produced, not tragedy, but only melodrama. Having already suggested the potential tragic justification by presenting the Duchess's marriage as a violation of Degree, he now runs the risk of causing Ferdinand to exact disproportionate retribution as a private agent; the nexus between crime and punishment is in danger of breaking. Webster's solution is to cement that nexus by an inversion of the process which led to the crime.

Throughout II v Ferdinand employs the imagery which will lead him from private to at least a semblance of public revenge. From the beginning his mind dwells upon purgation:

> We must not now use balsamum, but fire,
> The smarting cupping-glass, for that's the mean
> To purge infected blood, such blood as hers:
>
> (24–6)

If the sin is of the blood, as Vittoria's was in *The White Devil*, the blood must pay for it. But this medical imagery, which suggests an impulse towards impersonal action – Ferdinand as agent of society, the physician-priest who will restore order by destroying disorder – is unconvincing in light of the private animus manifest in Ferdinand's outbursts. But there is, as we noted, a shift of tone following the Cardinal's remonstrance about 'deaf men's shrill discourse', a shift of tone which mirrors Ferdinand's shift in self-consciousness. After the Cardinal's next speech, which concludes with an exhortation to order – 'Come, put yourself | In tune' – Ferdinand, already sobered by self-doubt, returns a premeditated answer:

> So – I will only study to seem
> The thing I am not.
>   (62–3)

To pause briefly here, we should note the verbal echo from Act I where the Duchess, lamenting the inhibitions imposed by greatness, spoke of 'simple virtue, which was never made|To seem the thing it is not' (447–8), just before she 'put off all vain ceremony'. Here, however, Ferdinand intends just the reverse – to submit passion to order, or at least to the appearance of order. He continues:

> I could kill her now,
> In you, or in my self, for I do think
> It is some sin in us, heaven doth revenge
> By her.
>   (62–5)

This is an entirely new turn of thought, to which the Cardinal can only react with amazement: 'Are you stark mad?' But this is a far cry from madness. If we have been correct in gauging his growth of self-awareness, Ferdinand's acknowledgement of 'some sin in us' which requires expiation employs the plural 'us' merely as a cover: the sin is within him alone, and he knows it. More significant, however, is his identification of his with the Duchess's sin, the linking of his latent desire with her realized desire; for here is precisely the association needed to justify his revenge upon her and to expiate his own latent sin: he can now truly quench his 'wild-fire' with her 'whore's blood'. What would have been merely a private act of violence now assumes the status of ritual purgation, with the Duchess as sacrificial scapegoat and Ferdinand, already her judge, as physician-priest-executioner who seeks the purgation of his own tainted blood in the purging of hers. Before the scene closes, Ferdinand reverts to the language of violence once more, but it is clear that he has found his solution. His final speech reveals an attitude far more terrifying than his earlier bluster, for it portends not merely an uninhibited, formless act of revenge but a patient, controlled, impersonal ceremony which will culminate with the Duchess's execution.

All of this is not of course to suggest that the highly ceremonialized murder of IV ii is justified merely because it is ceremonial, nor that

Ferdinand is genuinely identified with moral order merely because he converts an essentially private vengeance into the appearance of public justice. Ferdinand's role is obviously synthetic, an attempt to dignify incestuous frustrations that urge him to retaliation. Yet by restraining his desire for immediate vengeance, and, more important, by transforming it and his sexual desires as well into elements of a formal process, he makes a gesture of sublimation which, even though synthetic, suggests a confirmation of order. It is a gesture entirely appropriate to the nature of the Duchess's marriage, for if the crime is against society, the punishment must in some sense proceed from society. It is owing to this ritualization of vengeance that we apprehend the inevitability of disaster so important in tragedy, an inevitability which arises only from our consciousness of extra-personal forces working out the fate of the protagonist.[1]

In IV i the ritual begins. The Duchess has been imprisoned for an indeterminate period. Ferdinand consults Bosola about her behaviour, seems satisfied to learn of her nobility. But when Bosola remarks that her blood is not altogether subdued, indeed that her very imprisonment away from Antonio 'Makes her too passionately apprehend| Those pleasures she's kept from', Ferdinand responds with his own brand of passion:

> Curse upon her!
> I will no longer study in the book
> Of another's heart: inform her what I told you.
>
> (15–17)

The nature of his feelings and the difficulty with which he keeps them subjected to the demands of ceremony are always most apparent when some sensual reference to the Duchess's 'whore's blood' reignites his 'wild-fire'. But he always manages to regain control, to depersonalize the issue. When Bosola remonstrates with him (117–21) and unfortunately mentions the Duchess's 'delicate skin', Ferdinand's reply again reveals a momentary breakdown of his role: 'Damn her, that body of hers . . .'. He resolves upon further torments: so long as the

1 For the relationship between private action and communal order, I am indebted to Professor Robert B. Heilman's excellent book on *Othello – Magic in the Web* (Lexington, Kentucky, 1956) – and especially to his chapter, 'Othello: Action and Language', pp. 137–68.

sacrificial victim lives, so long as the Duchess's blood remains unregenerate, the latent sin within himself continues unpurged. More drastic purgatives having been planned, he resumes his role: '*Intemperate agues make physicians cruel*' (142).

In IV ii a new development occurs. The increasing imbalance of Ferdinand's mind is suggested by his changing to a form of homeopathic treatment in which the mad are to heal the mad. He is still attempting to purge himself by proxy, but his employment of madmen symbolizes his own approaching madness. His identification of his own sin with that of the Duchess has led him to impute to her, not just sensuality, but all of his aberrations. The strain of holding in balance the conflicting demands of the synthetic role and private passion, the inevitable self-injury involved in destroying the object of desire, and the impossibility of genuinely purging himself by means of another – all are contributing to Ferdinand's mental disintegration. As the Duchess grows more confirmed in her personal identity (142), he begins to lose all sense of identity in that 'wilderness' within him.

The conclusion of the ritual is the Duchess's sacrificial death. Bosola engages in his own form of depersonalization, assuming the role of bellman both to conceal and to dignify his participation in what he has come to regard as an extravagant cruelty. Ironically enough, the ceremony designed to purify Ferdinand has served to purify Bosola, for by experiencing the Duchess's integrity of self it is he who has metamorphosed from an impersonal agent of Ferdinand's malice to a responsible individual capable of the independent action he performs in the last act of the play.

In the dialogue with Bosola over the Duchess's body, Ferdinand, rapidly nearing madness, achieves what appears to be a form of *anagnorisis*. He acknowledges both the fact and the injustice of the private act of vengeance: 'I bade thee, when I was distracted of my wits,|Go kill my dearest friend, and thou hast done't' (279–80). But the admission of injustice is in the abstract, and, qualified by the emphasis upon Bosola as efficient cause and by the claim of mental distraction, it is in effect merely a denial of personal responsibility. Appeals to justification on the grounds of ritual authority – Ferdinand as physician-priest serving society – are conspicuously absent. For evaluation from that point of view, however, we have only to wait a few lines, until Ferdinand says:

By what authority did'st thou execute
This bloody sentence?
BOSOLA: By yours –
FERDINAND: Mine? was I her judge?
Did any ceremonial form of law,
Doom her to not-being?

(298–301)

The denial of 'any ceremonial form of law', of any communally
sanctioned process by which revenge was executed, is aimed at depriv-
ing Bosola of reward, but instead deprives Ferdinand himself of that
superficial ennoblement of motive which he had sought through an
alliance with the forms of order. It is one of Ferdinand's last rational
utterances, and it is thoroughly appropriate that as he approaches the
disaster of mind which is correlative with the Duchess's death, Webster
chooses to illumine the nature of Ferdinand's revenge by the same
dramatic technique with which he illumined the nature of her offence:
it is Webster's final use of ceremony as an 'internal scale to measure
depravity'.

(133–47)

Clifford Leech

[Distancing in *The Duchess of Malfi*] from *Webster: 'The Duchess of
Malfi'*   1963

The deliberateness of *The Duchess of Malfi* is brought home to us, too,
in the different modes of distancing that Webster uses. And of course
we must recognize that such distancing is necessary for two reasons.
The Greek dramatists had a chorus, which both generalized from the
particular instance of the play's action and, by referring to the past
that lay behind the play's events or by invoking a setting and an
atmosphere remote from the immediate issue, sketched a total image
of the world which was the context of the play's being. The Elizabethans and Jacobeans had no such ready device, but they could switch
the attention by an interjaculated scene or by a speech that looked
back or forward or in its manner was remote from everyday usage,

so that the play's individual story was not merely (though it was also) a special case. In *Antony and Cleopatra* we may think of the scene on Pompey's galley, where the three masters of the world in their cups are, without knowing it, at the mercy of Pompey's reluctant honour, or of the scene in Asia Minor where Ventidius dare not do too well on Antony's behalf lest the victory of a subordinate should gall the general, or of Enobarbus's speech on Cleopatra, which both looks to the past and justifies the present. At such moments we are not immediately involved with the passing event: we have the leisure to consider, we see the framework of space and time within which the event takes place. The interventions of the story-teller in Brecht's *The Caucasian Chalk Circle* operate in much the same way. Webster had particular need, however, for some devices of this sort. In this play and in *The White Devil* he had stories of peculiar intimacy and dreadfulness to tell. He wanted to assert the general truth of the action – that is, he wanted to suggest that his tragic conflict and its consequences were emblems of things known to man as part of his condition – and he wanted to interpose moments of relaxation to avoid the numbing effect of a persistent pageant of woe. We know well enough in actuality that, when misfortunes come in full battalions, their edge is blunted. The high points of misfortune in tragedy may effectively take an audience unaware but not when they are unready. So-called 'comic relief' is of limited use for this purpose, though, if the absurdity is in tune with the tragic event, if it has the right acrid quality, it will in some measure do. Webster uses it in Bosola's railing at the Old Lady and Castruchio in Act II. But this in plenty will defeat itself, becoming expected and blunted, and it may overwhelm the tragic event in frivolity. So other devices had to be found. Webster's solutions to the problem were not all equally successful, but at least we should recognize their purpose.

The first method we may notice is the use of interposed fables, which Rupert Brooke called 'long-winded, irrelevant, and fantastically unrealistic tales'.[1] Webster had used the device in *The White Devil* – in II i, where Francisco tells Camillo a story of Apollo's projected wedding and the general protest caused by the fear that the sun might beget many suns, and in IV ii, where Flamineo tells Brachiano and Vittoria the tale of the ungrateful crocodile and the bird that flies

[1] *John Webster and the Elizabethan Drama*, 1916, p. 130.

into its mouth to relieve it of pain. In both these instances the fable is a roundabout way to persuade without over-blunt speaking: Camillo is to see to it that his wife Vittoria does not become pregnant; Brachiano is to remember with gratitude the services Flamineo has done him. The indirectness of the communication is underlined when, in the later instance, Flamineo produces an alternative explanation. But the device is used not merely for tact. The extended narration, the turning to another story (however much of an allegory it is), take us away from the immediate presence of lust and murder and revenge. In *The Duchess of Malfi* we also have two instances of the device, more surprisingly but more tellingly used. The meeting of Ferdinand and the Duchess in her bedchamber in III ii is the play's central point, the moment of reversal in that thereafter the brother and sister change places, and the end of the slow climb to discovery and the beginning of the plunge to disaster. As Ferdinand is about to leave her, he breaks off his imprecations to tell her of how Reputation, Love, and Death came to journey through the world and planned to take separate paths – Death to battlefields and plague-stricken cities, Love to the dwellings of 'unambitious shepherds' and penniless orphans – but Reputation urged the others not to leave him, for, once he had parted company with a man, he was never to be found again. It is a twelve-line intermission from the direct encounter of the two characters: the audience is invited to think in general terms, in allegorical abstracts, on a subject that is only tangential to the Duchess's story. Yet, though tangential, it is relevant enough: the Duchess has defied Reputation, the world's good word, the world's and the word's power over her. Listening, we lean away from the joined conflict, but are not allowed to forget it. Then suddenly we are plunged back, with Ferdinand's departure and the disturbed reappearance of Antonio and Cariola. The second instance of the device comes almost at the end of Act III, when the Duchess has been arrested by Bosola and his guards. She breaks from straightforward protest to tell the story of a salmon and a dog-fish. The rough fish of the sea rebukes the salmon for leaving its river and venturing to the sea without showing a proper respect for its native-born citizens. The salmon replies that their respective worths will not be known till they are both netted and sold for cooking. It is an allegorical challenge to the world's great, appropriate because in the following act the Duchess is to die and Bosola and his master will

then be led to death. In the immediate context it is in defence of
Antonio that the Duchess speaks, but her words have more powerful,
if grotesque, relevance to her own position. And, after the sadness of
her parting from her husband, we are given this opportunity to stand
back from the present before entering on the ceremony of woe that
will occupy Act IV.

There is no doubt that these interposed fables in Webster's tragedies
constitute an oddity for most modern readers. We can hardly guess
how they sounded in 1612–14. Yet we can see why they were used,
and in attentive reading (less certainly in performance) they can have
their proper effect today.

The next device of this kind to be mentioned is also foreign to a
modern audience. This is the use of the 'sentence' or *sententia*, commonly reinforced by rhyme. Thus in I i Antonio compares a prince's
court to a fountain from which 'Pure silver drops' should flow, and
he then gives the warning:

> ... but if't chance
> Some curs'd example poison't near the head,
> *Death, and diseases through the whole land spread.*[1]
>   (I i 13–15)

A modern audience is not used to rhyme, but will accept it when employed facetiously or in a fantastic situation (in *A Midsummer Night's
Dream*, for example): today rhyme will seem inappropriate in an utterance deliberately embodying wisdom or showing strong feeling. This
is partly because, of our older dramatists, Shakespeare alone dominates
the modern stage. He used rhyme frequently in his earlier plays but
moved from it later. So Webster's rhymes here will jar, seeming at
odds with the temper of the utterance. In fact, Webster probably uses
rhyme less frequently than Chapman, whose tragedies were written in
almost the same years as Shakespeare's: the Jacobeans had not read that
rhyme was a sign of early dating. Moreover, the sentence is generally
less directly employed in the mature Shakespeare. It can be a facetious
utterance, as with Iago in *Othello*, II i, where he improvises verses on
the natures of women, or it is given a personal impress and an impress

---

1 In the original Quarto a sentence-line is commonly preceded by quotation-
marks and, in addition, is sometimes printed in italics. In J. R. Brown's Revels
edition, italics are uniformly used for the purpose.

appropriate to the situation. Macbeth, contemplating the nature of life in v v, speaks in terms fitting himself and his situation when his wife is dead and power is slipping away. Chapman and Webster, on the other hand, use the generalized utterance in an impersonal, unparticularized form. There is nothing to tell us, save the speech-heading, who the speaker is. That does not make it poor drama: if a playwright wishes, he can depersonalize a character as Shakespeare did with Casca in *Julius Caesar*, I iii. Unlike Shakespeare, Webster will use such a de-personalized speaker for a direct choric utterance. And he will use the sentence, with its clanging rhyme, even at a point of emotional inten-sity, as with the Duchess immediately she has cursed the stars and her brothers:

> Let them, like tyrants,
> Never be remember'd, but for the ill they have done;
> Let all the zealous prayers of mortified
> Churchmen forget them! –
> BOSOLA: O, uncharitable!
> DUCHESS: Let heaven, a little while, cease crowning martyrs,
> To punish them!
> Go howl them this: and say I long to bleed:
> *It is some mercy, when men kill with speed.*
>   (IV i 103–10)

The employment of this device grows more frequent, indeed, in *The Duchess of Malfi* and *The White Devil* as they move towards a peak. Just as Webster's use of locality was a varying one, shifting between constriction, contrast, and dispersal, so in his use of dialogue he moved from the strongly personal and particularized to the generalized. The sentences are short, a single line or a couplet, but there are enough of them to give the impression of a tendency to change the dramatic focus. If a modern audience finds the varying technique a distraction, it should be reminded of the alternation of dialogue and chorus in Greek tragedy.

We [should notice] the distancing-effect in the use of theatre-images at IV ii 8, IV ii 36, IV ii 288–90, v v 95–6, and in the echo-device of v iii. But perhaps the strongest example of this kind of effect is to be found dispersed through Act v, coming into most direct expression through the echo-scene but inherent in the whole last movement of the play. It is a commonplace of Webster criticism that *The Duchess of Malfi* falls into anticlimax in Act v, with the Duchess dead and only a huddle of murders to follow. There is some truth in the criticism, for the presentation of Ferdinand's grotesque raving, Bosola's uneasy and fumbling pursuit of virtue, the Cardinal's sudden maladroitness, is more impressive as a scheme than as part of an acted play. But the intention is surely to suggest the presence of the dead Duchess haunting those who have lived along with her. She is mentioned in every scene; her murder is the immediate cause of every detail of the action here; Ferdinand dies invoking her. Webster does not need her ghost – he is content to make a dubious echo speak for her, borrowing Antonio's words – but her presence is meant to be felt as that of the dead Julius Caesar in the concluding scenes of Shakespeare's play. And the effect of this is to reduce the stature of those still alive in the fifth act: they are haunted men who cannot escape the disembodied judgement that hangs in the air. So, in their loss of stature, in the now patent impotence of the individual will, they become almost the 'maggots' that Rupert Brooke believed to be the only inhabitants of a Webster play.[1] That was a short-sighted view of the two major tragedies when seen as wholes, but it will do, approximately, for the last act of *The Duchess*. These men acting out their doom are, to change the image, seen through the wrong end of the telescope. We may at moments find the horrible and the pitiful in what happens to them, but we are not properly involved in the immediate event. We ceased to feel such an involvement at the end of Act IV, and we cannot much doubt that this effect was deliberate.

(35–40)

Elizabeth Brennan

'The Relationship between Brother and Sister in the Plays of John Webster', *Modern Language Review*, vol. 58   1963

Although the importance of the code of honour in sixteenth- and seventeenth-century England has long been recognized, the extent to which its influence was reflected in the drama has only recently been

1 op. cit., p. 158 (see above, p. 94).

studied.[1] It was, indeed, as a result of the dramatists' interest in a code which governed the behaviour of a large proportion of their audience that the theme of revenge tragedy changed from revenge for murder to revenge for honour, and consequently this type of play flourished on the English stage till 1642. One may now reconsider *The Duchess of Malfi*, not in the manner of E. E. Stoll which so irritated Rupert Brooke, but in the light of the relation between John Webster's use of the theme of revenge for honour in it and his use of the same theme in his two other major plays.

Webster, like Ford, was interested in the dramatic possibilities of a variation in the normal relationship between brother and sister: a variation which is as obvious in the abnegation of brotherly consideration and protection as in hints of or the realization of incestuous feelings. His major works show how the real or imagined dishonour of his heroines affects their brothers at least as much as it affects the men who love them. In *The White Devil*, which has the dramatic form of a tragedy of blood revenge, Flamineo gains promotion in the service of the Duke of Brachiano by acting as the Duke's pander to his sister. Flamineo even tricks his brother-in-law into being safely locked up while Vittoria cuckolds him. Flamineo's complete lack of honour is emphasized by his attitude to Cornelia, who pleads on honour's behalf against his actions. Vittoria shows some regret at their mother's words, but Flamineo is unmoved, and Brachiano dismisses Cornelia as mad. Yet Brachiano, who ignores murder, becomes conscious of dishonour when he suspects Vittoria of being unfaithful to him. Finding a letter addressed to her by Francisco de Medicis, he exclaims:

Ud's death, I'll cut her into atomies
And let th'irregular north-wind sweep her up
And blow her int' his nostrils. Where's this whore?

(IV ii 42–4)

Thus berated, Vittoria also prates of honour, saying to her lover:

1 E. M. Wilson, 'Othello, a Tragedy of Honour', *The Listener*, vol. XLVIII, no. 1214 (5 June 1952) and 'Family Honour in the Plays of Shakespeare's Predecessors and Contemporaries', *Essays and Studies* 1953, pp. 19–40; C. L. Barber, *The Idea of Honour in the English Drama*, 1591–1700 (Gothenburg, 1957); Curtis Brown Watson, *Shakespeare and the Renaissance Concept of Honor* (Princeton, 1960).

What have I gain'd by thee but infamy?
Thou hast stain'd the spotless honour of my house,
And frighted thence noble society:

> (IV ii 107–9)

Similarly Flamineo, blunt and coarse as he is in his references to Brachiano's dealings with his sister, professes to consider honour when it suits his purpose, saying to her of the Duke's offer of marriage:

> ... you are blemish'd in your fame, my lord cures it.
> (IV ii 238–9)

Flamineo's lack of scruple for his sister's honour is equalled by that of Romelio in *The Devil's Law-Case*. When Jolenta tells him that she is with child, Romelio does not respond as a man of honour might, and Jolenta cries,

If you had lov'd or tendered my dear honour,
You would have lock'd your poniard in my heart,
When I nam'd I was with child; ...

> (III iii 97–9)

Jolenta is not pregnant, but Romelio persuades her to continue the pretence in order that she may inherit the lands of her supposedly dead lover and, at the same time, conceal the birth of Romelio's child by the nun Angiolella. Meanwhile their mother, Leonora, tries publicly to dishonour Romelio by proclaiming him a bastard. But neither Romelio nor Leonora, any more than Flamineo, Vittoria or Brachiano, is really concerned with honour. Flamineo uses an argument of honour to win his sister to the marriage that will bring him advancement. Vittoria, herself a destroyer of her family's honour, is motivated by rage and spite. Brachiano is moved by jealousy at the thought of his mistress (whom he has dishonoured) preferring another to himself. Romelio stains his sister's reputation so that he may gain the kind of honour that he most values: land, wealth, and noble connexions (IV ii 18–23; 119–23). Leonora wants to cheat Romelio of his inheritance because she believes that he has murdered her beloved Contarino.

It appears, therefore, that Webster was interested not so much in honour or revenge for honour as in their use as disguises for other passions. This is illustrated in his finest study of the conflict between unexpected and conventional behaviour, *The Duchess of Malfi*.[1] The story of Giovanna, Duchess of Amalfi, was first recounted by Matteo Bandello without comment, though he had exclaimed in his introduction against murders motivated by revenge for honour. William Painter, deriving his version of the Duchess's history from Belleforest, endorsed the French writer's moral fervour in stressing repeatedly the dishonour of the Duchess in marrying beneath her and thus staining the noble blood of Arragon. In *El Mayordomo de la Duquesa de Amalfi* Lope de Vega grounded the brothers' motives explicitly on revenge for honour. For Webster, however, revenge for honour was only a cloak to cover a passion which was, in Ferdinand at least, more horrible and unnatural.

It has been suggested that the reason for the difference between Lope's tragedy and Webster's lies in the difference between the Spanish and English codes of honour; that, unlike Lope de Vega, Webster could not expect his audience to accept the brothers' motives without question and, therefore, had to interpret them in terms of a deep psychological derangement.[2] Though the Spanish code was governed by stricter rules than the English, the idea of a brother being the guardian of his sister's honour or even the selector of her husband was found in English plays from *The Spanish Tragedy* onwards. It is seen in Laertes's attitude to Ophelia's relationship with Hamlet. It is probable that Webster could and did expect his audience to understand the brothers' behaviour in terms of the code of honour, and for that reason chose to examine it in order to demonstrate how this code could conceal deeper motives.

Thus Webster not only gives a detailed picture of the young Duchess through her own words and actions; he shows both how well and how little her brothers know her and themselves. In the first scene

1 This conflict is at the centre of the tragedy. It is the Duchess's unexpected but wise and natural choice of a virtuous and humble man for her second husband that sets her in opposition to the conventional, unnatural and corrupt world of the court. An analysis of the means whereby Webster presents Antonio as the ideal husband is given by Frank W. Wadsworth in 'Webster's Duchess in the Light of Some Contemporary Ideas on Marriage and Remarriage', *P.Q.*, vol. 35 (1956), p. 401.

2 J. E. Housman, *Parallel Plots in English and Spanish Drama of the Early Seventeenth Century*, unpublished Ph.D. thesis of the University of London (1951), pp. 87, 89.

they reveal their interpretation of her inclinations and declare their own:

FERDINAND: You are a widow:
You know already what man is: and therefore
Let not youth, high promotion, eloquence –
CARDINAL: No, nor any thing without the addition, *honour*,
Sway your high blood.

(I i 293–7)

Ferdinand would not have his sister remarry at all. He speaks of the luxuriousness of those who wed twice. He warns her against the deadly honey dew, found in the rank pasture of the court, which will poison her fame. He tells her,

Your darkest actions – nay, your privat'st thoughts –
Will come to light.

(I i 315–16)

The Cardinal's reference to the possibility of the Duchess contracting a secret marriage makes Ferdinand condemn the 'lustful pleasures' of such a marriage. Finally, he leaves his sister with an obscene allusion to women's preferences which she cannot mistake, though he tries to excuse it.

This conversation reveals that the brothers' picture of the Duchess is a projection of the evil in their own minds. Far from being, as Ferdinand calls her, a 'lusty widow', she is one whose purity and virtue – an active, Christian virtue – both forbid all lascivious hopes and make her behaviour an example to other ladies (see Antonio's speech, I i 187–205). Ferdinand may later question whether her children have ever been christened, but we see that one of her last earthly concerns is that her daughter be brought up to pray. Facing danger and death the Duchess is able to think and speak of Heaven. She accepts persecution as a necessary means of divine guidance:

Must I like to a slave-born Russian,
Account it praise to suffer tyranny?
And yet, O Heaven, thy heavy hand is in't.
I have seen my little boy oft scourge his top,
And compar'd myself to't: naught made me e'er
Go right but heaven's scourge-stick.

(III v 76–81)

She meets death kneeling, in an attitude of Christian humility. In contrast, her brothers' last hours reveal their consciousness of the hell awaiting them.

Though the Duchess realizes that her brothers have probably studied their speech about marriage she does not understand that their apparent warning about her actions coming to light is, indeed, a threat. They have already prepared a trap. Bosola has been hired to

> ... observe the duchess,
> To note all the particulars of her 'haviour:
> What suitors do solicit her for marriage
> And whom she best affects.
>
> (I i 252–5)

Nevertheless, the Duchess knows her brothers well enough to recognize both the impossibility of reconciling them to her remarriage and the danger to be incurred by crossing their determined wills.

Marrying in secret, the Duchess commits into the hands of Antonio and Cariola the honour that consists in her good name. What is more important, she falls into her brothers' trap, though not all the facts of her situation become known. Bosola discovers that she is pregnant and, later, that she has borne a son. It never occurs to him that she might be married. Bosola's response to this knowledge is conditioned by the corrupt world about him.[1] The letter which he sends to the Arragonian brothers gives their sister the reputation of a 'notorious strumpet'.

Yet, as the Cardinal himself recognizes, not even this justifies the excessive rage to which the letter drives Ferdinand. The Cardinal, thinking of family honour as consisting in noble blood, exclaims:

> Shall our blood
> The royal blood of Arragon and Castile
> Be thus attainted?
>
> (II v 21–3)

---

1 The only other marriage that we are allowed to see in the play is the sterile union of Castruchio and Julia. The very nature of this 'conventional' marriage of a young woman to an old, diseased, and impotent courtier leads to Julia's immoral relationship with the Cardinal (II iv 27–36) and to her attempt to establish a similar relationship with Bosola. It also provokes immoral desires and obscene jests in the otherwise upright Delio.

Ironically, noble blood is theirs, not by legitimate right, but by the lust of their grandparents.[1] Ferdinand, however, is one who, as Clifford Leech has said of Flamineo, cannot get the act of sex from his mind.[2] He is, moreover, obsessed with the image of his sister's body.[3] When he next meets the Duchess he shows a remarkable restraint, quietening her mind when she boldly tackles him on the subject of the rumours current concerning her honour. When he surprises her in her chamber, however, Ferdinand's mind is once again filled with images of lust. Before speaking he presents her with a poniard, probably the same that earlier pointed his obscene jest. Though the Duchess protests that she is married, Ferdinand refers to her husband as her lecher, and warns her never to reveal his identity. Nothing that she can say will make Ferdinand explain why she should not have remarried. Whatever his real feelings are, he hides them behind a fable of Reputation, Love, and Death, concluding:

> And so, for you:
> You have shook hands with Reputation,
> And made him invisible: – So fare you well.
> I will never see you more.
>
> (III ii 133–6)

When her husband's identity is known the Cardinal banishes the Duchess, Antonio and their family. Tearing her wedding ring from her finger, he publicly declares that he will sacrifice it to his revenge. Despite what Ferdinand has said, he is unable to keep away from his sister. In order not to break his vow of never seeing her, he speaks to her in darkness. This gives him the opportunity of frightening her with a dead hand to kiss and then with wax figures of Antonio and her children. Bosola would have Ferdinand stop tormenting her when she is brought to despair. Unfortunately, he suggests that Ferdinand send her

> ... a penitential garment to put on,
> Next to her delicate skin.
>
> (IV i 119–20)

---

1 *The Duchess of Malfi*, ed. F. L. Lucas (1958), p. 17.
2 *John Webster, A Critical Study* (1951), p. 49.
3 He will hew her to pieces (II v 42); he can think of her suckling her child (II v 46); he would have her and her lover's bodies burnt (II v 66–73).

To Ferdinand's sex-ridden mind this immediately recalls 'that body of hers' and spurs him on to devise fresh cruelties. He determines to torture the Duchess and to pursue Antonio. Within her brother's hearing the Duchess is afflicted with the noise of madmen, but Bosola's promptings purposely bring her back from her unchristian despair to assert that she is Duchess of Malfi still. Most touchingly, she is also the mother of a little boy with a cold, of a little girl who likes to pray. Yet, as the Duchess lies strangled, she is to her brother Ferdinand the woman whose beauty dazzles him; his dearest friend. He confesses at last that the meanness of her match meant nothing to him. He says, perhaps to deceive Bosola, but not himself, that he had hoped to gain treasure by her death if she had remained a widow. This seems unjustifiable if she were to be survived by her eldest son, the young Duke of Amalfi.[1] Ferdinand's true reason seems to lie in the words:

> . . . her marriage! –
> That drew a stream of gall, quite through my heart.
>
> (IV ii 286–7)

It has been questioned whether Ferdinand, or Webster himself, understood Ferdinand's obviously incestuous passion.[2] It has been denied that there is any satisfactory human motivation for what Ferdinand does.[3] Yet, as it appears that Webster was especially interested in the relationship between brother and sister, it seems unlikely that he should not have considered all the possible variations of feeling within this relationship. Ferdinand's obsession with the image of his sister's body suggests the attitude of a lover. More than this, Webster alters historical facts to stress the extent of Ferdinand's subconscious rejection of his natural relationship with her, making Ferdinand appear so like the Cardinal that Delio asks if they are twins; to which Antonio replies that they are so in quality. As Ferdinand's appearance and behaviour suggest that he is close to the Cardinal and his sister's senior, we are surprised by his revelation after she has been strangled:

1 Leech, op. cit., p. 68; Webster: 'The Duchess of Malfi' (1963), pp. 23–4.

2 Leech, John Webster, pp. 101–4; but see his Webster: 'The Duchess of Malfi' (1963), pp. 57–60, and J. R. Mulryne in 'The White Devil and The Duchess of Malfi', Stratford-upon-Avon Studies 1: Jacobean Theatre (1960), pp. 222–3.

3 Travis Bogard, The Tragic Satire of John Webster (Berkeley and Los Angeles, 1955), p. 53; Gunnar Boklund, 'The Duchess of Malfi', Sources, Themes, Characters (Cambridge, Mass., 1962), pp. 99–102, 138–40.

She and I were twins:
And should I die this instant, I had liv'd
Her time to a minute.
BOSOLA: It seems she was born first:
You have bloodily approv'd the ancient truth,
That kindred commonly do worse agree
Than remote strangers.

                                                    (IV ii 267-72)

But Ferdinand's closeness to the Cardinal springs rather from a rejection of any sense of brotherly affinity with or deference due to the twin sister who is his senior. If Flamineo could detach himself from brotherly feelings to the extent of becoming his sister's bawd and could instruct her lover how to fondle her, speaking of her sexual appetite with a coarse understanding possibly based on his imagination of her in the position of a responsive mistress, there is no reason to assume that Ferdinand, with a mind at least as coarse, could not imagine his sister's similar responses – but to himself.

It is important for the understanding of each of Webster's major plays that his audience be acquainted with a certain pattern of behaviour of a brother with regard to his sister's honour, for in each play the audience is to be surprised by Webster's treatment of that pattern. Flamineo's degeneracy is most evident in his disregard of family honour. Romelio would exchange his sister's honour for a false honour proceeding from wealth. His failure to avenge her supposed dishonour surprises Jolenta. Throughout The Duchess of Malfi it is clear that the Arragonian brothers desire to preserve their family honour. For the Cardinal that honour consists in a good reputation and untainted blood. Indeed, he appears to think more of his sister's injury to family honour than of her transgression of the Church's laws in her marriage. Our knowledge that the real Cardinal used his ecclesiastical authority in his tyrannous purposes against his sister[1] supports the implication of Webster's characterization of her: that it is her brothers' tyranny which forces the otherwise Christian Duchess to marry outside the Church. In accordance with a brother's authority over his unmarried sister on questions of honour he could cure even the dishonour of rape by marrying her to her injurer. As the Duchess was already Antonio's

1 Ed. F. L. Lucas (1958), pp. 19-20.

wife her brothers had no cause for an honourable quarrel with Antonio or with her other than that, while the marriage remained secret, her reputation, and her family's, had been laid open to common scandal.

Ferdinand, no less than the Cardinal, is intent to avenge a wounded family honour; but with Ferdinand it is the wrong kind of family honour. His attempt to catch the Duchess in her chamber with Antonio, the torture and killing of her, the murder of her children and her maid, and the final pursuit of Antonio do not constitute a brother's revenge for his sister's dishonour but the revenge of a husband for his wife's adultery. A knowledge of other revenge tragedies confirms this, for the wife trap and at least one of the features of Ferdinand's treatment of the Duchess – torture, murder of a witness of the liaison, pursuit of the lover – are found in *Alphonsus, Emperor of Germany*; *Lust's Dominion*; Chapman's *Bussy D'Ambois* and Ford's *Love's Sacrifice*.

It must be stressed, however, that an examination of the concept of revenge for honour was not Webster's main interest in writing the play. In such an examination Ferdinand becomes the most interesting person, whereas it is the Duchess herself who commands our interest; it is her marriage to Antonio that is the play's most important human relationship.[1] Indeed, the last act suffers from anticlimax by the Duchess's absence as well as by the contrivance in Bosola's accidental killing of Antonio.

That Webster's portrayal of the effects of her death on her brothers is not entirely successful on the modern stage is due partly to a lack of understanding of Elizabethan and Jacobean notions of psychology and partly to the difficulty of presenting the lycanthropic form of madness in a serious character. Medical treatises translated into English as well as Burton's *The Anatomy of Melancholy* show that a corrupted mind, obsession with the image of one's mistress, and madness were accepted symptoms of love sickness. In *Theatrum Mundi*, which first appeared in English *c.* 1566, Pierre Boaistuau declared that if lovers were jealous they became mad and played the lycanthrope. In his *Erotomania*, published in France in 1612, Jacques Ferrand wrote of lovers becoming wolf-mad. Thus Ferdinand's lycanthropia was undoubtedly intended by Webster as a final confirmation of his characterization as

1 J. R. Mulryne, op. cit., pp. 219–22, gives an excellent examination of the importance of this relationship.

a jealous lover.[1] We also see the effects of sin on the Cardinal's conscience. He is puzzled about the nature of hell fire. The thing armed with a rake which he sees in the fishponds suggests the devil of the Mystery Plays who, at the Judgement, would herd the bad souls into that hell fire.

In *The Duchess of Malfi* John Webster showed, as Shakespeare had done in *Othello*, how considerations of honour could be used to cloak an insane jealousy. Yet if Webster was a follower of Shakespeare, he was also a leader of later Jacobean dramatists. The illustration, in his major plays, of the way in which individuals could adapt the code of honour to suit their own purposes prepared the way for Middleton and Ford, who made this one of their own important dramatic studies.

(488–94)

William Empson

'Mine Eyes Dazzle', a review of Clifford Leech's *Webster: 'The Duchess of Malfi'*, *Essays in Criticism*, vol. 14   1964

This handbook by Professor Clifford Leech on *The Duchess of Malfi* is scholarly and up to date, and also betrays a certain delicacy of feeling. As he is strictly bound by our ridiculous fashion, he has to argue that the author and the first audiences were jeering at the Duchess for her carnal lust, and the book gives the horrid little 'proofs' of it, but one feels that he dislikes the duty and mitigates it so far as he can.

Since this view of the Duchess cannot be presented on the stage, because an audience rejects it, the academic critics can give no help to the dramatic producers, so the dramatic critics, when the play is revived, usually praise the production for guying the sensationalism of the Elizabethans. There is a bit of tradition behind this idea, so that it gives a useful hint; the trouble about having learned the neo-Christian tradition, on the other hand, is that it cuts you off from any real tradition. Webster may sensibly be regarded as a precursor of Monk Lewis and Mrs Radcliffe, and what they were being 'sensational' about was the

1 Lawrence Babb, *The Elizabethan Malady, A Study of Melancholia in English Literature from 1580 to 1642* (East Lansing, 1951), pp. 136–7. Earlier in his study, however, Babb interprets Ferdinand's lycanthropia as the result of remorse for the murder of his sister (p. 112).

wickedness of Roman Catholic southern Europeans. Neo-Christian critics have to pretend that everybody has always been an Anglo-Catholic, so they have no idea of what the play meant to its first audiences.

We are commonly told that Webster and Tourneur, with their characters like 'coiling asps' (Mermaid edition), were describing the harm often done by loss of religious faith to the Londoners around them. But an Elizabethan would say of *The White Devil* what a Victorian did of *Antony and Cleopatra*, 'How unlike the domestic life of *our* beloved Queen!' The English felt culturally and socially inferior beside Italians and Spaniards, and felt it a duty to try to catch up; but also took comfort in remembering that we were good and they were very wicked, partly because they had such a wicked religion. Webster would be astonished to have his Italians taken for Englishmen. Not long ago [the] Student Drama Society at Sheffield put on *The Revenger's Tragedy*, and I was reflecting how innocent the young people seemed, as they threw themselves into their parts with all the pleasure of fancy, when I realized with a jolt that this was what Tourneur had done too. His aristocratic villains felt to him very remote; indeed I suspect they are often just unlifelike.

I realize that Belleforest and Painter, the French and English pedants who report the story, scold the Duchess for marrying her butler (unlike the Italian source); Mr F. L. Lucas showed a firm grasp of tradition by remarking that this was ungentlemanly of them. The theatre usually backs the young lovers against the Arranged Marriage, and the Globe Theatre, having a mass audience, was ready to rebuke the pride of lineage of Arragon. Thus the Duchess is a heroine; Painter or Clifford Leech would have been hooted in that theatre if they had voiced their sentiments about her. One character in a play for the Globe, indeed, does talk about a romantic marriage as we are now told that everybody in the audience would have talked; it is Iago, and the playwright does not assume that the audience will agree with him. However, as Miss Bradbrook said long ago, the play is also in part a Discussion Drama, like those of Bernard Shaw, questioning whether the Duchess ought to have married the butler. I know this sounds very Philistine, after the great anti-intellectual movement, but any good theatre discusses matters of current interest. Still, a play can give the pleasure of debate without leaving any doubt which side the author is on. The moral of this play, driven home as with the sledge-hammer of Dickens I should have thought, is not that the Duchess was wanton but that her brothers were sinfully proud.

My opponents argue that the Duchess and her husband make a number of anticlerical or free-thinking remarks, which would turn the audience against them; and though she becomes pious just before her death, accepting her punishment, this only gives a further indication that we are meant to think of it as partly deserved. Rather an interesting bit of historical background is needed here. Aquinas lays down (*Sum. Theo.*: Q. 42.1, Q. 45.5, Q. 63.2) that marriage, even the second marriage of a woman, is a sacrament, and its sufficient cause is consent 'expressed in words of the present' (that is, not a bethrothal); the priest's blessing does not validate a marriage, and indeed is not given at the second marriage of a woman. However, not to solemnize a marriage is a sin. A footnote to the translation by the English Dominicans explains that Aquinas was giving the Canon Law of his time, but that clandestine marriages were declared invalid by the Council of Trent. This Council, during the middle years of the sixteenth century, tightened up a number of points of discipline by way of inaugurating the Counter-Reformation, and was of course not accepted by Protestants. The events of the play had taken place before the change in the law, but probably most of the audience would be vague about these dates. When her brother tells her that her children are bastards, and she answers:

You violate a sacrament o' th' church
Shall make you howl in hell for't

(IV i 39–40)

she is in the right, considering her date; but anyhow a legal Discussion is going on, and only the horrible flabby aestheticism of our present fashion would refuse to recognize it. A fanatical Protestant, I suppose, would say that the new law arrogated power to priests and encouraged breach of promise in seducers, but the Church of England was rather inclined to favour it; a play which treated the question as open was not likely to frighten the licensing authority. The Duchess and her husband are presented as reasonable and practical – 'Our sort of people', as Professor Leech rightly puts it (though the Duchess is aristocratic in her exceptional courage), so the audience would think of them as souls naturally Protestant. All the phrases which have been found irreligious, and therefore likely to make the audience condemn the Duchess and her husband (for example, the assumption that pilgrimages deserve no reverence), are simply Protestant. Antonio, though a cautious speaker, also contrives a reference to one of the major disputed points of doctrine. Asked what he thinks of marriage, he says:

I take't, as those that deny purgatory –
It locally contains, or heaven, or hell

(I i 393–4)

This crack of course is meant to make him seem charming, as well as sturdily sensible and right-thinking; the idea that the Globe audience would expect him to be punished for his flippancy is very overstrained.

Modern critics usually call him cowardly, because he is so aware of his wife's danger, just as they call her irresponsible for her courage. But it was standard bourgeois opinion that a second husband should not be dashing or flashy; with a sober businesslike man, the theoretical objections would not be raised. Thus, in a way, his character is sacrificed to make the audience accept the Duchess. To allow the separation when she goes to her brothers alone was fatal in the result, but Ferdinand loves her and has demanded to have Antonio kept out of his sight, so the plan is worth trying as a last chance; when it goes wrong, Antonio follows her with courage ('very near my home').[1] In the [first] scene of the play we are told he has won the ring at jousting, to prove that he is a gentleman in all but his origins. A play intended as a warning against marrying a social inferior would have to be constructed quite differently.

Professor Clifford Leech has an argument of his own to prove that the Duchess is an irresponsible ruler; as usual, it goes bang in the opposite direction as soon as you examine the text. The Duchess is so devoted to her city state that we never hear her personal name, and she marries the man who is already administering it in the way she approves. Naturally he spends rather more as her husband. Later on she asks him what people say; he says they think she is letting him get hold of a lot of her own money, unwillingly no doubt, but on the calculation that then he won't squeeze money from the people. That is,

1 Probably means 'close to my eternal home – heaven'. [Ed.]

the people know that they are unusually well governed, or at least lightly taxed, and try to invent some amusingly bad reason for it, but even in doing so confess they realize that the Duchess wishes them well. If she had married a grand husband, he would be pretty sure to squeeze Malfi for his private vanity or his quarrels. As the case stands, the only person who seems politically irresponsible is the Professor.

Modern critics often claim that the Duchess admits, shortly before she dies, that she was wrong to marry Antonio, or at least the Imagery there, having so much Hell about it, makes her remarks amount to that. Such critics would also claim to be defending the high old moral tradition, now all but lost; whereas any ordinary citizen could tell that they are being quaintly low-minded. A number of people in the seventeenth century actually did meet death with saintly impertinence towards the tyrant who killed them, thanking him for the gift of martyrdom, which had done them all the good in the world: 'Minds innocent and quiet take That for [an] hermitage'. If anything could have knocked them off their perch, poor creatures, it would have been to have a modern neo-Christian come up and say how pleased he was to find them licking the boots of the tyrant at the last, as it made a very edifying picture. I can't tell you how old it makes me feel, to have lived on into this eerie cultural twilight.

When the Duchess proposes marriage to her major-domo, we are usually told that he betrays ambition by accepting, but Clifford Leech is inclined to think that she tricked him into the fatal marriage; his luke-warm polite answer would not have bound him if she had not hidden a witness behind the curtain. So far from that, knowing that she is asking him to accept a post of danger, she hides the witness to make him free to refuse; in the presence of her maid, he might well feel that a refusal would make her lose too much face. We have already heard him tell a friend that he loves her, so we need not doubt it when we hear him hesitate because of the danger to her, not to himself. Both the lovers in this scene show delicacy of feeling, and the struggle of modern critics to display high-mindedness by finding something dirty in it strikes me as very queer.

We may now approach the famous Incest Problem, which arose because Freud expected audiences to be unconscious and English critics did not know what an Elizabethan audience would be conscious of. Elizabethans believed that Lucrezia Borgia went to bed with her brothers because, owing to her intense family pride, which was like that of the Pharaohs, she could find no fit mate elsewhere. The incestuous reflections of Ferdinand would thus be obvious to the first audiences, as a standard expression of the insane pride which is almost his only characteristic (at the start of the play, he forbids his courtiers to laugh unless he laughs first); no wonder he turns into a wolf in the last act, as one hoped he would. In short, the play has a popular Dickensian moral, against the wicked rich; whereas our critical attempt to recover the ethics of a nobler age has been limited to recovering subservient or boot-licking morals.

You may answer that, although many spectators would feel an easy sentiment in favour of the lovers, their serious conviction would be that the Duchess was wrong to marry her major-domo. Some would think so, no doubt; the idea that everyone held the same opinion at a given date, 'the opinion of the time', is disproved as soon as you open a history book and find a lot of them killing each other because they disagreed. But there was a reason why this question was especially open to doubt, so that hardly anyone could feel the whole truth lay with Painter and Belleforest. Many subtle pages in the Variorum edition of *Twelfth Night* offer meanings for *Strachey* in 'There is example for it; the lady of the Strachey married the yeoman of the wardrobe'; the answer is that Shakespeare had hunted for a meaningless word because the meaning which would be presumed was dangerous. The widow of the national hero Prince Hal, whether or not she actually married her Gentleman of the Wardrobe, in their brief and harried life together, had made him the ancestor of the entire Tudor Dynasty. It would strike the groundlings as probable that the Duchess too had made a momentous decision, and I think this explains what is usually called one of the mistakes of the play, the unhistorical choice of her surviving son by Antonio as the next Duke of Malfi. English critics tend to regard Dukedoms as ancestral, but the first husband of the Duchess had merely been given the job, presumably through the influence of her brothers. Now that they are both dead and discredited the normal influence of the town council may carry some weight, and Delio is speaking for them when he pronounces that this boy deserves the position. His horoscope would no doubt be right in predicting an early end, but I expect Webster thought of him as lasting long enough to establish a dynasty.

Perhaps I should try to make clear my assumptions about the audience. It was predominantly artisan, and the real Puritans would not come. Such an audience, like most of the population, would readily admire aristocratic courage and independence; but they would be especially prone to blame the family pride which destroys the lovers. Readily, again, they would side with their own Protestant Government against wicked Spanish grandees; but the nagging theoretical Puritanism of our present mentors would be remote from their sympathies. They would welcome the detail about keeping down the taxes.

(80–86)

J. R. Brown

[The Stage Effect of *The Duchess of Malfi*] from the Introduction to his edition of *The Duchess of Malfi* 1964

Many details have to be held in the mind in order to discuss Webster's characters. And, indeed, there is a careful ingenuity in every element of the writing – all except one, which is not verbal: the large and sweeping impression of the play in performance.

In the first three acts, crowded court scenes alternate with private scenes. The focus moves incessantly, illuminating briefly a whole court, groups, couples, individuals; no one person holds the stage for long. The birth of the first child in Act II is attended by alarms and followed by a still darkness. In Act III the flight from Malfi leads the Duchess and her husband to the open country where they separate and the Duchess becomes a prisoner. In Act IV, the prison provides the one consistent setting and a steady dramatic focus: it is dark, and alternately frighteningly still and frighteningly wild. The Duchess dies separated from everyone she loves or knows. Then the last act is a mixture of slow cunning and sudden moves. Entries seem timed by some manipulating fate: there is a sharp decisiveness ('O, my fate moves swift!'), and elaborate involvement ('you'll find it impossible To fly your fate'), and a contrivance ('Such a mistake as I have often seen In a play'). In a tragedy where appearances and judgements change like quicksilver, and the plot has many by-paths and hesitations, and some irreducible contradictions (the neglect of the son of

the first marriage, and perhaps, Bosola's long failure to find the
Duchess's husband), the simple eloquence of the shape of the action is
especially impressive. The dramatist's silent handling seems to have
something like a 'meaning': a suggestion that the Duchess had to die,
and her impermanent world to be destroyed.

And, briefly, in the last silent homage to the son of the Duchess,
there is a hint that men may, perhaps, wish for some renewal and
order.

(liv–v)

A. W. Allison

[The Two-Fold Plot of *The Duchess of Malfi*] from 'Ethical Themes
in *The Duchess of Malfi*', *Studies in English Literature*, vol. 4   1964

'There is no poet morally nobler than Webster,' wrote Algernon
Swinburne in a moment of high enthusiasm; that 'instinctive righteousness' of which Aeschylus is the classic exemplar 'is shared no less
by Webster than by Shakespeare.'[1]

For all its excesses of manner, this estimate of Webster seems to me
just in kind, especially as touching his most soberly considered play,
The Duchess of Malfi. And, though I do not propose that all other
critics of that work have wandered in darkness until now, I find some
deficiencies in the understanding of it which a straightforward consideration of its ethical design might serve to supply. There is, first, a
general disposition – the legacy of E. E. Stoll's reaction against nineteenth-century mawkishness – either wholly to moralize the Duchess
or wholly to sentimentalize her.[2] Secondly, the several villains have
not been clearly enough differentiated from one another, and then,

---

1 *The Age of Shakespeare* (London, 1908), pp. 36–7 (see above, p. 68).
2 Stoll found Webster the 'stern justicer of human error – of the folly of
Antonio and the Duchess', *John Webster* (Boston, 1905), p. 192. Dr Dyce had
found that 'we mourn the more over the misery that attends [Antonio and the
Duchess] because we feel that happiness was the natural and legitimate fruit of
so pure and rational an attachment', *The Works of John Webster* (London,
1857), p. xiv. An informative recent note is Frank W. Wadsworth's 'Webster's
The Duchess of Malfi in the Light of Some Contemporary Ideas on Marriage
and Remarriage', *P.Q.*, vol. 35 (1956), pp. 394–407.

modern critics in particular have been too nearly spellbound by
Bosola. Thirdly, the fifth act, being judged aesthetically inferior, has
been written off as hardly a part of the whole. These and other flaws
in understanding or perspective are partly mended when we see how,
as the plot unfolds, the local and particular concerns of the play are
subsumed into larger ethical configurations and at length form general
statements of fitting dignity.

The Duchess has a two-fold plot with separate strands of action and
separate catastrophes for the title character and her adversaries. Herein,
like most Elizabethan tragedy, it partakes of the nature of melodrama
or what Aristotle calls tragedy of the second rank,[1] differing from it
chiefly in that the catastrophes befalling the good characters and the
bad are parallel rather than opposed. It further contains an ambivalent
character, Daniel de Bosola, whose role, though partly contingent
and choric, is partly independent; Bosola's ethical hesitations may be
said to constitute an action of their own.

The manner in which these strands of action are united into a single
plot appears when we examine them seriatim. The Duchess's story is
set in motion when she secretly marries Antonio, rises to crisis when
she is confronted with her supposed immorality (III ii), and declines
to catastrophe as she is separated from her husband and harried to her
death (IV ii). The story of her adversaries – her brothers Ferdinand and
the Cardinal – is set in motion when they oppose her desire to marry,
reaches its crisis when they have her murdered (IV ii), and declines to
catastrophe as they suffer the consequences of their crime. The story
of Bosola, who is at first merely the brothers' agent, takes an independent turn when he finds that the Duchess is married to the admirable Antonio and is moved to sympathize with her (III ii); this strand
of action reaches its crisis when he is denied reward for presiding over
her persecution (IV ii) and declines to catastrophe when he seeks, at the
eventual cost of his own life, to frustrate the further malice of the
brothers and avenge the wrongs in which they have already involved
him.

These actions, we observe, are so organized that the play falls into
three approximately equal parts, related by causal necessity. The first
part shows the Duchess marrying in the face of her brothers' opposition; in this part of the play Bosola is oriented toward the brothers.

1 Poetics, xiii 7.

The second part shows the brothers breaking up her marriage and eventually bringing about her death; Bosola becomes ambivalent. The third part shows the brothers demoralized by their crime and inviting their own destruction; Bosola, now in active revolt against them, is an agent of their downfall.

(263–4)

Modern Productions and Adaptations

We have, in previous sections, discussed the earlier theatrical records and rewritings of Webster's tragedies (such as were known to us). From 1890 onward these become more frequent and pursue a course separate from that of the now increasingly professional world of literary criticism. We have thought best to treat them in an independent section.

William Poel's 1892 production has always been regarded as an occasion when Webster's text was restored to its integrity; compared with Horne's version, and even with George Daniel's, Poel's prompt-books show a great deal of the original Webster; but Poel was not here, any more than elsewhere, a textual purist. The original is very much cut about; and it provides an interesting document of the taste of the nineties. The opening of Act II may give some indication of his freedom:

[*Enter* BOSOLA]

BOSOLA: The sin of youth is the very patrimony of the physician, makes him renew his footcloth with the spring and change his high-prized courtesan with the fall of the leaf. And yet some would the souls of princes were brought forth by some more weighty cause than those of meaner persons – they are deceived; there's the same hand to them; the like passions sway them. The same reasons weigh with the great as with the base. Observe our Duchess now. When she grew sick and contrary to the Italian fashion wore loose-bodied gowns the cunning doctor gave out that the baths of Lucca would cure her aches. It was a good stratagem.

[*Enter* ANTONIO *and* DELIO]

Poel has not simply got rid of the Old Lady (constantly cut, by producers and critics alike), but has made a new opening speech out of odd lines (for example, II i 40–43, 101–4) and scraps picked up from all over the play – the 'baths of Lucca' comes from III ii 314 – padded out with Elizabethan-ese tid-bits out of Poel's own invention or memory. The final phrase seems to come from *King Lear*. The whole play is intercut in this complex way. Thus the dialogue which

begins at Act II, scene i, ll. 96 ff. is followed by the beginning of
Act III, scene iii, followed by II iv 41–64, II v, III i 37–56, II i 118–28,
III i 56–7, II iv 79–81. In the sense that a majority of Webster's lines
turn up at some point or other, the prompt-book is faithful to the
original; but the structure that emerges, and many of the individual
effects, are Poel's own.

In the scene of the Duchess's torment Poel's hooded friars and
half-clothed skeletons (not to mention 'Mr Brunton's groan') made
a considerable effect. The horrors are interestingly stylized in a
wholly modern, quite un-Elizabethan, manner. Cariola's strangling
is omitted (as often); the children are strangled on stage, in
accordance with Dyce's text; and a ninetyish curtain-effect is
contrived to end the scene:

*While Ferdinand is looking at body the three madmen enter and stand
staring vaguely at Ferdinand. He raises his eyes and shudders and ex-
tends his hands towards them. Bosola goes up and touches Ferdinand
on shoulder. Ferdinand makes no movement. Bosola, withdrawing
his hand, speaks*
BOSOLA: [*with horror*] He is distracted.
  Slow curtain

The last Act tries to keep the idea of the Duchess before the
audience by various theatrical devices. The echo-scene (for which a
special choir was deployed) is recalled whenever a significant line
needs to be emphasized; and the 'shadow of the Duchess' is thrown
across the stage for further emphasis. When Bosola says

The weakest arm is strong enough that strikes
With the sword of justice – still methinks the Duchess
Haunts me
                              (V ii 344–6)

the echo repeats 'with the sword of justice', and there is a
Stage-direction 'shadow thrown at Bosola's feet'. Likewise when

the Cardinal says 'I would pray now: but the devil takes away my heart' (v iv 27), the echo repeats 'take away my heart'. At the end of the play Bosola is given Delio's lines

To establish this young, hopeful gentleman
In's mother's right.

This is then followed by '*Echo*. In his mother's right' and then

Bosola at the sound of the Echo gives a slight shudder and makes the sign of the cross.
BOSOLA: [*to Delio*] Farewell. Mine is another venture.
As Bosola is going out guarded the figure of the Duchess is seen between the cypress trees at the back. She is looking sadly towards her son. Music.

At such moments Maeterlinck seems quite as close as Webster.

The next production, the Phoenix Society's performance of *The Duchess of Malfi* in 1919, provoked reviews from William Archer (p. 94) and T. S. Eliot but it seems to have been, theatrically speaking, an unmitigated disaster. The audience could not be kept from giggling as the corpses hit the floor; and when we hear that Ferdinand died standing on his head – for lack of space on the floor it was suggested – we are bound to wonder how far the production was designed to keep them from giggling.

Less documented than the Phoenix Society production but probably more influential were the Cambridge (Marlowe Society) productions of *The White Devil* in 1920 and of *The Duchess of Malfi* in 1924. An extraordinary number of those who would acquire importance in Elizabethan studies in the following decades were involved in these. The lead seems to have come from King's College, where Rupert Brooke had written his fellowship dissertation on Webster – Brooke was the first President of the Marlowe Society – and where F.L.Lucas was preparing his great edition of Webster's

Complete Works. *The White Devil* was directed by J. T. Sheppard, later the Provost of King's. *The Duchess of Malfi* was directed by T.H.Marshall the economist, had George Rylands as the Duchess, Theodore Spenser as Ferdinand, John Hayward as one of the madmen. Henri Fluchère who adapted the play for the Comédie des Champs Elysées in 1937 has said that his interest in the play 'was raised by the performance in Cambridge'.

The most successful production of *The Duchess of Malfi* in the century may be said to be a result of this 1924 event; for the 1945 Haymarket Theatre production was directed by George Rylands, Fellow of King's and mainstay of the Marlowe Society. It had a superb cast, with John Gielgud as Ferdinand and Peggy Ashcroft as the Duchess; but even these famous performers seem to have been overshadowed by the Bosola of Cecil Trouncer. It was remarked at the time that Bosola should have shared the final curtain-call with the other two. The idea of Bosola's centrality in the play raises an interesting general question. Phelps wanted to play Bosola when first organizing his 1850 revival. He played Ferdinand instead only because he could not find anyone else to play it. We should remember also that Richard Perkins, singled out for praise by Webster, probably played Flamineo. Genest, the historian of the English stage, thinks that Flamineo *is* the white devil. But, leaving this general question on one side, we should notice how ripe the time was in 1945 for an acceptance of Bosola as raisonneur. The real world at that moment seemed not at all unlike the world of greed and horror he projects, foul but true; Belsen and Buchenwald had just been discovered by the public. Gielgud emphasized the modernity of Webster's vision in other terms: by playing-up Ferdinand's incestuous feelings as a central factor, he brought the play into obvious relationship with the post-Freudian vision of human motivation.

Two direct results of the success of *The Duchess of Malfi* in 1945 should be mentioned. In March 1947 *The White Devil* was given its first purely commercial performance since the seventeenth century. For one spectator at least the great triumph of the production was the controlled and stylized violence of Flamineo, played by the dancer Robert Helpmann. There was also a fine public vindication of the staging: the play ran for an unheard-of four months. The second result of the 1945 *Duchess* was a production of the same play in New York in 1946. The main moving force behind this seems to have been the actress Elizabeth Bergner who had long desired to play the title-role. Both Brecht and Auden seem to have been involved in adapting the original for her. Mr Rylands was flown across the Atlantic to repeat his directoral triumphs of the year before. The text he found when he arrived was, he informs us, some kind of conflation of *The Duchess of Malfi* with *The White Devil*. This he rejected; but some rewriting remained. There was an Auden soliloquy in which Ferdinand revealed his incestuous passion for his sister. There was also some re-arrangement of the events in the last Act; but I have not been able to recover the detail of this. The waxworks had gone from Act IV, and the dead children (usually, Mr Rylands says, the children of local policemen) fell out of an enormous cupboard at the right moment. The obvious and perhaps fatal eccentricity in the casting was Bosola; he was played by the negro actor Canada Lee, wearing pink make-up. There was music by Benjamin Britten. The galaxy of international talent assembled round this production was unable to prevent it from being a crashing failure.

The success of the 1945 *Duchess* was re-assayed with greater effect in 1960 when the Royal Shakespeare Company chose this play to open their new London home – the Aldwych theatre. The other plays in this opening repertory were John Whiting's *The Devils* and Anouilh's *Becket*. The combination of cruelty on the stage and psychological evocation of the past that these imply suggest a theatrical context in which Webster finds a natural place. Peggy Ashcroft again played the Duchess, with even more effect than in

1945, according to the critics. The scene that was most highly praised was the wooing of Antonio in Act 1. When we learn that in her performance 'gentle raillery, tremulous passion, melting womanliness and utter certainty are blended into something of fragile and almost touchable beauty' it should not surprise us that this was the moment of highest definition. The production was praised on one side for being 'fluent and austere'; but on the other side was represented as 'a forthright noisy affair' in which 'nothing is lacking . . . save finesse and originality'. The text used was fairly close to the original; but a great deal of the specific texture of Webster's poetry was (once again) removed. Bosola's speeches suffered most. His tendency to indulge in strange metaphysical comparisons was curbed, as was his equally strong tendency to moral generalization; he became more business-like but less the creator of the specific atmosphere in which the action moves and by by which it is explained. Webster has not appeared on the professional stage in England since this time, though he has been produced in America.

One further adaptation deserves some mention. The Granada television network produced on 27 April 1964 a play by Kingsley Amis called *A Question of Hell*. This showed very little verbal connexion with Webster, but the story is based on *The Duchess of Malfi*, modernized in some interesting ways. The brothers are now rich white landowners in a Caribbean island. Their sister Angela, recently widowed, is secretly engaged to Sam, her coloured chauffeur. The claustrophobia of a society obsessed by the colour-bar provides a realistic modern equivalent for the Spanish pride of blood with which Webster dealt. There is a parallel attempt to find through Voodoo ceremonies an access to the supernatural which does not offend against the social realism of the modern play; but this works much less well; in the absence of poetry the magic can have no general effect. The brothers arrange for a waterfront bar-keeper and crook to kill Sam and then to silence their sister. The imprisonment of the sister in the bar, amid the brawling of drunks, provides a modern version of the Masque of Madmen. The denouement is given a realistic motivation: the coloured murderer finds that the 'crime' for which he kills Angela is a crime against the colour-bar. In a final blood-bath, brothers, murderers, and all are liquidated.

This play interestingly indicates the real capacity of the story of *The Duchess of Malfi* to hold continuous attention, just as a story, and to catch at basic obsessions of individuals and of society.

Acknowledgements

For permission to use copyright material acknowledgement is made to the following:

For the poem by T. S. Eliot from *Collected Poems* 1909–1962 to Faber & Faber Ltd, Harcourt, Brace & World Inc. and the Estate of the late T. S. Eliot; for the article by W. A. Edwards to the editors of *Scrutiny* and Cambridge University Press; for the extract from U. Ellis-Fermor, *The Jacobean Drama*, to A.B.P. International and Random House Inc.; for the article by James Smith to the editors of *Scrutiny* and Cambridge University Press; for the article by M. C. Bradbrook to the editors of the *Modern Language Review* and the author; for the extract from Edmund Wilson, *Europe Without Baedeker*, to the author, Laurence Pollinger Ltd and Rupert Hart-Davis Ltd; for the extract by Lord David Cecil, *Poets and Story-Tellers*, to the author; for the article by Ian Jack to the author, the editors of *Scrutiny* and Cambridge University Press; for the extract by Gabriele Baldini, *John Webster e il linguaggio della tragedia*, to Edizioni dell'Ateneo, Rome; for the extract by Travis Bogard, *The Tragic Satire of John Webster*, to the University of California Press and Russell & Russell Ltd; for the article by Hereward T. Price to the Modern Language Association of America; for the article by Inga-Stina Ekeblad to the editors of *Review of English Studies* and The Clarendon Press, Oxford; for the extract from R. W. Dent, *John Webster's Borrowing*, to the University of California Press; for the extracts from J. R. Brown's editions of *The White Devil* and *The Duchess of Malfi*, to A.B.P. International; for the extract from G. K. Hunter's article to Edward Arnold (Publishers) Ltd; for the extract from Harold Jenkins' article to the author and Cambridge University Press; for the article by James L. Calderwood to the editors of *Essays in Criticism*; for the extract from Clifford Leech, *Webster's The Duchess of Malfi*, to Edward Arnold (Publishers) Ltd; for the article by Elizabeth Brennan to the editors of the *Modern Language Review* and the author; for the article by William Empson to the editors of *Essays in Criticism*; for the extract from A. W. Allison's article to the editors of *Studies in English Literature*.

Select Bibliography

Editions

Elizabeth Brennan (ed.), *The Duchess of Malfi*, Edward Arnold, 1964.
Elizabeth Brennan (ed.), *The White Devil*, Edward Arnold, 1966.
F. L. Lucas (ed.), *The Complete Works of John Webster*, 4 vols., Chatto and Windus, 1927.
   Slightly revised editions of *The White Devil* and *The Duchess of Malfi* were issued as separate volumes in 1958.
J. R. Brown (ed.), *The White Devil*, Methuen, 1960.
J. R. Brown (ed.), *The Duchess of Malfi*, Methuen, 1964.

General Works on Elizabethan Drama

M. C. Bradbrook, *Themes and Conventions of Elizabethan Tragedy*, Cambridge University Press, 1935.
E. K. Chambers, *The Elizabethan Stage*, 4 vols., The Clarendon Press, 1923.
Una Ellis-Fermor, *The Jacobean Drama*, Methuen, 1936.
Robert Ornstein, *The Moral Vision of Jacobean Tragedy*, University of Winsconsin Press, 1960.
Moody E. Prior, *The Language of Tragedy*, Columbia University Press, 1947.
Irving Ribner, *Jacobean Tragedy*, Methuen, 1962.
F. P. Wilson, *Elizabethan and Jacobean*, The Clarendon Press, 1945.

Webster

Gabriele Baldini, *John Webster e il linguaggio della tragedia*, Edizioni dell'Ateneo, 1953.
Travis Bogard, *The Tragic Satire of John Webster*, University of California Press, 1955.
Gunnar Boklund, *The Sources of 'The White Devil'*, Lundeqvist, 1957.
Gunnar Boklund, *'The Duchess of Malfi': Sources, Themes, Characters*, Harvard University Press, 1962.
R. W. Dent, *John Webster's Borrowing*, University of California Press, 1960.
Dennis Donovan, *Elizabethan Bibliographies Supplements: John Webster*, The Nether Press, 1967.
D. D. Moore, *John Webster and his Critics 1617-1964*, Louisiana State University Press, 1966.
Norman Rabkin (ed.), *Twentieth Century Interpretations of 'The Duchess of Malfi'*, Prentice-Hall, 1968.

C. J. Sisson, *The Lost Plays of Shakespeare's Age*, Cambridge University Press, 1936. Chapter 2 deals with the scandal behind *Keep the Widow Waking*.

E. E. Stoll, *John Webster: The Periods of his Work Determined by his Relation to the Drama of the Day*, Harvard Cooperative Society, 1905.

S. A. Tannenbaum, *John Webster: A Concise Bibliography*, Tannenbaum, 1941.

Index

The Duchess of Malfi has not been included in the following Index.
Since reference to this play is made in most pages of the book it
would be time-wasting and unhelpful to document this fact in detail.
Obscure works cited in the text without author's name are given a
cross-reference; but it seemed too cumbrous to do this in every case.
Harbage's *Annals of English Drama* or Chambers's *Elizabethan Stage*
provide complete cross-reference for plays.

Extracts included in this anthology are indicated by bold page
references.